THE PENGUIN CLASSICS

EDITED BY E. V. RIEU

L81

THE LIFE OF
ALEXANDER
THE GREAT

BY

ARRIAN

Translated by Aubrey de Sélincourt

PENGUIN BOOKS
BALTIMORE · MARYLAND

Penguin Books Ltd, Harmondsworth, Middlesex
U.S.A.: Penguin Books Inc., 3300 Clipper Mill Road, Baltimore 11, Md
AUSTRALIA: Penguin Books Pty Ltd, 762 Whitehorse Road,
Mitcham, Victoria

—

This translation first published 1958
Reprinted 1962

—

Copyright © Aubrey de Sélincourt, 1958

—

Made and printed in Great Britain
by Richard Clay & Company, Ltd,
Bungay, Suffolk
Set in Monotype Bembo

CONTENTS

MAP	vi
INTRODUCTION	ix
BOOK ONE	21
BOOK TWO	60
BOOK THREE	91
BOOK FOUR	126
BOOK FIVE	163
BOOK SIX	193
BOOK SEVEN	225

The Route of Alexander's Expedition

INTRODUCTION

ARRIAN – Flavius Arrianus, to give him the name he was known by as an official of the Roman Imperial government – was a Greek, born at Nicomedia, in the province of Bithynia, during the last few years of the first century A.D. In his youth he had the inestimable advantage of studying under Epictetus, the pagan philosopher and friend of the Emperor Hadrian, in whose teaching was so much of the early Christian spirit of other-worldliness and contempt for the fugitive splendours of wealth and power. Arrian's respect for his master was, luckily for us, so great that he kept and subsequently published verbatim notes of his discourses; the *Encheiridion* ('manual') which he compiled from them was much used in the Middle Ages as a guide to the principles of monastic life, and is still extant.

Taking service in the Roman army, Arrian won rapid promotion and at the age of forty or thereabouts was appointed by Hadrian governor of the province of Cappadocia. Such a post was a most unusual honour for a Greek. He saw some fighting during his term of office, and the experience was to be useful to him later as a military historian. He did not, however, hold office long; seven years after his appointment Hadrian died (A.D. 138), whereupon Arrian retired into private life, spending his remaining forty years partly in the town where he was born, partly in Athens, and occupying himself with the pursuits of a gentleman of leisure and with his literary work. He was Archon (chief magistrate) at Athens in 171. He died about the year 180.

Arrian was a fairly prolific writer; in addition to his records of Epictetus he published books of travel and treatises on military tactics, but the work of his life on which he lavished all his powers was his History of Alexander – his *Anabasis*, as he called it, or *Journey Up-Country*, a word intended, one supposes, to recall Xenophon's great story of the Ten Thousand, but somehow strangely inadequate to describe the explorations and campaignings of Alexander, which were, indeed, a very considerable journey up-country, away from the familiar Grecian sea.

How important to Arrian was this book, how long and how intensely he had brooded upon his subject and laboured to make it as perfect as he could, he tells us himself in one of the few brief passages where he drops the role of impersonal historian and gives us a glimpse of his private feelings. 'There is no need for me,' he exclaims, 'to say who I am, though my name is not obscure; there is no need for me to speak of my country, or my family, or the public offices I have held: it is enough to say that this book, now and since my earliest years, has, for me, taken the place of all these things.' The history of his great hero was his life's work and justification; if it was well done, he would not, he felt, have lived in vain.

After the end of the Alexandrian age, from early in the second century before Christ, Greek literature rapidly declined, and during the hundred years – say from 50 B.C. to A.D. 50 – when Latin literature was at its height, it had almost petered out. It had had a long run, having been one of the glories of the world for not much less than a thousand years. However, it was not yet finished, and the second century of our era had hardly begun when there was a renaissance of the Greek spirit, and Greek began once again to be used as a literary language – it had, of course, never ceased to be spoken over great tracts of the eastern Roman empire, and educated Romans were as familiar with it as educated Englishmen are with French today. The beginning of no literary movement can be precisely fixed in time, and there were eminent Greek writers, of whom Plutarch was one, in the first century of the Christian era; but it is convenient to date the beginning of the Greek renaissance from the accession of Hadrian to the Imperial throne in A.D. 117. Much of its force and vigour was, indeed, due to this remarkable man, himself something of a poet and steeped in the literature of the ancient world. The patronage he gave to the Greek sophists of the day was responsible for their great and increasing influence, and that influence, in its turn, acted as a spur to the revival of Greek letters. The Emperor Marcus Aurelius, it will be remembered, wrote his famous little book in Greek.

Arrian was very much in the movement, which included such other contemporary writers as Appian, the Greek historian of Rome; Pausanias, whose *Tour of Greece* is a mine of antiquarian information; Galen the writer on medicine; and – in many ways the most readable of them all – the shallow but brilliantly amusing Lucian.

All these writers were employing an idiom very different from the Greek speech current at the time. They were deliberately *archaizing*, consciously imitating, or trying to imitate, the literary language and style of three or four hundred years ago. This could not but affect the quality of their work. All art is largely artifice, and there is no such thing as a 'natural' style, nevertheless we have come to believe, especially of late, that the best literary style is that which best achieves the effect of naturalness, and employs all the power of artifice to subdue the current spoken idiom to its purpose. The Greek writers of the second century thought otherwise; for them, the best literary style had been fixed by the great writers of the classical age, four or five hundred years before their time, and the only way to achieve distinction was to copy their idiom as closely as they could. The only two books we possess of which the language approaches the *koinê*, or contemporary spoken Greek of Syria and Asia Minor, are the New Testament and the records taken by Arrian of the lectures of Epictetus. For centuries scholarship and pedantry, too often the same thing, supposed that the Greek of the New Testament was barbarous and debased – Nietzsche's notorious jibe about God having learnt Greek, and having learnt it so badly, is a case in point. But today most of us are wiser, and the beauty of New Testament Greek and its power of expressing what its users wanted it to express make us wish that the professional literary men, too, of that epoch had taken their language warm from contemporary lips instead of seeking it in the written pages of the past. An instance of the lengths to which this artificiality could go is provided by Arrian himself. In one of his books – the *Indica*, a short piece in which at Hadrian's request he wrote up Nearchus' account of his voyage from the Indus to the Persian Gulf – he uses, apparently for a change, or simply to show that he could manage it, the Ionic dialect of Herodotus.

This strange convention imposes an almost intolerable burden upon the writers of the period. Lucian alone of them manages to carry it gracefully; the rest, including Arrian, show inevitable signs of strain, as might a modern Englishman who, admiring the coloured, supple, and racy idiom of Elizabethan prose, elected to write historical portraits in the style of Sir Thomas North.

From the point of view of style, therefore, Arrian is not a writer of the first rank. In some ways this is an advantage to his translator; for a translator of the great Greek classics is perpetually humbled by a sense of inadequacy, while a translator of Arrian is warmed from time to time by a flush of self-satisfaction, almost pardonable, as it is borne in upon him that, instead of flattening and dimming his author by what even Shelley, speaking of his beautiful version of Plato's *Symposium*, called 'the grey veil of his own words', he may, here and there, even have improved him. However, Arrian is, in the main, clear and easy to understand; and that is a virtue.

But though we are unlikely to read Arrian for his style, we do read him for his matter, which is of the highest interest and importance. Alexander's twelve years of unparalleled endeavour and achievement are poorly documented for so momentous a period in history, and Arrian's account of them is the best and fullest we possess. His History, like the only other two ancient histories of Alexander still extant – that contained in the relevant parts of the immense universal history of

Diodorus, written just before the beginning of the Christian era, and the account by the Latin historian Curtius, written in the reign of Claudius – is, by the necessity of things, derivative; but he had good sources and made, so far as we can judge, good use of them. Happily for posterity, he had to draw upon a number of memoirs written by men who themselves played an active part in Alexander's campaigns. Chief among these were Aristobulus and Ptolemy, the latter of whom became King of Egypt, when Alexander's empire was divided after his death. Onesicritus, Alexander's pilot, or shipmaster, also wrote his story, and so did the philosopher Callisthenes – though the work of that bold but tactless man was cut short by his execution for high treason. It is said to have been subsequently much enlarged and embellished by anecdotes, fabulous or otherwise, and to have become one of the most popular books of antiquity. Nobody, of course, can guarantee the fidelity of any of these contemporary memoirs; but it is fairly safe to say that a collation of them by as conscientious an historian as Arrian undoubtedly was, is likely to have produced a good solid groundwork of fact. He tells us himself at the opening of his history that wherever he finds the accounts of Aristobulus and Ptolemy, his two most trusted authorities, in agreement, he has assumed the truth of what they say. The two reasons which he appends to justify his confidence are not, perhaps, quite in accord with modern critical standards. They are: (i) that, as Alexander was dead when they wrote their memoirs, neither of them had anything to gain by falsifying the facts, and (ii) that Ptolemy was a king himself, and it is shameful for a king to tell lies.

In his admiration for his hero, Arrian is passionate and whole-hearted; at the same time, remembering, it may be, the teaching of his old master Epictetus, he is not afraid of censuring where he feels that censure is due. Like most of the serious authors of antiquity, he was very conscious of his moral responsibility to his readers; his morality is severe, with all the dignity and purity of the best Stoic doctrine, though he is always eager, when he can, as in the case of Alexander's tendency to excessive drinking, to find a reason which will excuse or justify a fault.

We cannot but be grateful for what Arrian has given us; at the same time we cannot but regret his omissions. He is obsessed with the military aspect of Alexander's story, and his book, though it contains much else, is primarily a record of successful fighting. Enough for him, or almost enough, is the spectacle of this extraordinary boy, who, at the age of twenty, finding himself King of Macedon with no money and a load of debts, surrounded at home by a pack of jealous and turbulent nobles and hemmed in by hostile tribes on the north and on the south by a Greece torn with faction and uncertain whether to submit or to fight for the shadow of its ancient liberties, first set his own house in order, got himself acknowledged as master and leader of all Greece, and then set out, with an army he could not afford to pay, to the conquest of the world. It is a dazzling story, enough in itself to make a book of fascinating interest. Arrian tells it methodically, competently, quietly, avoiding almost always the temptation to colour it up with those elements of the miraculous which legend, even in his day, had associated with Alexander's name. When his imagination is touched, he can paint a vivid scene; few readers of his book are likely to forget his description of the siege and capture of Tyre, that almost impregnable island stronghold, or his account of Alexander's quarrel at dinner with his friend Cleitus and its fatal issue – an account rendered so much more moving by his grave but humane judgement upon the guilty King. The death of Calanus, the Wise Man of India, on the funeral pyre; the fleet setting out for the passage down the Jhelum river, and its negotiation of the rapids (all Greeks, unlike most Englishmen, write accurately and well upon nautical matters), and its first startling encounter with the fierce tides of the Indus estuary; the beautiful story (surely true) of the helmetful of water brought to Alexander in the parched sands of the Gedrosian desert; the meeting in the tent with the mother and wife of Darius after the defeat of the Persian army at Issus; the death of Hephaestion and Alexander's grief: such tales and incidents, and many others like them, are memorable; all have life and actuality, and make one feel, for the moment at least, that Arrian might have been a first-rate writer of history, had not Herodotus and Thucydides written before him.

What we miss in Arrian's book is any real sense of Alexander's greatness, of the quality in him which sets him apart from other distinguished men of action. The great soldier, the great commander who won not the confidence only, but the adoration of his men by his contempt of danger and constant sharing of their worst hardships, who, like Caesar with his barrack-room jokes before a battle, spoke to them in their own idiom and as man to man; the irresistible conqueror, and adventurer into lands where Greek feet had never trod and into seas which Greek ships had never sailed: all this Arrian brings out to the full; but of Alexander's vision of the ultimate and controlling purpose of his career of conquest he has nothing to say. *Why* did this young man set out to conquer the world? We, too, no doubt, can answer this question only by inference, and even then only partially. But we are concerned to answer it; Arrian was not – the question does not seem to have occurred to him. Nevertheless we can find hints in Arrian's narrative, and the hints set us thinking. There is his account, for instance, of the banquet at Opis on the river Tigris. Nine thousand guests were invited, chosen from all the nations of the old Persian empire which Alexander had conquered. When the moment for the toast-drinking came, to what did Alexander drink? He drank to his vision of Persians and Macedonians sharing their imperial power like 'friends of one mind'. Arrian records the fact, but he makes no comment.

Alexander had many tutors when he was a boy, among them Aristotle, one of the acutest and most curious minds of the ancient world. What precisely Aristotle taught him we do not know, though Plutarch (whose sketch of Alexander is a valuable supplement to Arrian's narrative) tells us that Alexander was angry with his old master in later years for publishing his 'more secret, hard, and grave doctrine', which he had hitherto kept for his private pupils. One thing, however, we do know, and that is that in one branch of speculation, namely politics and statecraft, the elderly philosopher was a mere child compared with the young Alexander. Aristotle never moved from the accepted Greek notion of city-state politics; for him the city-state, the tiny unit of perhaps 20,000 citizens and as many slaves, was the only proper community for free and civilized men. For him, too, the only civilized men were the Greeks, while all other peoples in the world, gabbling an unintelligible lingo which appropriately conferred upon them the name of ba-ba-ba-barians, were fit only for slaves. He is said to have advised Alexander, after his career of conquest had begun, to use his native Macedonians and Greeks 'like a leader', but the conquered Persians 'like a master'. Alexander knew better. He ignored the stupid advice. He knew, as Aristotle never knew, or would never admit, that the day of small independent communities violently quarrelling among themselves or linked in unstable associations, was gone for ever. A new idea was to dawn upon the world, and Alexander was to embody it.

That idea has been called by historians the 'marriage of East and West'. It is as good a name as any. The point to remember is that Alexander broke down for the first time the old Greek assumption that the earth was peopled by two sorts of people only: Greeks – and the rest. He soon discovered, and rejoiced in the discovery, that the noblemen of Persia were not savages, but had an old and rich civilization from which the Greeks might learn much. India opened his eyes still further; he did not penetrate far into that fabulous country, but he found there one ruler, at any rate, who had all the attributes of a King. Conquest must come first, and conquest came; but Alexander kept the vision of a larger and richer unity which was to succeed it, many disparate but complementary parts contributing to a vast and varied whole. The parts were to contribute not only by cultural but by commercial means; for when Alexander had a new harbour, capable of accommodating 1,000 ships, constructed on the Euphrates at Babylon, and sent his admiral Nearchus to survey the ocean coast from the Indus to the Persian Gulf, his object can only have been to establish shorter and better trade routes between East and West, while many of the seventy new towns he is said to have founded were without doubt sited to serve as trade centres or clearing stations. His sense of geography was almost uncanny in an age without maps, and he was one of the great pioneers of exploration. Though a Macedonian, he was, in his passion to know, a Greek of the Greeks. His distress and anger when his troops refused to accompany him across the Ganges to the eastern shores of India were due to disappointed curiosity as much as to the knowledge that his military campaign was incomplete. India was *terra incognita* to the Greeks: was her further coast indeed the end of the world, and did the Stream of Ocean flow round it northward and westward, to unite at last with the ocean of the west? And was the Caspian Sea a gulf of that ocean? Alexander wanted to know, as he wanted to know all things. But his men had had enough and would go no further.

Arrian in his competent, workmanlike, and factual narrative gives us little or no sense of these deeper purposes and motives, which do, after all, constitute the greatness of Alexander. He tells us, for instance, of Alexander's increasing tendency, as his power and empire grew, to adopt oriental manners in dress, in luxury, in the vexed question of 'prostration' or obeisance, even in the fashion of punishments for treasonable offences; and this tendency he, like Alexander's own Macedonian troops, strongly deprecates, as if it were a mere unfortunate departure, due to human weakness under too great a load of success, from the simpler and severer manners of Greece. But it was undoubtedly much more than this, and here, as elsewhere, Alexander saw further than his contemporaries and successors, and it is surely fair to surmise that all this was part of a deliberate policy to blur the hard distinctions between East and West and to lead the conquered countries to feel that they were not mere subject races under an alien King. Possibly Alexander's assumption of a divine origin, after his mysterious visit to the shrine of Ammon at Kiwa in the Egyptian desert, was directed to a similar purpose. But that is guesswork. There was a queer, half mystical streak in Alexander, and it would be absurd for us to pretend to understand it. Genius works in hidden ways.

One world: an association of nations enriched by commerce, with facilities for intercommunication by land and sea, each member retaining its ancient learning and culture and at the same time (an essential, this, in the vision of a man who knew his Homer by heart and fancied that Achilles' blood ran in his veins) purified and enlightened by the clear flame of Greek thought, and all subject to a single King – it was a grand conception. The idea still exercises us, in one form or another, and it is still unrealized. We owe it to Alexander more than to any other single man.

*

A word may be added here about Alexander's army organization and Arrian's military terminology. To the very end of his life Alexander was making experimental changes and developments in army organization, and all the changes were in the direction of increased mobility, and away from the tactical supremacy of the phalanx of heavy infantry armed with pikes. His pitched battles he won (like Cromwell, as historians have already pointed out) by rapid flanking cavalry movements, keeping the heavy infantry in reserve; his sieges by breaching the enemy defences with siege artillery, followed by a rush of light infantry through the breach.

Arrian's terminology is not always clear. It is likely enough that, writing 400 years after the epoch he describes, he did not himself know the precise meaning in every case of the terms he found in his authorities. Such terms are liable, in any case, to shift their meaning as time passes and conditions change, and it is always difficult to recover it exactly for any given epoch. An English translator has to make do with approximate equivalents. Where the original is vague, a translator can hardly be precise; and, even where the original is clear, it is probably more convenient for an English reader to find the terms he is familiar with – brigade, company, battalion, and so on. But such terms are never more than approximate. One or two terms present a special problem to the translator: the chief of these is the Hetaeri – 'Companions', as the word literally means. These 'peers' or 'companions' were young Macedonian noblemen who, in Alexander's time, formed a permanent part of the King's household; they were brought up in the King's service, both as personal attendants upon him and also with a view to forming his household brigade of both horse and foot guards. They were the pick of his fighting force. All that is clear enough; but Arrian, unfortunately, appears to use the same word in other senses, sometimes to describe troops who were acquainted with one another because they came from the same part of the country, and sometimes in the direct and untechnical sense to describe someone who was a member of the King's inner circle of friends. A translator can only do his best in each particular case. Where the word means the picked troops of the household brigade, I have left it as it is – Hetaeri.

The reader will find frequent mention of the Longshields. These troops were the light infantry, the second most important unit after the Hetaeri. They carried the long, not the round, shield; hence their name. Some English historians of the period refer to them as the 'hypaspists', transliterating the Greek word; but the term suggests nothing to an English reader and is so ugly that I have called them Longshields, which is a fairly literal equivalent of the Greek.

The ubiquitous Agrianes were recruited from the mountains of Paeonia in southwestern Thrace. Very lightly armed, they were used to rough ground, and invaluable skirmishers.

The famous 'phalanx' needs a word of explanation. The actual word occurs frequently in the Greek text, but I have used it only occasionally in my translation. Phalanx, in English, suggests a body of troops massed solid. This in fact it sometimes was, but by no means always. The troops which composed the Macedonian phalanx were heavy armed infantry, their distinctive weapon being the pike, but, especially under Alexander, who, as I have said, was always experimenting for the purpose of giving his army greater and greater suppleness of movement, the actual formation of the phalanx was variable. It could be formed in line or in column, with varying depth to suit the circumstances. It could be packed close or strung out thin. Sometimes it was in wedge formation, to penetrate an enemy's front. This being so, to keep in an English rendering the term 'phalanx' for every occasion would be misleading.

THE LIFE OF
ALEXANDER THE GREAT

BOOK ONE

WHEREVER Ptolemy and Aristobulus in their histories of Alexander, the son of Philip, have given the same account, I have followed it on the assumption of its accuracy; where their facts differ, I have chosen what I feel to be the more probable and interesting. There are other accounts of Alexander's life – more of them, indeed, and more mutually conflicting than of any other historical character; it seems to me, however, that Ptolemy and Aristobulus are the most trustworthy writers on this subject, because the latter shared Alexander's campaigns, and the former – Ptolemy – in addition to this advantage, was himself a King, and it is more disgraceful for a King to tell lies than for anyone else. Moreover, Alexander was dead when these men wrote; so there was no sort of pressure upon either of them, and they could not profit from falsification of the facts. Certain statements by other writers upon Alexander may be taken to represent popular tradition: some of these, which are interesting in themselves and may well be true, I have included in my work.

If anyone should wonder why I should have wished to write this history when so many other men have done the same, I would ask him to reserve judgement until he has first read my predecessors' work and then made some acquaintance with my own.

Philip of Macedon died when Pythodemus was archon at Athens. He was succeeded by his son Alexander, then about twenty years of age. The story goes that Alexander, upon his succession to the throne, went into the Peloponnese, where he assembled all the Greeks in that part of the country and asked them for the command of the campaign against Persia, which they had previously granted to Philip. The only people to refuse his request were the Lacedaemonians, who declared that the tradition of their country forbade them to serve under a foreign commander. At Athens, too, there was a certain amount of trouble; but resistance collapsed the moment Alexander approached, and he was granted even greater authority than his father Philip before him. This settled, he returned to Macedonia and prepared for his Asian campaign.

The following spring he marched towards Thrace, having learned that the Triballi and Illyrians were up to mischief. The territories of these two peoples bordered upon Macedonia, and since his expedition would take him so far from home he did not think it wise to leave them in his rear, unless they were first thoroughly crushed. Starting from Amphipolis he entered the territory of what are known as the free Thracians, leaving Philippi and Mount Orbelus on his left; then, crossing the Nessus, he reached Mount Haemus, according to all accounts in ten days. Here, where the lower slopes of the mountain rise through a narrow defile, he was met by a large force of natives under arms and the free Thracians, who had occupied the high ground which he would have to pass, with every intention of stopping his advance. They had collected a number of carts, which they intended to use, if they were hard pressed, as a sort of defensive palisade, with the further idea of sending them crashing down upon the Macedonian phalanx as the men were climbing the steepest part of the slope; their hope was that the impact of the vehicles would cause damage to the enemy troops in proportion to the closeness of their order.

Alexander had now to consider how to cross the ridge with least loss, for cross it he must, as there was no way round. His orders were that those sections of the heavy infantry which had room enough were to break formation when the carts came tearing down the slope, and so let them through; any sections, on the other hand, which were caught in the narrow pass were to form in the closest possible order, such men as were able lying prone on the ground with shields locked together above their bodies, so as to give the heavy wagons, as they careered down the hill, a chance to bounce over the top of them without doing any harm. Alexander accordingly gave his orders, and the result was what he expected: those who had room left a space between their ranks, and as for the rest, the carts passed harmlessly over their locked shields. There were no casualties. The wagons had been the most serious cause of apprehension; so, when they proved ineffectual, the Macedonian troops plucked up their courage, raised a cheer, and charged. Alexander brought his archers across from the right wing to a more convenient position in front of the main body of his troops, and instructed them to meet with a volley any attack the Thracians might make; he himself took charge of the Longshield * division and

* So called from their equipment. They were the principal light infantry troops in the Macedonian army. (Translator's note.)

the foot guards, together with the Agrianes, and moved across to the left, where the archers checked the Thracian attacks, and the infantry battalions, moving up to close quarters, had no difficulty in dislodging the inadequately armed and equipped enemy. Indeed, even before the troops under Alexander on the left wing came into contact with them, they flung down their arms and fled in a *sauve-qui-peut* down the mountainside. Some 1,500 were killed, but only a few captured; for most of them were too quick, and knew the country too well, to fall into their enemies' hands. The women, however, who had followed the fighting men were all taken, together with the children and all the gear and stores.

The captured material was sent back to the coastal towns, with orders to Lysanias and Philotas to dispose of it, and Alexander crossed the ridge. He then proceeded across the Haemus range to the Triballians, and arrived at the river Lyginus, three days' march, on this route, from the Danube. His movements had been known for some time to Syrmus, the King of the Triballians, who had taken steps accordingly, sending the women and children on to the Danube with orders to cross over to an island in the river called the Pine Tree. The neighbouring Thracians had also taken refuge on this island upon Alexander's approach, together with Syrmus himself and his personal entourage, though the majority of the Triballians hurriedly retreated to the river from which Alexander had started the previous day.

The moment the news of the Triballians' move reached him, Alexander set off to engage them. He turned in his tracks, retraced his steps, and found them already occupied in pitching camp. The tribesmen, caught napping, prepared to fight in the shelter of the wood by the river, and Alexander, forming his infantry in column, advanced against them, with orders to the archers and slingers to proceed in front at the double and discharge their missiles, in the hope of drawing the enemy from the shelter of the wood into open ground. The tribesmen, once they felt the effect of the missiles, came surging forward to get to grips with the lightly armed Macedonian archers, whereupon Alexander, having succeeded in drawing them out of cover, ordered Philotas to attack their right wing, which was well ahead of the rest of them, with the cavalry from upper Macedonia. At the same time he instructed Heraclides and Sopolis to advance against the enemies' left with the cavalry from Bottiaea and Amphipolis. The main body of infantry, preceded by the rest of his cavalry, he led against the enemy centre.

The Triballians held their own while the fighting was at long range; but once they had felt the weight and drive of the Macedonian infantry in close order, and the cavalry, instead of shooting at them, had begun actually to ride them down in a fierce assault all over the field, they broke and ran, in an endeavour to make their escape through the wood to the river. Three thousand were killed. Only a few were taken alive, because the wood along the river-bank was very thick, and there was not enough daylight left for the Macedonians to finish the job properly. According to Ptolemy, the Macedonian losses were eleven men from the cavalry and about forty from the infantry.

Three days after the battle Alexander reached the Danube. This river is the largest in Europe; it drains a greater tract of country than any other, and forms the frontier to the territories of some very war-like tribes. Most of them are of Celtic stock – indeed, the source of the river is in Celtic territory – the most remote being the Quadi and the Marcomanni; then, flowing east, it passes through the country of the Iazyges, a branch of the Sauromatae, of the Getae ('the immortals'), of the Sauromatae themselves, and finally of the Scythians, where it reaches the end of its course and debouches through five mouths into the Black Sea. On the river Alexander found warships awaiting him: they had come up across the Black Sea from Byzantium. He manned them with heavy infantry and archers, and, sailing for the island to which the Triballians and Thracians had fled for refuge, attempted to force a landing. Circumstances, however, were against him: the ships met with resistance at every point where they tried to run ashore; they were few in number and not strongly manned; in most places the island shore was too steep for a landing, and the current, sweeping past it through the narrows, was strong and very awkward to deal with. Alexander accordingly withdrew the ships, and determined in-stead to cross the river and attack the Getae who lived on the further side. A large force of them – some 4,000 cavalry and more than 10,000 on foot – was already assembled on the river-bank, evidently prepared to resist a crossing, and the sight of them was one reason for his change of plan. Another was the fact that the idea of landing on the further side of the Danube suddenly seemed attractive. He joined the fleet in person, having left instructions for the tents under which the men bivouacked to be filled with hay, and for all available dug-outs to be collected. There were a great many of these boats in the neighbourhood, for they are used by the natives for fishing, and for visiting neighbouring tribes up the river, and – fairly generally – for plundering expeditions. As many as possible of them were collected, and the troops, or as large a part of them as was practicable with this sort of transport, were ferried across. Actually, the number which crossed with Alexander was about 1,500 cavalry and 4,000 infantrymen.

The crossing took place at night, and the landing on the river-bank was more or less concealed by a tract of land in which the grain stood high. Just before dawn Alexander moved forward through the grainfield, having given orders that the infantrymen should lead the way to the open ground, clear of crops, beyond, carrying their spears parallel with the ground and obliquely to their line of march, to flatten the grain as they advanced. The mounted troops followed the infantry through the cornfield, but once they were out in clear ground Alexander took charge of them and led them over to the right wing, at the same time ordering Nicanor to proceed with the infantry in close formation on an extended front.

The very first cavalry charge was too much for the Getae; the crossing of the Danube, greatest of rivers, so easily accomplished by Alexander in a single night, without even a bridge, was an act of daring which had shaken them profoundly; and added to this there was the violence of the attack itself, and the fearful sight of the phalanx advancing upon them in a solid mass. They turned and fled to their town, which was about four miles from the river; but as soon as they saw that Alexander, with his mounted troops ahead, was pressing on along the river-bank to avoid ambush or encirclement, they abandoned the town, which had few defences, and, taking with them as many women and children as their horses could carry, continued their flight into uninhabited country, as far from the river as they could go. Alexander took the town, together with anything of value which the Getae had left behind. This material was removed to the base by Meleager and Philip, after which the town was razed to the ground, and Alexander offered sacrifice on the banks of the Danube to Zeus the Saviour and Heracles, not omitting the River himself, for allowing the passage. The same day he led his whole force to camp, safe and sound.

At this point Alexander was visited by envoys from Syrmus, the King of the Triballians, and from the various other independent tribes along the Danube. The Celts from the Ionian Gulf also sent representatives – men of haughty demeanour and tall in proportion. All professed a desire for Alexander's friendship, and mutual pledges were given and received. Alexander asked the Celtic envoys what they were most afraid of in this world, hoping that the power of his own name had got as far as their country, or even further, and that they would answer, 'You, my lord.' However, he was disappointed; for the Celts, who lived a long way off in country not easy to penetrate, and could see that Alexander's expedition was directed elsewhere, replied that their worst fear was that the sky might fall on their heads. None the less, he concluded an alliance of friendship with them and sent them home, merely remarking under his breath that the Celts thought too much of themselves.

He then made for the territory of the Agrianes and Paeones, where a message reached him that Cleitus, the son of Bardylis, was in revolt, and had been joined by Glaucias, the prince of the Taulantians, and, further, that the Autariates intended to attack him on the march. For these reasons Alexander thought fit to get on the move without delay.

Langaros, King of the Agrianes, who had made no secret of his respect for Alexander even in Philip's lifetime, had already been on an embassy to him in person, and on the present occasion attended him with his bodyguard, the finest and best-equipped troops he possessed. Hearing that Alexander wanted to know who the Autariates were and what their strength was, he advised him to think no more about them, as they were the least warlike tribe in that part of the country. He offered to keep them occupied by invading their territory himself, and, with Alexander's consent, actually did so, causing severe losses. For these services Langaros received from Alexander every mark of honour, including such presents as are considered in the Macedonian court to be of the highest value. Alexander also promised that if Langaros visited him at Pella, he would give him his sister Cyna in marriage. Langaros, however, after his return home, fell ill and died.

Alexander now proceeded along the river Erigon on his way to Pelium, a town which had been occupied by Cleitus as the most defensible in the district. Arriving there, he halted by the river Eordaicus with the intention of making his assault the following day. The town

was ringed with commanding heights, thickly wooded, which were
held by Cleitus' troops, who were thus enabled, in the event of an
assault, to attack the Macedonian forces from every side. Glaucias, the
King of the Taulantians, had not yet come upon the scene. Alexander, however, lost no time, and the enemy, on his approach to the
town, having sacrificed three boys, three girls, and three black rams,
made a movement as if with the intention of engaging the Macedonians at close quarters; but no sooner had the latter come within striking distance than they abandoned their defensive positions, strong
though they were. The bodies of the victims they had sacrificed were
found still lying where they fell.

Alexander now shut them up in the town, and taking up a position
close to the walls, proposed to establish a blockade; but on the following day Glaucias appeared with a large force. As a result of this Alexander abandoned his project of taking the town; for his own force
was comparatively small, many fine fighting men had withdrawn
within the walls, and many more, under Glaucias' command, would
be ready to attack him should he make an attempt upon the defences.
Accordingly he dispatched Philotas on a foraging expedition with the
baggage animals and a small squadron of mounted troops to act as
guard. The movement did not escape Glaucias; he went forward to
the attack, and seized the high ground which ringed the stretch of
country where Philotas and his men intended to collect their forage.
The danger which threatened both the mounted troops and the pack-
animals should they be overtaken by darkness was reported to Alexander, who at once marched to their rescue with a force composed of
the Agrianes, the archers, and the Longshields, and a squadron of
cavalry 400 strong. His remaining troops he left near the town; for had
he withdrawn his entire force the enemy who were shut up within it
might well have broken out and joined Glaucias. Glaucias, however,
abandoned his position on the high ground as soon as he saw Alexander coming, and Philotas' party returned to camp in safety.

Nevertheless it still seemed that the forces under Glaucias and Cleitus had caught Alexander in an awkward position. They held the
commanding heights strongly, both with mounted troops and with
other detachments armed with javelins and slings, in addition to a
considerable force of heavy infantry; those at present confined within
the town were all ready to attack the moment Alexander withdrew;

and the country through which the withdrawal would have to be
made was in the nature of a narrow wooded pass, with the river on
one side and a lofty range with precipitous foothills on the other, so
that it would hardly be practicable for his army to get through even
four abreast. Such being the situation, Alexander drew up the main
body of his infantry in mass formation 120 deep, posting on either
wing 200 cavalrymen with instructions to make no noise, an order
they implicitly obeyed. Then he gave the order for the heavy infantry
first to erect their spears, and afterwards, at the word of command, to
lower the massed points as for attack, swinging them, again at the
word of command, now to the right, now to the left. The whole
phalanx he then moved smartly forward, and, wheeling it this way
and that, caused it to execute various intricate movements. Having
thus put his troops with great rapidity through a number of different
formations, he ordered his left to form a wedge and advanced to the
attack.

The enemy, already shaken by the smartness and discipline of these
manœuvres, abandoned their position on the lower slopes of the hills
without waiting for the Macedonians to come to grips with them.
Thereupon Alexander called on his men to raise the war-cry and clash
their spears upon their shields, with the result that the din was altogether too much for the Taulantians, who hastily withdrew to the
town.

A small party of enemy troops were still in possession of a hill by
which Alexander would have to pass; he gave orders, accordingly, to
the Hetaeri and the men of his personal guard to prepare for action
and ride to the attack. Their instructions were that if the enemy who
had occupied the hill should hold their ground, half their number
should dismount and fight on foot in close support of their mounted
comrades. The hill, however, was not held; the enemy, as a result of
this movement of Alexander's, abandoned it and went off at a tangent
towards the mountains. Alexander with the Hetaeri then occupied the
hill, sent for the Agrianes and archers – a force of some 2,000 men –
and ordered the Longshields to cross the river, followed by the other
Macedonian units, and, on reaching the further side, to form up towards the left in order to present a solid front to the enemy immediately they were across the river. Meanwhile he kept a careful watch
from the hill upon any movement the enemy might make.

Seeing the Macedonian troops crossing the river, the natives moved down from the high ground with the intention of falling upon Alexander's party which would form the rear of the army as it withdrew; and Alexander countered by a rapid sally of his own, while the main body of his infantry, coming to the attack through the river, raised the war-cry. The enemy, under the combined onslaught, broke and fled, and Alexander ordered the Agrianes and archers to advance at the double to the river. He himself was the first across, and, setting up his artillery on the river-bank, he gave orders for every sort of missile it would take to be discharged at long range against the enemy, whom he could see pressing hard upon those of his own troops who were bringing up the rear. The archers, too, who were already part-way over, were ordered to shoot from mid-stream. Glaucias' men refused to venture within range, and the Macedonians got across safely, without a single casualty during the process of withdrawal.

Three days later information came in that the troops under Cleitus and Glaucias were encamped without adequate precautions: no regular sentries had been posted, and no palisade or trench constructed for their protection; their line, moreover, was perilously extended. Alexander at once took advantage of this carelessness – which was due, presumably, to the assumption that he had retreated in panic. Under cover of darkness he took the Longshields, the Agrianes, the archers, and the troops of Perdiccas and Coenus back across the river, with orders to the rest of the army to follow. The moment was ripe for attack; so, without waiting for the entire force to concentrate, he sent into action the Agrianes and the archers, who made a surprise assault on a narrow front – a formation likely to fall with greatest effect upon the enemy at his weakest point. Some they killed in their beds, others they took without difficulty as they tried to escape. Many were caught and killed on the spot, many more as they fled in panic and disorder. Not a few were captured alive. The pursuit was pressed as far as the mountains in Taulantian territory. None escaped except at the cost of throwing away their weapons. Cleitus' first move was to the town; later he set fire to it and made his way to the Taulantians, where he sought refuge with Glaucias.

Meanwhile events were taking place in Thebes. Certain persons, with a view to overthrowing the government, had invited a number of political exiles to return; these men, having slipped into the city during the night, had seized and murdered Amyntas and Timolaus, two of the men who were holding the Cadmeia and had no suspicion of any danger outside. They then presented themselves in the Assembly and incited the Thebans to rebel against Alexander, making great play with the grand old words 'liberty' and 'free speech', and urging them at long last to throw off the burden of the Macedonian yoke. They made their appeal more attractive to the Thebans in general by insisting that Alexander had died in Illyria—which was, as it happened, a common rumour at the time and fairly widely disseminated, because he had been long absent without communicating with them. In these circumstances they did what most of us do, and, being ignorant of the truth, persuaded themselves into believing what they wished to believe.

The news of these events caused Alexander considerable concern. For a long time past he had had doubts about Athens, and now had come this attempt from Thebes. He could not but take it seriously, for the danger clearly was that the spirit of disaffection might spread to the Lacedaemonians, who already, in any case, silently resented Macedonian control, and to other states in the Peloponnese, and even to the Aetolians, who were by no means to be trusted. He therefore decided to act, and, proceeding by way of Eordaea and Elimiotis and the mountain ranges of Stymphaea and Paravaea, arrived within seven days at Pelinna in Thessaly. Six days later he entered Boeotia, and the news that he had passed the Gates did not reach the Thebans until his whole force was at Onchestus. Even then the organizers of the revolt continued to maintain that Alexander was dead: an army of Antipater's, they declared, had arrived from Macedonia, and anyone who reported that Alexander himself was in command they met with an angry denial – if it was Alexander at all, they insisted, it was another Alexander, Aeropus' son.

The following day Alexander left Onchestus and marched to Thebes. He halted by the enclosure of Iolaus, waiting there in order to give the Thebans time to think things over, in case they should change their minds and decide to treat with him. Nothing, however, was further from their thoughts than coming to terms or yielding a single inch; on the contrary, their mounted troops and a considerable force of light infantry made a rapid sortie and attacked the outposts of the Macedonian army with missile weapons at long range, and not altogether without effect. Alexander ordered out parties of light infantry and archers to check them, which they did without difficulty, though they had already advanced almost within striking distance of his main position. Next day he moved round with his entire force to the gates which lead to Eleutherae and Attica. Here, still refraining from an assault upon the city's defences, he took up a position not far from the Cadmeia, to provide support for the Macedonians who were holding it. The Thebans had ringed it with a double palisade and were watching it closely, so that no outside help could reach the besieged garrison, or any sudden attack from within interfere with their own operations against their enemies elsewhere. Alexander, however, made no move, but continued to wait; for he still hoped to remain on terms with the Thebans and to avoid action against them.

In these circumstances all who had their city's interest most at heart were anxious to approach Alexander and gain from him a general pardon for the revolt; but the exiles and the party responsible for their recall, especially as some of them were officers of the Boeotian Confederacy, refused to recognize the possibility of humane treatment by Alexander, and urged war by every means in their power. But still Alexander waited and did not attack.

Ptolemy, the son of Lagus, states in his account of these operations that Perdiccas, who, as officer in charge of the guard, was posted with his own detachment not far from the enemies' palisade, began the assault on his own initiative and without waiting for the word of command from Alexander. Forcing a breach in the palisade, he burst in upon the Theban advanced troops, followed by Amyntas, the son of Andromenes, who with his own troops, which formed a part of the same contingent, moved forward immediately he saw that Perdiccas had got inside. It was to prevent them from being cut off and being placed at the mercy of the Thebans that Alexander ordered a general advance, sending his archers and the Agrianes through the breach in the palisade, but still keeping the Longshields and the main body of his infantry outside.

Perdiccas was wounded while he was trying to break through the second palisade; he was carried back to the base, but the wound was serious and it was only with difficulty that his life was saved. His men, joined by Alexander's archers, boxed the Thebans up in the sunken road which runs down by the Heracleum, pressing on them hard so

long as they retreated towards that temple; but the moment came
when they turned to face their pursuers with a yell of rage, and then
it was the Macedonians who gave ground. About seventy of the
archers were killed, together with their commander, Eurybotas the
Cretan; the rest hurriedly sought the protection of the King's Guards
and the main body of the Macedonian army.

The sight of his men in full retreat, with the Thebans straggled out
in chase of them, soon brought a counter-blow from Alexander, who
launched an infantry attack in close order, and drove the enemy inside
the city gates. The rout became a panic – so much so, indeed, that they
failed to shut the gates behind them in time. The result was that the
men of the Macedonian army closest on their heels passed with them,
in the general scramble, inside the fortifications, which the need for so
many advanced posts had left undefended. One party, joining up with
the garrison of the Cadmeia, passed thence by way of the Ampheum
into the actual town, while the troops by the walls, which were already held by the men who had got in during the rout, swarmed over
the top and made at the double for the market square.

For a short time the Theban armed forces stood firm by the Ampheum, until, attacked from every side by the Macedonians, with
Alexander himself apparently ubiquitous in the field, they broke
Their mounted troops, forcing a way through the streets, fled to the
open country, and the infantry endeavoured to save their skins as best
they could. In what followed it was not so much the Macedonians as
the Phocians, Plataeans, and men from other Boeotian towns who, in
the lust of battle, indiscriminately slaughtered the Thebans, who no
longer put up any organized resistance. They burst into houses and
killed the occupants; others they cut down as they attempted to show
fight; others, again, even as they clung to temple altars, sparing
neither women nor children.

The violence of the action, the size and importance of the fallen
city, above all, perhaps, the unexpectedness of the event both to vic-
tors and vanquished, all made the horror of this disaster to men of
Grecian blood hardly less shattering for the rest of Greece, than for
those who were actually involved. The Sicilian expedition, measured
merely by the number of dead, brought a comparable disaster to
Athens; but that, it must be remembered, took place far from home:
the army which perished was not a native army, but consisted largely

of troops from allied states; Athens herself remained untouched, still able to hold out for a number of years against Persia and the Lacedaemonian confederacy; and for all these reasons her defeat in Sicily did not bring to Athens the same sense of overwhelming calamity, or to the rest of Greece a comparable thrill of horror. Again, the collapse at Aegospotami was at sea, and though Athens by that defeat suffered humiliation in the destruction of her Long Walls, the surrender of the greater part of her navy, and the loss of her sovereignty, she nevertheless retained her former shape and quickly recovered her former strength; indeed, the Long Walls were rebuilt, her sea-power was regained, and she was actually able subsequently to reverse the position and save from great danger those very Lacedaemonians who had once been so formidable and had come so near to destroying her. The Lacedaemonians themselves, after the defeat at Leuctra and Mantinea, were shaken rather by the unexpectedness of the disaster than by the magnitude of their losses; and it was the strangeness of the sight when the Boeotians and Arcadians under Epaminondas launched their attack upon Sparta, much more than the immediacy of the danger, that struck terror into them and their allies. Again, the capture of Plataea cannot be considered a major disaster; for the town was a small one, and, as most of its people had already fled to Athens for refuge, very few were taken when it fell; and, lastly, the capture of Melos and Scione was hardly more important: they were merely island communities, and their destruction, though a disgrace to its perpetrators, could scarcely be called a severe shock to Greece as a whole.

With Thebes, on the contrary, it was a different matter: the lack of planning, the rapid movement of events which led to the revolt, the suddenness and ease with which the city fell, the slaughter, so appalling and so inevitable where men of kindred stock are paying off old scores, the complete enslavement of a city pre-eminent in Greece for power and military prestige, were, not unnaturally, all put down to the wrath of God. People felt that Thebes, at long last, had been punished for her treachery – she had paid the penalty for her betrayal of Greece in the Persian war, her capture of Plataea during the truce, the merciless enslavement of its population, and the massacre, for which she alone was responsible, of men who had surrendered not to her, but to Sparta, and the devastation of a countryside in which the united armies of Greece had driven back the Persian invader, and, lastly, for the murderous malignancy she showed towards Athens when she voted in favour of the suggestion, put forward by the Lacedaemonian confederacy, that the people of Athens should be sold into slavery. Everyone now declared that the calamity had been preceded by many warning signs from heaven – signs ignored at the moment, but remembered now, long afterwards, and clearly proved by the event to have been prophetic of the coming doom.

The allied troops who took part in the fighting were entrusted by Alexander with the final settlement of the fate of Thebes. They decided to garrison the Cadmeia, but to raze the city itself to the ground. All its territory but the places hallowed by religious associations was to be divided among the allies; the women, the children, and all the men who survived were to be sold into slavery – the only exceptions being priests or priestesses and such as had either personal ties with Alexander or Philip or official connexions with Macedon. It is generally believed that Alexander's reverence for Pindar induced him to spare the poet's house and all his living descendants. In addition to this, the allies determined to rebuild and fortify Orchomenus and Plataea.

When the news of the Theban *débâcle* became generally known, the Arcadians who had started out in order to assist in the rising condemned to death those of their compatriots who had urged them to do so; the Eleans granted a pardon to their political exiles, simply because they were on good terms with Alexander; the various branches of the Aetolians all sent representatives to beg forgiveness on the ground that they had supported the revolt only because of the news from Thebes. In Athens the arrival of Theban refugees straight from the fighting coincided with the celebration of the Great Mysteries; the shock of the news induced the Athenians to cut short the ceremony and begin at once to get all movable property into the city from the surrounding country. The Assembly was convened, and on the motion of Demades ten men, all known to be on friendly terms with Alexander, were sent to him to represent the city's attitude and to assure him, somewhat unseasonably, that the Athenian people rejoiced to see him safely returned from Illyria and the Triballians, and thoroughly approved his punishment of the Thebans for their revolt. Alexander's reply to these representations was in general friendly enough; he did, however, demand, in a letter to the Athenians, the surrender of the supporters of Demosthenes and Lycurgus, and, in addition, of Hypereides, Polyeuctus, Chares, Charidemus, Ephialtes, Diotimus, and Moerocles, all of whom he held responsible for the defeat at Chaeronea and for certain errors in policy, detrimental to Philip's interest and his own, subsequently committed upon Philip's death. He declared moreover that these men were as responsible for the rebellion as were the Thebans themselves, who had actually carried it out. The Athenians, instead of giving the men up, sent again to Alexander and begged him to relent – which he did, perhaps out of regard for Athens, perhaps simply because he was in a hurry to proceed with his Asian campaign and unwilling to leave behind him in Greece any cause for mistrust. He did, however, give orders that one of the men whose surrender he had unsuccessfully demanded – Charidemus – should be exiled. The sentence was carried out, and Charidemus took refuge in Asia at the court of Darius.

Alexander now went north again to Macedonia, and offered to Olympian Zeus the form of ceremonial thanksgiving which had been in use since the time of Archelaus. He also celebrated the Olympian games at Aegae, and, according to some accounts, held games in honour of the Muses. During the ceremonies a report came from Pieria that the statue of Orpheus, son of Oeagrus of Thrace, had been constantly sweating, a phenomenon which was variously interpreted by the seers; one of them, however – Aristander of Telmissae – told Alexander that he had no cause for alarm: it merely signified that the writers of odes and the epic and melic poets had hard work coming to celebrate Alexander and his exploits in verse and song.

At the start of the next campaigning season Alexander left Antipater in charge of affairs in Macedonia and Greece, and made for the Hellespont with a force composed of not much more than 30,000 infantry, together with light troops and archers, and over 5,000 cavalry. His route lay past lake Cercinitis, in the direction of Amphipolis and the mouth of the Strymon, which he crossed, and proceeded by way of Mount Pangeon towards Abdera and Maroneia, two Greek settlements on the coast; continuing from there to the Hebrus, which he also crossed without difficulty, he marched through Paetica and across the river Melas to Sestus, which he reached twenty days after leaving home. At Elaeum he offered sacrifice upon the tomb of Protesilaus, who was supposed to have been the first man of Agamemnon's army to set foot upon the soil of Asia when the Greeks sailed against Troy. His purpose in performing the ceremony was to ensure better luck for himself than Protesilaus had.

The task of getting the mounted troops and most of the infantry across the Hellespont from Sestus to Abydos was entrusted to Parmenio, and the crossing was carried out in 160 triremes and a large number of merchant vessels. It is generally believed that Alexander sailed from Elaeum to the Achaean harbour, himself at the helm of the admiral's ship, and that half way over he slaughtered a bull as an offering to Poseidon and poured wine from a golden cup into the sea to propitiate the Nereïds. There is a further tradition that, fully armed, he was the first to leave the ship and set foot upon the soil of Asia, and that he built an altar on the spot where he left the shore of Europe and another where he landed on the other side of the strait, both of them dedicated to Zeus, the Lord of safe landings, Athena, and Heracles. Once ashore, he travelled inland to Troy and offered sacrifice to Athena, patron goddess of the city; here he made a gift of his armour to the temple, and took in exchange, from where they hung on the temple walls, some weapons which were still preserved from the Trojan war. These are supposed to have been carried before him by his bodyguard when he went into battle. He is also said to have offered sacrifice to Priam on the altar of Zeus Herceius, to avert his anger against the family of Neoptolemus, whose blood still ran in his own veins.

At Troy his sailing-master, Menoetius, crowned him with gold, as did Chares the Athenian, who came from Sigeium with a number of others, either Greeks or natives. One account says that Hephaestion laid a wreath on the tomb of Patroclus; another that Alexander laid one on the tomb of Achilles, calling him a lucky man, in that he had Homer to proclaim his deeds and preserve his memory. And well might Alexander envy Achilles this piece of good fortune; for in his own case there was no equivalent: his one failure, the single break, as it were, in the long chain of his successes, was that he had no worthy chronicler to tell the world of his exploits.

No prose history, no epic poem was written about him; he was not celebrated even in such choral odes as preserve the name and memory of Hiero or Gelo or Thero, or many other men not in the same class as Alexander, with the result that the wonderful story of his life is less familiar today than that of the merest nonentities of the ancient world. Even the march of the Ten Thousand under Cyrus against Artaxerxes, the fate of Clearchus and his fellow prisoners, and the return under Xenophon's command to the sea, are, thanks to Xenophon's history, much better known than the grand achievements of Alexander; yet, unlike Xenophon, Alexander did not hold a mere subordinate command; he was not defeated by the Persian King, or victorious only over the force which tried to stop his march to the sea. On the contrary, there has never been another man in all the world, of Greek or any other blood, who by his own hand succeeded in so many brilliant enterprises. And that is the reason why I have embarked upon the project of writing this history, in the belief that I am not unworthy to set clear before men's eyes the story of Alexander's life. No matter who I am that make this claim. I need not declare my name – though it is by no means unheard of in the world; I need not specify my country and family, or any official position I may have held. Rather let me say this: that this book of mine is, and has been from my youth, more precious than country and kin and public advancement – indeed, for me it *is* these things. And that is why I venture to enter the company of the great masters of Greek literature, as Alexander, of whom I write, was the great master of the profession of arms.

From Troy, Alexander marched to Arisbe, where his entire force had taken up its position after crossing the Hellespont; next day he proceeded to Percote, and the day after passed Lampsacus and halted by the river Practius, which has its source in Mount Ida and flows into the sea which connects the Black Sea with the Hellespont. From there his route led past Colonae to Hermotus. On the march he had scouts ahead of the army, under the command of Amyntas, son of Arrabaeus, with the squadron of native mounted troops from Apollonia under Socrates, son of Sathon, and four squadrons of what were known as Pathfinders. The town of Priapus, which lay on his route, surrendered to him, and he sent a party under Panegorus, son of Lycagorus, one of the Guards, to take it over.

The Persian forces were commanded by Arsames, Rheomithras, Petines, and Niphates in association with Spithridates, the satrap of Lydia and Ionia, and Arsites, the governor of northern Phrygia. They had taken up a position near the town of Zelcia with the Persian cavalry and the Greek mercenary troops. On receiving the report that

Alexander had crossed into Asia, they met to discuss the situation. Memnon of Rhodes advised against risking an engagement: the Macedonian infantry, he pointed out, was greatly superior in numbers; Alexander was present in person, while Darius was not. It would be better, therefore, to proceed at once to burn all growing crops, trample down and destroy grass and horse-feed, and even gut the towns, to prevent Alexander, by lack of supplies, from remaining in the country. Arsites, however, is said to have replied to this proposal that he would not consent to the destruction by fire of a single house belonging to any of his men. The other commanders supported him – no doubt because they had their suspicions of Memnon, and guessed that he was afraid of losing the position he held from Darius, if fighting started too soon.

Alexander meanwhile was advancing in battle order upon the river Granicus. His infantry was massed in two groups, both wings protected by cavalry, while all transport had orders to follow in the rear. The reconnaissance parties were under the command of Hegelochus, with the lancers and about 500 light troops. Just short of the river the scouts galloped back to report that the Persian army had taken battle positions on the further bank, whereupon Alexander gave all necessary orders in preparation for an engagement. Parmenio, however, was opposed to this; presenting himself before Alexander, 'My lord,' he said, 'in my view our best plan in the present situation is to halt here, on this side of the river. The enemy infantry is heavily outnumbered by ours, and I do not think they will run the risk of remaining so close to us throughout the night; so if they withdraw, we can get across at dawn without opposition – indeed, we shall be over before they have a chance of getting into position to meet us. But to attempt the crossing in the present circumstances would, I think, be a grave risk. We cannot manage the crossing in line on a broad front, because in many places the river is obviously deep, the banks very high and, here and there, almost sheer. We should have to cross, therefore, in column, and in loose order at that, with the result that their massed cavalry will be upon us just as we are struggling out of the water and at the greatest possible disadvantage. A failure at the outset would be a serious thing now, and highly detrimental to our success in the long run.'

Alexander had his answer: 'Yes, Parmenio,' he said; 'but I should

be ashamed of myself if a little trickle of water like this' (a very dero-
gatory way of referring to the Granicus!) 'were too much for us to
cross without further preparation, when I had no difficulty whatever
in crossing the Hellespont. Such hesitancy would be unworthy of the
fighting fame of our people and of my own promptitude in the face
of danger. Without doubt it would give the Persians added confidence; nothing has yet happened to them to cause them alarm, and
they would begin to think they were as good soldiers as we are.'

Without further delay he sent Parmenio to take command of the
left wing, and himself moved over to the right. Command of the
right had already been given to Philotas, Parmenio's son, with the
mounted troops of the Hetaeri, the archers, and the Agriane spearmen; Amyntas, son of Arrabaeus, was attached to him with the lancers, the Paeonians, and Socrates' squadron. On the left of these divisions were the infantry of the Hetaeri, commanded by Parmenio's
son, Nicanor; next came the infantry divisions of Perdiccas, son of
Orontes, of Coenus, son of Polemocrates, of Craterus, son of Alexander, of Amyntas, son of Andromenes, in that order: finally the troops
under Amyntas' son, Philip. The advance position of the left wing
was held by the Thessalian cavalry under Calas, son of Harpalus, and
these were supported – in the following order – by the allied cavalry
under Philip, son of Menelaus, and the Thracians under Agathon.
Immediately on their right was infantry – the divisions of Craterus,
Meleager, and Philip, extending to the centre of the army as a whole.

The Persians had about 20,000 cavalry and nearly the same number
of foreign mercenaries fighting on foot. Back from the river the
ground rose steeply, and they had taken up a position with their
mounted troops along the bank on a very broad front and with the infantry in the rear. At one point on the river-bank they had massed
their squadrons in strength – for here it was that, threatening their
left, they could see Alexander himself, an unmistakable figure in
magnificent armour, attended by his suite with an almost ecstatic
reverence.

There was a profound hush as both armies stood for a while motion-
less on the brink of the river, as if in awe of what was to come. Then
Alexander, while the Persians still waited for the crossing to begin,
that they might fall upon his men as they were struggling up the
further bank, leapt upon his horse and called upon his bodyguard to

follow and to play the man. His orders were that Amyntas, son of
Arrabaeus, should lead off into the water with the mounted skirmishers, the Paeonians, and one infantry company, preceded by
Ptolemy, son of Philip, with Socrates' squadron, which was the leading cavalry squadron for that day; then he himself, at the head of the
right wing of the army, with trumpets blaring and the shout going up
to the God of Battle, moved forward into the river. He kept his line
oblique to the pull of the current as the troops went over, to prevent a
flank attack as they emerged from the water, and to enable him to
engage the enemy with a front as solid as he could make it.

The leading files under Amyntas and Socrates were met as they
gained the river bank by volleys of missiles from the Persians, who
kept up a continuous fire into the river both from their commanding
position on the high ground above, and also from the comparatively
flat strip right down by the water's edge. A hand-to-hand struggle
developed, the Greek mounted troops trying to force their way out
of the water, the Persians doing their utmost to prevent them. Persian lances flew thick and fast, the long Macedonian spears thrust and
stabbed. In this first onslaught Alexander's men, heavily outnumbered, suffered severely; their foothold was insecure, and down there
in the water they had to contend with an enemy in a strong position
on the bank above them – not to mention the fact that they met there
the fine flower of the Persian horse, with Memnon and his sons brav-
ing the fortune of battle in its midst.

The first to engage the Persians were cut down and died a soldier's
death, though some of the leading troops fell back upon Alexander,
who was now on his way across: indeed, he was almost over, at the
head of the army's right wing. A moment later he was in the thick of
it, charging at the head of his men straight for the spot where the Persian commanders stood and the serried ranks of enemy horse were
thickest. Round him a violent struggle developed, while all the time,
company by company, the Macedonians were making their way over
the river, more easily now than before. It was a cavalry battle with, as
it were, infantry tactics: horse against horse, man against man, locked
together, the Greeks did their utmost to thrust the enemy once for all
back from the river-bank and force him into open ground, while the
Persians fought to prevent the landings or hurl their opponents back
into the water.

Things soon turned in favour of Alexander's men; their experience and the weight of their attack began to tell, added to the advantage of the long cornel-wood spear over the light lances of the Persians.

During the fight Alexander's spear was broken. He called on Aretis, one of his grooms, for another, but Aretis was himself in difficulties for the same reason, though still fighting gallantly enough with the remaining half of his weapon. Showing it to Alexander, he called out to him to ask someone else, and Demaratus the Corinthian, one of Alexander's personal bodyguard, gave him his spear. The fresh weapon in his hand, he caught sight of Mithridates, Darius' son-in-law, riding with a squadron of horse in wedge formation far ahead of the main body; instantly he galloped out in front of his men, struck Mithridates in the face with his spear, and hurled him to the ground. Rhoesaces then rode at Alexander with his scimitar and, aiming a blow at his head, sliced off part of his helmet, which nevertheless dulled the full force of the impact. A moment later Alexander was on him, and he fell with a spear-thrust through his cuirass into his breast. Now Spithridates had his scimitar raised, ready for a blow at Alexander from behind; but Cleitus, son of Dropides, was too quick for him, and severed his shoulder with a single stroke. Meanwhile Alexander's party was being steadily reinforced by the mounted troops as one after another they succeeded in getting up out of the river and joining him.

The Persians were now in a bad way: there was no escape for horse or rider from the thrust of the Macedonian spears; they were being forced back from their position and, in addition to the weight of the main attack, they were suffering considerable damage from the lightly armed troops who had forced their way in among the cavalry. They began to break just at the point where Alexander in person was bearing the brunt of things.

Once the centre had failed to hold, both wings of the Persian cavalry broke too, and the rout was complete. About 1,000 were killed – not more, because Alexander soon checked the pursuit of them in order to turn his attention to the foreign mercenaries, who had remained in their original position, shoulder to shoulder – not, indeed, from any deliberate intention of proving their courage, but simply because the suddenness of the disaster had deprived them of their wits. Ordering a combined assault by infantry and cavalry, Alexander quickly had them surrounded and butchered to a man, though one or two may have escaped notice among the heaps of dead. About 2,000 were taken prisoner. Among the killed were the Persian commanders Niphates, Petines, and Spithridates, satrap of Lydia; Mithrobuzanes, governor of Cappadocia; Mithridates, son-in-law of Darius; Arbupales, son of Darius and grandson of Artaxerxes; Pharnaces, brother of Darius' wife, and Omares, commander of the foreign contingent. Arsites escaped to Phrygia, where he is said to have died by his own hand, because the Persians held him responsible for the defeat.

The Macedonian losses were small: about twenty-five of the Hetaeri were killed during the first assault. Their statues in bronze now stand at Dium, executed, on Alexander's instructions, by Lysippus, who was chosen from a number of competitors to make a statue of Alexander as well. Rather more than sixty of the other mounted troops were killed, and about thirty infantrymen. By order of Alexander all the dead were buried with their arms and equipment on the day after the battle, and their parents and children were granted immunity from local taxes and all forms either of personal service or dues payable on property. For the wounded he showed deep concern; he visited them all and examined their wounds, asking each man how and in what circumstances his wound was received, and allowing him to tell his story and exaggerate as much as he pleased. He also gave rites of burial to the Persian commanders and the Greek mercenaries who fell fighting in the enemies' ranks; the Greek prisoners he sent in chains to hard labour in Macedonia, as a punishment for the outrage they had committed against Greek sentiment by fighting in a foreign army against their own countrymen. As an offering to the goddess Athena, he sent to Athens 300 full suits of Persian armour, with the following inscription: *Alexander, son of Philip, and the Greeks* (*except the Lacedaemonians*) *dedicate these spoils, taken from the Persians who dwell in Asia.*

Alexander appointed Calas to the satrapy previously held by Arsites, with orders to maintain the taxes at the same level as before; all natives who came out of hiding in the hills and surrendered he allowed to return to their homes; to the people of Zeleia he gave a free pardon, because he knew that they had fought with the Persians only under pressure. He sent Parmenio to take over Dascylium; and this was done without trouble, as the guards had abandoned the town.

His next objective was Sardis. He was still some eight or nine miles away when he was met by Mithrines, the officer in command of the inner fortress; with him were the leading men of the town, who had come to surrender it to Alexander, while Mithrines did the same for the fortress and the treasure. Alexander halted on the Hermus, a river about two and a half miles from Sardis, and sent on Amyntas, son of Andromenes, to take over the fortress; Mithrines he kept with his own suite, treating him in a way suitable to his rank, while the people of Sardis and the other Lydians he permitted to observe the old customs of their country and gave them their freedom.

While he was in Sardis he went up into the acropolis, where the Persian garrison was stationed, and saw at a glance that this fortress, built as it was on a lofty and precipitous hill and defended by a triple wall, was an extremely strong position.

It occurred to him to build here a temple and altar in honour of Olympian Zeus, and while he was considering the best site a summer storm, breaking suddenly with violent thunder and a fall of rain over the palace of the Lydian kings, persuaded him that Zeus himself had indicated the spot where his temple should be raised; so he gave his orders accordingly.

He left Pausanias, one of the Hetaeri, in charge of the fortress, and made Nicias responsible for the collection of taxes and tribute; the governorship of Lydia and the other territory formerly controlled by Spithridates was given to Asander, son of Philotas, with an adequate force of light infantry and mounted troops. Calas and Alexander, son of Aeropus, were sent to Memnon's part of the country with the Peloponnesians and most of the other allied troops, with the exception of the Argives, who were left in Sardis to garrison the fortress.

Meanwhile, news of the cavalry engagement had reached Ephesus. The mercenaries who formed the garrison of the town seized two warships and made their escape, accompanied by Amyntas, son of Antiochus, who had left Macedonia in order to avoid Alexander. He had not, to be sure, anything to complain of in Alexander's treatment; he merely disliked him and was disinclined to be made uncomfortable by his presence.

Alexander took three days to reach Ephesus; on his arrival he recalled everyone who had been expelled for supporting him, stripped the small governing clique of its power, and restored democratic institutions. All dues previously paid to Persia he transferred to the temple of Artemis. The people of the town, freed from the fear of their political masters, promptly murdered the men who had been responsible for calling in Memnon, and everybody else who had either ransacked the Temple, or helped to smash up the statue of Philip which stood there, or break open in the public square the tomb of Heropythes, the liberator. They dragged from the temple and stoned to death Syrphax and his son Pelagon and all his nephews. Alexander, however, who was well aware that the Ephesian populace, given the chance of continuing the hunt for guilty men and indulging its lust for revenge, would, out of personal hatred or greed, kill many who were innocent as well, firmly called a halt, with the result that his popularity never stood higher than it did on this occasion by his handling of the situation at Ephesus.

During the same period representatives came from the towns of Magnesia and Tralles to offer their submission; he accordingly dispatched Parmenio with a force consisting of 2,500 allied foot, 2,500 Macedonians, and about 200 mounted men of the Hetaeri, giving instructions for a similar force under Alcimachus, son of Agathocles, to proceed to the Aeolian towns and all the Ionian ones still subject to Persia. Throughout the country he dispossessed the ruling cliques and established popular government in their place, allowing every community to enjoy its own laws and customs and to continue to pay taxes on the same scale as it had previously paid to the Persians. Meanwhile he remained in Ephesus, offered sacrifice to Artemis, and held a ceremonial parade of his troops, fully equipped and in battle order.

On the following day he marched for Miletus with a force made up of all the infantry not otherwise engaged, the archers, the Agrianes, the Thracian cavalry, the Royal Squadron of the Hetaeri, and three other squadrons. What is known as the Outer City fell into his hands without a blow, as the garrison had withdrawn, whereupon he called a halt and proposed to establish a blockade of the inner defences, where Hegisistratus, who had been entrusted by Darius with the defence of the town, was still hoping to hold out. This officer had, some time before, written to Alexander to offer submission, but the proximity of the Persian fleet had subsequently encouraged him to make an effort to save the city for his masters. Nicanor, however, was too

quick for him; he brought the Greek fleet to Miletus three days ahead
of the Persians, and anchored, with 160 ships, at Lade, the island just
off the town. The Persians had missed their opportunity; and the
commanders, as soon as they found that Nicanor's fleet had put in at
Lade before their arrival, brought their own ships to anchor under
Mount Mycale. Alexander had, indeed, already made sure of Lade
not only by anchoring his fleet there: he had also put ashore on the
island his Thracian contingent and some 4,000 other mercenary
troops.

The Persians had about 400 ships, but Parmenio, in spite of their
numerical superiority, urged Alexander to engage. He did, undoubtedly, believe that a sea-fight would go in favour of the Greeks,
but the real reason for his confidence was a sign from heaven – an
eagle which had been seen on the beach just astern of Alexander's
ships. He pointed out that a victory in present circumstances would
be of great strategic advantage, while a defeat would not be very
serious, as Persia in any case had command of the sea. He was fully
prepared, he said, to go aboard himself and share the perils of the day.
Alexander replied that Parmenio was mistaken, and that he had
wrongly interpreted the omen. In the first place, it was absurd to rush
blindly into a naval engagement against greatly superior forces, and
with an untrained fleet against the highly trained Cyprian and Phoenician crews; the sea, moreover, was a tricky thing – one could not
trust it, and he was not going to risk making a present to the Persians
of all the skill and courage of his men; as to defeat, it would be very
serious indeed and would affect profoundly the general attitude to the
war in its early stages, above all by encouraging the Greeks to revolt
the moment they got news of a Persian success at sea. Secondly, having given his reasons for not risking an engagement, he went on to
say that his interpretation of the omen was different from Parmenio's:
the appearance of the eagle was, without doubt, a favourable sign;
but the fact that it had been seen on shore surely indicated that it was
his army, not his navy, which would render the Persian fleet power-
less – he would, as it were, win his sea battle from the land.

At this juncture a distinguished Milesian named Glaucippus appeared before Alexander with a proposal from the people of the town
and the foreign mercenaries who were chiefly responsible for guarding it in the Persian interest: this was that they were willing to grant

free use of their harbours, and free entry within their walls, to Alexander and the Persians alike, and that on these terms the siege should be raised. Alexander's reply to this suggestion was to order Glaucippus to get back to his friends at the double and tell them to be ready to defend themselves at dawn next morning. He then proceeded to order up his siege engines; the walls were bombarded at close range, long stretches of the fortifications breached with battering-rams; he then brought his men up, to be ready to get a foothold at any point where the defences were sufficiently gapped or weakened to allow an entry, while the Persians at Mycale were so near that the progress of operations against their friends was almost visible to their eyes.

When Nicanor's men in Lade saw that Alexander's assault had begun, they got their ships under way and, rowing along shore, made for the harbour at Miletus, where they brought up in the narrowest part of the entrance, each vessel close aboard its neighbour, so that the harbour was effectively closed to the Persian fleet and the Milesians could no longer hope for assistance from that quarter. The Milesians and the mercenary troops in the town were already hard pressed by Alexander's attack; and now, at this fresh development, some of them plunged into the sea and paddled themselves over on their upturned shields to an islet (it has no name) just off the town, while others made a desperate effort to escape in boats before the Macedonian warships arrived; but they were too late and were caught at the harbour entrance. Most of them, however, were killed within the walls.

The town was now in Alexander's hands, and his next move was to turn his attention to the men who had escaped to the little island. Its shore was steep, and landing on it would be much like scaling a wall; so to facilitate the operation he had scaling-ladders fixed in the bows of his ships – when, however, he saw that the fugitives were preparing to fight to the death, he was moved to pity by their courage and loyalty and refrained from action on condition of their serving in future under his own command. They were Greek mercenaries, about 300 in number. All the Milesians who had not been killed when the town was taken he let go free.

The Persians continued for a while to use Mycale as a base for annoying the Greek fleet at Miletus. Every day they made a movement towards it in the hope of provoking a conflict; at night they remained in their station, which was not, however, a comfortable one, because they were obliged to water their ships from the Maeander, which was a long way off. Alexander, still keeping his fleet on guard in the harbour, to prevent the Persians from forcing an entrance, sent Philotas round by land to Mycale with the mounted troops and three companies of infantry, with orders to stop the Persians getting ashore. The result was that lack of water and other supplies reduced the Persian crews to what was, to all intents and purposes, a state of siege; so they sailed for Samos, filled up there with whatever they needed, and returned to Miletus. Off the harbour they took up battle stations with the main body of their fleet, hoping to lure the Macedonians out into deep water, while five of their ships carried on into the sheltered water between Lade and the Macedonian position on shore. There was a chance, they thought, of surprising Alexander's ships with no one aboard, because they had been told that most of the crews had gone off on various jobs, such as collecting firewood or foraging or fetching supplies. Some of the men were actually away, but there were enough left on duty for Alexander, when he saw the five enemy vessels approaching, to man ten of his own and send them out on the instant with orders to ram. The five Persians found the hostile approach of the Greek ships by no means according to plan; at first sight of them, still some way off, they put about and hurried back to rejoin the fleet. One of them, manned by Iassians, was a slow ship and failed to get away; she and her crew were taken, but the other four kept ahead of the pursuers and safely rejoined the fleet. As a result of this episode the Persian fleet left Miletus, with nothing to show for the time it had spent there.

Alexander now decided to disband his fleet. He had not, at the moment, the money for maintaining it; he knew that it was no match for the Persian navy, and he had no wish to subject any part of his strength, in ships or men, to the risk of disaster. Moreover, now that his army was master of the continent, he was well aware that a fleet was no longer of any use to him: by seizing the coastal towns he could reduce the Persian navy to impotence, for they would then have no port on the Asian coast which they could use, and no source of replacement for their crews. Here, then, was the point of his interpretation of the omen of the eagle – it meant that he would 'conquer the ships from the land'.

Having settled affairs at Miletus, he started for Caria on a report that the Persians were in Halicarnassus with a considerable force of native and mercenary troops. The towns which lay upon his route surrendered without resistance, but on arriving at Halicarnassus he took up a position rather more than half a mile from the town in expectation of a long siege; for apart from the natural strength of the place, due to its geographical situation, any deficiencies in the means of assuring its safety had long before been supplied in person by Memnon, who had already been appointed by Darius controller of lower Asia and commander of the fleet; a powerful force of Persian troops and mercenaries had been left to garrison the town, and the presence of warships in the harbour meant that the sailors, too, could lend a helping hand, should the need for action arise.

On the first day Alexander moved up towards the fortifications on the side of the town which faces Mylasa. As he approached the gates the defenders made a sortie and flung weapons at long range. A counter-attack by Alexander's men checked them without difficulty, and they were driven back within the walls. A few days later, with a force consisting of the Longshields division, the mounted troops of the Hetaeri, and the infantry commanded by Amyntas, Perdiccas, and Meleager, supported by the Agrianes and archers, Alexander moved round to the part of the town which faces Myndus, his intention being to reconnoitre the state of the defences in that sector in the hope of finding that they offered an easier approach. There was also, he thought, a chance that by an unexpected raid he might take Myndus, the possession of which would greatly facilitate the siege of Halicarnassus. The plan was all the more attractive because some people in Myndus had suggested that they might open their gates to him if he came under cover of darkness. He accordingly took them at their word and approached the town about midnight. There was, however, no sign of surrender. Alexander, who had expected the place to be betrayed into his hands, was not prepared for a siege: he had brought with him neither rams, nor artillery, nor ladders; nevertheless, ill-equipped as he was, he ordered the Macedonian infantry to advance and begin sapping operations. They destroyed one fort, but its fall did not leave the wall defenceless; the troops in the town put up a vigorous resistance and, with the help of strong reinforcements which arrived by sea from Halicarnassus, successfully frustrated the surprise attack. Alexander accordingly, forced to withdraw with his object unaccomplished, turned his attention once more to the siege of Halicarnassus.

To enable him to bring into position his siege-engines – the towers from which to bombard the defenders of the wall, the artillery and battering-rams for breaching the defences – Alexander began by filling in the trench, about 45 feet wide and 23 feet deep, which had been dug outside the town. The work was done without difficulty and the towers soon brought into position. After dark a party of Halicarnassians made an attempt to set fire to the Macedonian siege artillery, including the towers, which were either already in position or about to be brought up; but the Macedonians on guard duty, with the help of others who were awakened by the noise during the action and joined them, had little trouble in driving them back within the town's defences. They lost 170 men, including Neoptolemus, who, among others, had deserted to Darius. He was the son of Arrabaeus and brother of Amyntas. Alexander's losses were about 16 killed and 300 wounded – the comparatively large number of wounded being due to the fact that the attack took place in the dark, when it is more difficult to defend oneself.

A few days after this incident two Macedonian infantrymen of Perdiccas' battalion were drinking together in their tent and telling each other what stout fellows they were; as they warmed up with the drink, each bragging as hard as he could go, it soon developed into a competition between the pair of them, until at last they seized their weapons and, without any serious intention of risking their lives in a fight, but simply to prove to each other what mighty fellows they were, sallied out on their own to attack the wall of the town on the high ground facing Mylasa. Some soldiers in the town saw the foolish pair coming and promptly went for them; both were killed close outside the fortifications, and the party who had come out to the attack then proceeded to harass with missiles at long range the Macedonian lines farther to the rear. This they were emboldened to do by their local superiority in numbers and the fact that the lie of the land was greatly to their advantage and they could both shoot and move forward to the assault from high ground. More men from Perdiccas' battalion soon came hurrying to meet this threat, and, on the other side, reinforcements from the town. There was a sharp struggle, until once again the Macedonians succeeded in driving the attacking force back within their gates. Indeed, the town itself was very nearly taken; the walls, at the moment, were inadequately defended, and the collapse of two towers together with the intervening stretch of wall would have offered an easy entrance, had the assault been made in strength. Moreover a third tower had been badly damaged and might easily have been brought down by mining; but before anything could be done, the men in the town made good the breach in their defences by building, from inside, a crescent-shaped wall of brick – and many hands made light work of it.

On the following day Alexander brought up his siege artillery to attack it, and his move was promptly countered by a party from the town. Their object was to set fire to his assault machines, and they succeeded in burning a part of the screen near the walls and of one of the wooden towers, though everything else was saved by the men under Philotas and Hellanicus, who were on guard there. During the raid Alexander appeared upon the scene in person, and the result was that the raiding party dropped their firebrands – most of them throwing away their weapons as well – and beat a hurried retreat into the town.

In spite of this set-back, in the first phases of the ensuing struggle the defenders had the advantage: their position, on the higher ground, was a commanding one; the troops forming a screen in front of Alexander's assault machines could be met by volleys of missiles not only in the direct line of their advance, but also from the flanks, where they could be enfiladed from the towers still standing on both sides of the breach in the original wall; indeed, as they approached the newly built section, they could be shot at practically from the rear as well.

A few days passed before Alexander renewed his assault on the new brick wall inside the town. This time he took personal charge of the operation. His move was met by a counter-attack in full force from the town, by one division at the breach in the wall, where Alexander was, and by another at the Tripylum, or Triple Gate, where the Macedonians least expected it. Flaming brands and other inflammable material were flung at the assault machines to set them alight and spread the blaze; but the men under Alexander's immediate command made a strong counter-attack; the catapults mounted on towers kept up a continuous pressure by hurling heavy stones; javelins flew thick and fast, and the defenders of the town were without difficulty beaten back and forced to withdraw once more within their defences. The attempt had been a bold one, carried out with a considerable force, and their losses were, in proportion, heavy: some were killed in hand-to-hand fighting with the Macedonians, others among the debris of the breached wall: they could not get through because the gap was too narrow for such a press of men, and they could not get over because the fallen blocks of stone were an almost insuperable impediment.

The force which had made its sortie at the Tripylum was met by Ptolemy, Captain of the Royal Guard, with the troops under Addaeus and Tinander, supported by light infantry. These had no greater trouble than the others in repelling the attack from the town. Like that of their comrades, the retreat of this force, too, was disastrous: for as they withdrew across a narrow bridge over the dyke, the bridge collapsed under the excessive weight. Many were flung into the dyke and were either trampled to death or shot from above by the Macedonians. But the worst slaughter was at the gates of the town, which were shut too soon in blind fear of letting in the Macedonians on the heels of the fugitives; in this way the defenders shut out large numbers of their friends, who were cut down by the Macedonians right under the walls. Once again the town was almost in Alexander's hands; but even in this extremity he wished to save it, if only the people gave any sign of willingness to come to terms. So he called off the assault.

In this action Halicarnassus lost about 1,000 men, Alexander about forty, among whom were Ptolemy, Captain of the Royal Guard, Clearchus, in command of the archers, Addaeus, a chiliarch – or battalion commander – and other well-known Macedonians.

The Persian commanders Orontobates and Memnon now met to discuss the situation. It was clear that in present circumstances it would not be possible to hold out much longer; part of the wall was already gone, other parts were seriously damaged, and in the recent sorties they had lost heavily, many men having been either killed or put out of action by wounds. Accordingly, somewhere near midnight they had the magazines set on fire together with the wooden tower which had been constructed as a counter to the enemy assault machines. The houses near the wall were also fired, while flames from the fiercely burning tower and magazines were spread by the wind to other buildings, which were soon ablaze as well. Their own surviving forces withdrew to the Arconnese, an island stronghold, and the high ground known as Salmakis.

These events were reported to Alexander by some Halicarnassians who had deserted after the fighting; accordingly, as the fire was still spreading before his eyes, he ordered up his Macedonian divisions, in spite of the fact that it was nearly midnight, with instructions to kill every man they could catch in the act of setting fire to buildings. Any of the townspeople found indoors were, on the contrary, to be rescued from the conflagration.

Daylight revealed the occupation by the Persians and their mercenaries of Salmakis and the Arconnese. Alexander, however, decided not to lay siege to these strongholds, because in addition to the fact that they would be awkward to take and much time would be wasted, he knew that, with the town itself already in his hands, they would not bring him any great advantage. So he buried the men killed in the night's fighting, ordered the troops in charge of the assault engines to move them to Tralles, and then razed the town to the ground. To garrison the place, together with the rest of Caria, he left a force of 3,000 infantry – mercenaries – and about 200 mounted troops under their commander Ptolemy. Then he made his preparations to move on into Phrygia.

He appointed Hecatomnos' daughter Ada to the governorship of Caria as a whole. This woman was the wife of Hidrieus – and also his sister, a relationship in accordance with Carian custom; Hidrieus on his death-bed had bequeathed her his power, government by women having been a familiar thing in Asia from the time of Semiramis onward. She was subsequently deposed by Pixodarus, who seized power, and was succeeded after his death by his son-in-law Orontobates, who had been appointed to the position by a warrant from the King. Ada meanwhile remained in control of Alinda only, one of the most strongly defended places in Caria, and when Alexander invaded Caria she presented herself before him, surrendered the town, and offered to adopt him as her son. Alexander did not refuse the offer. He restored Alinda to her, and when, with the fall of Halicarnassus, he found himself master of Caria, he put the whole country under her control.

A number of the Macedonians serving in the campaign had been married just before the expedition started; feeling that some con-

sideration was due to these men, Alexander dismissed them from
Caria and sent them home to spend the winter with their wives; they
were put in charge of Ptolemy, son of Seleucus, an officer of the Royal
Guard, and of two other officers of high rank: Coenus son of Polemocrates, and Meleager son of Neoptolemus – both chosen because they,
too, were newly married men. The officers' instructions were to raise
levies of both horse and foot on as large a scale as possible on their rejoining the army with the party in their charge. No act of Alexander's ever made him better beloved by his native troops.

At the same time he sent Cleander, son of Polemocrates, to raise
troops in the Peloponnese, while Parmenio was dispatched to Sardis
with a force consisting of a squadron of the Hetaeri, the Thessalian
cavalry, the other allied contingents, and the baggage wagons. His
orders were to proceed from Sardis to Phrygia. Alexander himself
marched for Lycia and Pamphylia, to establish control of the coast and
so immobilize the enemy's fleet. On the way the first place he took
was the fortified town of Hyparna; it was held by a mercenary garrison, but on the offer of a truce they abandoned the citadel and
marched out to surrender. There was no battle. On entering Lycia he
took over Telmissa, the people agreeing not to resist him, after which
he crossed the Xanthus and accepted the surrender of Pinara, Xanthus,
Patara, and about thirty smaller places.

It was now midwinter, and Alexander's next move was into what
is known as Milya – which actually belongs to greater Phrygia, but
was reckoned at that period, by order of the Persian King, as part of
Lycia. Here he was met by representatives from Phaselis, bringing him
a gold crown and offers of friendship, and similar offers also reached
him from the greater part of lower Lycia. Alexander in reply instructed the envoys from Phaselis, as well as those from Lycia, to surrender their towns to the proper authorities, which was duly done in
every case. Soon afterwards he went in person to Phaselis and helped
the people of the town to reduce a fortress which the Pisidians had
built nearby as a base from which to annoy them – and annoy them
they did, men at work on the land often suffering severely from their
raids.

Before he had finished with Phaselis, a report reached him of the intended treachery of Alexander, son of Aeropus. This man was one of
the Hetaeri, in close contact with the King, and also, at the time, in

command of the Thessalian cavalry; he was also a brother of Hero-
menes and Arrabaeus, both of whom had been involved in the murder
of Philip. On the occasion of his father's murder, Alexander, in spite
of the fact that the evidence against his namesake looked black, did
not prosecute the charge, because he had been among the first to support him on Philip's death, accompanying him into the palace, armed
like his master; subsequently Alexander had given him an honourable
position in his personal suite, sent him to direct operations in Thrace,
and finally appointed him to the command of the Thessalian cavalry
in place of Calas, who had been transferred to a provincial governorship.

The plot was revealed to Alexander in the following way. Amyntas, who had deserted to the Persians, brought Darius certain written
proposals from this fellow Alexandros (as I shall now call him). Thereupon Darius sent down to the coast a trusted member of his suite
named Sisines, ostensibly on a visit to Atizyes, the satrap of Phrygia,
but in reality to get into contact with Alexandros and promise him the
throne of Macedonia and 1,000 talents of gold if he succeeded in assas-
sinating the King. Sisines, however, fell into Parmenio's hands, revealed the purpose of his mission, and was sent on under guard to
Alexander, to whom he repeated his story. Alexander called a meeting
of his friends to discuss the situation, and the members of the Hetaeri
most closely in his confidence expressed the opinion that it was a mistake in the first place to have put an untrustworthy officer in command of the best cavalry regiments, and that he should now be
summarily disposed of, before he became hand in glove with the Thessalians and plotted rebellion. Moreover, an ominous event had added
to their anxiety; for it so happened that while Alexander, during the
siege of Halicarnassus, was taking his siesta, a swallow flew round and
round over his head twittering loudly in a way that seemed to express
unusual alarm, and kept settling on various parts of his bed.

Alexander was too tired to wake up properly, but the noise the bird
made disturbed him, so with his hand he tried to shoo it gently away,
but without success; for, far from being scared off by the touch of
Alexander's hand, it came and perched on his head, and refused to
budge until he was fully awake.

Convinced that the incident was not without significance, Alexander reported it to the soothsayer Aristander of Telmissus, who de-

clared that it portended a friend's treachery; and, in addition, that the plot would be revealed, for swallows are domestic birds, friendly to man and exceedingly talkative.

This clearly corroborated Sisines' story; so Alexander sent Alexandros' son Amphoterus (he was brother to Craterus) to Parmenio, accompanied by some natives of Perga to act as guides. To avoid recognition on the journey, Amphoterus wore native dress, and succeeded in reaching Parmenio without detection; he had no written instructions, for Alexander felt that in an affair of this sort it would be dangerous to commit anything to writing – he merely delivered a verbal message, as directed. In this way Alexandros was arrested and put into custody.

Alexander now left Phaselis. Part of his forces he dispatched over the mountains towards Perga, along tracks made for him by the Thracians to facilitate what was otherwise a long and difficult journey. He himself marched with his picked troops along the coast, a route which is practicable only in northerly winds – during southerlies the beach is impassable. It had been blowing hard from the south before he started; but (by the grace of God, as both he and his staff felt) the wind went round into the north and made the passage quick and easy. Advancing from Perga he was met by plenipotentiaries from Aspendus, who offered to surrender the town, but begged, at the same time, that no garrison should be put in. As to the garrison, they got what they asked for; but Alexander demanded that the town should contribute fifty talents towards the men's pay and hand over all the horses bred there as tribute to Darius. Both demands were agreed to, and the envoys returned home.

The next objective was Side, a town whose people came originally from Cyme in Aeolia. There is a tradition among them that when the first settlers from Cyme sailed thither and landed from their ships to found a new home, they promptly forgot their native Greek and began to talk in a foreign tongue – not the language spoken by the people of those parts, but an entirely new dialect of their own; and from then on the men of Side had remained foreigners, distinct in speech, as in everything else, from their neighbours.

Alexander left a party of men to occupy Side and then proceeded to Syllium, a fortified town garrisoned by mercenaries and native troops. He was unable, however, to take this place by assault, without regular siege operations, and this fact, combined with a report which he had received during his march, determined him to return to Aspendus. The report stated that the people of Aspendus had backed out of their agreement; they were refusing to hand over the horses to the proper authorities and to pay the money; moreover, they had taken their movable property inside the town's defences, shut their gates against Alexander's men, and were at work upon all necessary repairs to their walls.

The main part of the town of Aspendus is built upon a very steep and easily defended hill, the base of which is washed by the river Eurymedon. There were also a number of houses on the level ground round this central stronghold, all of them enclosed within a wall of no great height. This wall, together with all houses on the flat ground which seemed impossible to hold, was abandoned by the people of the place the moment they were aware of Alexander's approach. They hurriedly withdrew and took refuge within the fortified centre on the hill. Alexander, as soon as he reached the town, led his men inside the outer wall – now defenceless – and took up his quarters in the deserted houses.

The shock of Alexander's presence and the sight of his army surrounding them were too much for the people of the town: they sent their spokesmen to him and begged to be allowed their original terms. Alexander, however, in spite of the fact that the position of Aspendus was obviously a strong one and he was not himself prepared for a protracted siege, refused the request; he demanded, in addition to the horses they had previously agreed to hand over, 100 talents instead of the original fifty and the surrender as hostages of the leading men of the community; further, they were forced to obey the governor appointed by himself, to pay an annual tribute to Macedon, and submit to an inquiry into the rightful ownership of the land, which they were accused of holding by force, when it was really the property of their neighbours.

When this was settled to his satisfaction, Alexander moved on to Perga, and thence, by a route which led past Telmissus, to Phrygia. The people of Telmissus are an Asiatic race of Pisidian blood; the town stands on a lofty and precipitous height, and the road which leads past it is an inconvenient one, because a ridge runs right down to it from the town above, breaking off short with the road at the bottom, while opposite to it, on the other side, the ground rises again in an equally steep ascent. The two cliffs make a sort of natural gateway on the road, so that quite a small force can, by holding the high ground, prevent an enemy from getting through. And this is precisely what the Telmissians did: they marched out with every available man and occupied the heights on either side of the road. Alexander, accordingly, gave the order to halt at once, convinced that when the enemy saw his men taking up a position for the night they would no longer hold the road in force but withdraw the majority of their troops into the town near by, leaving only a small party on the hills to keep a watch. His guess proved right: the main body retired, and only the outposts remained. Alexander then promptly moved to the attack with a force consisting of the archers, the javelin battalions, and the lighter infantry. The small force on the hills, unable to withstand the weight of his missiles, abandoned the position, and Alexander moved on through the narrow passage and took up a fresh position near the town.

It was at this juncture that representatives from the large town of Selga sought an interview with Alexander. The people of this place, too, are Pisidians – Asiatics – and are good soldiers. They were old enemies of Telmissus, and their object in sending to Alexander was to offer him their support. Alexander accepted the offer, and from that moment found them trustworthy in every respect.

Concluding that it would not be possible to reduce Telmissus without a long siege, he now proceeded to Sagalassus, another place of some size, belonging, like Telmissus, to people of Pisidian blood. The Pisidians are all fine soldiers, but the Sagalassians were conspicuous even among a nation of fighters. On this occasion they occupied the high ground in front of the town, a position no less good for defensive action than the wall itself, and there awaited the Macedonian assault. On the right wing of the attacking force Alexander had the Longshields division under his personal command. In touch with them were the foot-guards, forming the whole centre of the line and commanded by the various officers whose turn of duty happened to fall upon that day; command of the left he assigned to Amyntas, son of Arrabaeus. In advance of the right wing he stationed the archers and the Agrianes, while his left was screened by the Thracian javelin battalions under Sitalces. Cavalry was useless, as the nature of the ground

was unsuitable for it. The enemy were reinforced by troops from Telmissus who had come to offer assistance.

When Alexander's troops had reached the steepest part of the
ascent towards the Pisidians' position on the hill, they were attacked
on both wings by small parties of men, who took advantage of the
difficult ground to slip in where they best could and the enemy had
least chance to retaliate; in this they were partially successful, for the
archers who were leading the assault, and were, moreover, only
lightly protected, were forced to retreat. The Agrianes, however,
yielded nothing – encouraged, no doubt, by the fact that the Macedonian infantry divisions were already coming up, with Alexander in
full view at the head of them. A hand-to-hand struggle ensued; the
Pisidians, who had no defensive armour, found themselves matched
with fully equipped heavy infantry, with the result that they suffered
severe losses and finally broke. About 500 were killed; prisoners were
few, because their light equipment and knowledge of the country
made escape easy, while the Macedonians, for their part, with their
heavy gear and lack of local knowledge, were none too eager to pursue them. None the less Alexander hung on to the fugitives and
stormed the town. Cleander, who commanded the archers, was killed
during these operations, as were about twenty others.

Alexander then proceeded against the other Pisidian communities;
some of their fortified places he took by assault, others surrendered to
him without resistance.

His next move was into Phrygia. His route lay past lake Ascania –
a lake from which the people of the neighbourhood collect natural
salt, so that they have no need to depend on supplies from the sea.
Five days later he was at Celaenae.

The town of Celaenae has a lofty central stronghold, sheer all
round, and this was garrisoned by 1,000 Carian troops and 100 Greek
mercenaries, who took their orders from the Persian governor of
Phrygia. The garrison sent Alexander an offer to surrender the town
provided that no reinforcements arrived on a certain day on which
they had agreed to expect them – which date they specified; and it
seemed better to Alexander to accept this arrangement than to attempt the reduction by siege of such an unassailable position. Accordingly he left a force of some 1,500 men to watch the town, and after
a wait of ten days marched for Gordium. Before he left he appointed

Antigonus, son of Philip, to the governorship of Phrygia, promoting Balacrus, son of Amyntas, to the command of the allied contingents in his place. To Parmenio he sent orders to meet him at Gordium with the troops under his command – and the orders were duly carried out. The recently married Macedonians who had been sent home on leave also rejoined at Gordium with a force of freshly levied troops – 3,000 Macedonian infantry and about 300 horse, 200 Thessalian horse, and 150 men from Elis under their own commander Alcias. The whole force was commanded by Ptolemy son of Seleucus, Coenus son of Polemocrates, and Meleager son of Neoptolemus.

Gordium is in Hellespontine Phrygia; the town stands on the river Sangarius, which rises in Phrygia and runs through Bithynian Thrace into the Black Sea. During his stay there Alexander was visited by envoys from Athens with a request for the liberation of Athenian prisoners of war, who had been captured on the Granicus fighting for Persia and were at that time in Macedonia under close confinement, with the other 2,000 prisoners. But for the moment, at any rate, the request was not granted, and the envoys were forced to return with their mission unfulfilled. For Alexander felt that, with the war against Persia still on his hands, it would be dangerous to relax his severity towards anyone of Greek nationality who had consented to fight for Asia against his own country. Nevertheless he did tell the Athenian envoys that they might approach him again on the matter when circumstances were favourable.

BOOK TWO

AFTER the events just related the island of Chios was betrayed into the hands of Memnon, whom Darius had made supreme commander of the Persian navy and responsible for the defence of the Asiatic coast. The object of Memnon's move was the hope of diverting the war to Greece and Macedonia. He then sailed to Lesbos and made himself master of all the towns in the island except Mitylene, the inhabitants of which refused to treat with him. He accordingly made a landing at Mitylene and blockaded it with a double stockade carried right to the sea on both sides; in addition to this he constructed five blockhouses, and was thus enabled to control the island without difficulty. Part of his fleet guarded the harbour; other ships he sent to the promontory of Sigrium, the usual landing-place for merchantmen from Chios, Geraestus, and Malea, and was thus able to keep a watch on the coast and prevent any help from reaching Mitylene by sea.

Before his work was completed, however, he fell sick and died, and his death was the most serious setback which Persia received during this period of the war.

Memnon on his deathbed – and pending a further decision by Darius – had handed over his command to his nephew, Pharnabazus, Artabazus' son; and he and Autophradates vigorously prosecuted the siege. The people of Mitylene, finding themselves cut off on the landward side and blockaded by a powerful fleet, sent to Pharnabazus and agreed, first, to get rid of the mercenary troops sent to fight for them by Alexander; secondly, to rescind the pact they had made with him and enter into alliance with Darius according to the terms of the peace of Antalcidas, and, lastly, to allow their exiles to return and resume possession of half their original property. Such were the terms of the agreement; but Pharnabazus and Autophradates, once they had got inside the town, brought in a garrison under the command of Lycomedes of Rhodes and put one of the exiled party, named Diogenes, in general control with autocratic powers. At the same time they enforced the contribution of a sum of money, extorting a part of it from the wealthier men and raising the remainder by a general levy, after which Pharnabazus set sail for Lycia with the mercenary troops, while Autophradates proceeded to the other islands.

Meanwhile Darius sent Thymondas, son of Mentor, to fetch the mercenaries which were in Pharnabazus' charge and to order Pharnabazus himself formally to take over Memnon's command. The mercenaries were, accordingly, transferred to Thymondas, and Pharnabazus sailed to rejoin Autophradates and the fleet. On his arrival they first dispatched ten ships under a Persian named Datames to the Cyclades islands, and then sailed with a squadron a hundred strong for Tenedos, where they brought up in what is known as North Harbour. They then sent a demand to the islanders for the abrogation of their agreements with Alexander and the Greeks, and the observance of the terms of the Peace of Antalcidas, which they had concluded with Persia.

The people of Tenedos would have liked nothing better than to remain on good terms with Alexander and the Greeks; but in the circumstances they were forced to believe that their only hope of safety lay in accepting Persia's terms; even Hegelochus was a broken reed, for though he had had orders from Alexander once again to get a fleet together, he had not yet raised a sufficient force to give any prospect of speedy relief. One might say, therefore, that Tenedos was scared into surrender by Pharnabazus and his men, against the true wishes of the people.

About this time it so happened that Proteas, son of Andronicus, upon orders from Antipater, had assembled a number of warships from Euboea and the Peloponnese to afford protection to the Greek coast and the islands in the event of a Persian attack by sea, which report said was not unlikely. Information reached Proteas that Datames had brought up off Siphnos with a squadron of ten ships, so with fifteen of his own he sailed at night for Chalcis on the Euripus. It was dawn when he reached the island of Cythnus, and throughout the day he remained there at anchor in order to get more definite information about the ten enemy ships, and also to give himself the chance of attacking their Phoenician crews with more devastating effect during the hours of darkness. As soon as all doubt about Datames' presence at Siphnos was removed, he made sail just before dawn, while it was still dark, delivered a surprise attack, and captured eight of the ten ships, together with their crews. Right at the start of the encounter with Proteas' squadron Datamese slipped away with the remaining two vessels and succeeded in rejoining the rest of the fleet.

To return to Alexander at Gordium. Upon reaching this place he was irresistibly impelled to visit the palace of Gordius and his son Midas high up on the acropolis, in order to inspect the famous Wagon of Gordius and the Knot with which its yoke was fixed. There was a story about this wagon, widely believed in the neighbourhood. Gordius (so went the tale) lived in Phrygia in the ancient days; he was poor and had but two yoke of oxen and a small plot of land to till. With one pair of oxen he ploughed, with the other he drove his wagon. One day when he was ploughing an eagle perched on the yoke of his plough and stayed there until the oxen were loosed and the day's work done. Gordius was troubled, and went to the seers of Telmissus to consult them about what this sign from heaven might mean – for the people of Telmissus were skilled in interpreting God's mysteries, and their women and children as well as their men inherited the gift of divination. Near a village belonging to these people he fell in with a girl who was drawing water; he told her of the eagle, and she in reply, being herself sprung from a line of seers, advised him to return to the place where he had seen the sign and offer sacrifice to Zeus the King. Gordius urged her to go with him and show him the form the sacrifice should take, and he performed it as she directed, and afterwards married her, and they had a son whose name was Midas.

Now when Midas had grown to be a fine and handsome man there was trouble and strife among the Phrygians, and an oracle told them that a wagon would bring them a king, who would put an end to their quarrels. While they were still debating what to do about these things, Midas with his father and mother drove up in the wagon and came to a stop at their place of meeting. Taking this to be the fulfilment of the oracle, the Phrygians decided that here was the man whom the god had foretold that a wagon would bring. So they put Midas on the throne, and he made an end of their trouble and strife and laid up his father's wagon on the acropolis as a thank-offering to Zeus the King for sending the eagle.

There was also another traditional belief about the wagon: according to this, the man who undid the knot which fixed its yoke was destined to be the lord of Asia. The cord was made from the bark of the cornel tree, and so cunningly was the knot tied that no one could see where it began or where it ended. For Alexander, then, how to undo it was indeed a puzzle, though he was none the less unwilling to leave it as it was, as his failure might possibly lead to public disturbances. Accounts of what followed differ: some say that Alexander cut the knot with a stroke of his sword and exclaimed, 'I have undone it!', but Aristobulus thinks that he took out the pin – a sort of wooden peg which was driven right through the shaft of the wagon and held the knot together – and thus pulled the yoke away from the shaft. I do not myself presume to dogmatize on this subject. In any case, when he and his attendants left the place where the wagon stood, the general feeling was that the oracle about the untying of the knot had been fulfilled. Moreover, that very night there was lightning and thunder – a further sign from heaven; so Alexander, on the strength of all this, offered sacrifice the following day to the gods who had sent the sign from heaven and proclaimed the Loosing of the Knot.

Next day he started for Ancyra in Galatia, where he was met by a deputation of Paphlagonians, who expressed a wish to be on terms of friendship with him, offering the submission of their people, and begging him not to march his troops into their territory. Alexander in reply instructed them to take their orders from Calas, the governor of Phrygia, and then proceeded to Cappadocia, where he received the submission of all territory bounded by the river Halys and also of a large tract to the west and north beyond it. Then, leaving Sabictas as governor of Cappadocia, he advanced to the Cilician Gates. When he reached the position where Cyrus had once encamped in the campaign with Xenophon, he found the Gates strongly held; so he left Parmenio there with the heavy infantry, and marched under cover of darkness to the Gates with the Longshields and Agrianes, with the intention of delivering a surprise attack upon the defending force. Actually, his approach was observed, but the bold move was none the less successful; for the knowledge that Alexander was coming upon them in person was too much for the enemy, who abandoned their posts and fled. At dawn the following morning he passed the Gates with all his men and entered Cilicia, where a report reached him that Arsames had abandoned his original intention of holding Tarsus for Persia: now, it appeared, having learned that Alexander had passed the Gates, he meant to give up the town, and the townspeople were consequently afraid that he might strip the place before he left. Alexander, accordingly, brought up his cavalry and the most mobile of his infantry battalions with all possible speed, with the result that Arsames, the moment he was aware of his rapid approach, did not stop to plunder the town, but got out as fast as he could and made his way to the court of Darius.

About this time Alexander had a bout of sickness. The cause of it, according to Aristobulus' account, was exhaustion, but others say that he plunged into the river Cydnus for a swim, as he was sweating with heat and could not resist the pleasure of a bathe. The Cydnus runs right through Tarsus, and as it rises in Mount Taurus and flows through open country, its waters are clear and cold; the result was that Alexander was seized by a convulsion, followed by high fever and sleepless nights. All his doctors but one despaired of his life; but Philip of Acarnania, who attended him and was not only a trusted physician but a good soldier as well, proposed to give him a purgative. Alexander consented to take it, and just as Philip was preparing the draught, Alexander was handed a note from Parmenio. 'Beware of Philip,' the note read; 'I am informed that he has been bribed by Darius to poison you.' Alexander read the warning, and with the paper still in his hand took the cup of medicine and then passed the note to Philip. Philip read it, and while he was reading Alexander swallowed the dose. It was immediately clear that there was nothing wrong with Philip's medicine; he showed no alarm at Parmenio's warning, but simply advised Alexander to continue to follow his instructions – for, if he did, he would recover. The dose had its due effect and brought relief, and from that moment Philip knew that Alexander was his faithful friend; it was evident also to everyone else about his person both that he was firm in his refusal to suspect treachery in friends and could look unmoved upon death.

He now dispatched Parmenio to the other Gates which stand on the boundary between Cilicia and Assyria. Parmenio's orders were to seize and hold the pass with the troops entrusted to him – the allied infantry, the Greek mercenaries, the Thracians under Sitalces, and the Thessalian cavalry. Alexander himself, leaving Tarsus after Parmenio had gone, in one day's march reached Anchialus, a town supposed to have been built by Sardanapalus the Assyrian. It is clear from the extent of the surrounding walls and the solidity of their foundations that it was originally a large town and grew to great importance.

6]   DEFEAT OF ORONTOBATES   65

Close to the walls was the tomb of Sardanapalus, supporting a statue of him in the attitude of a man clapping his hands, with an inscription in the Assyrian character. According to the Assyrians the inscription was in verse, but, whether verse or not, the general sense of it was this: 'Sardanapalus, son of Anakyndaraxes, built in one day Tarsus and Anchialus. O stranger, eat, drink, and play, for everything else in the life of a man is not worth this' – and by 'this' was to be understood a clap of the hands. They also said that 'play' was something of a euphemism for the original Assyrian word.

From Anchialus Alexander proceeded to Soli, and imposed upon the town a fine of 200 talents of silver for its support of the Persian cause; then with three battalions of Macedonian foot, the Agrianes, and all his archers he marched against those of the Cilicians who were holding the hills. Some he drove from their positions; others surrendered; and within a week he was back in Soli, where the news reached him that Ptolemy and Asander had won a victory over the Persian commander Orontobates, who was holding the acropolis in Halicarnassus together with the towns of Myndus, Caunus, Thera, and Callipolis, and had also taken possession of Cos and Triopium. According to the dispatch, Orontobates had been defeated in a great battle; he had lost some 700 of his infantry and fifty of his mounted troops, with at least 1,000 prisoners.

To celebrate this success Alexander offered sacrifice to Asclepius and held a ceremonial parade of all his troops, followed by a torch race and games which included contests in music and verse as well as athletics. The town of Soli he permitted to retain its own popular government. He then started for Tarsus and gave orders for the cavalry to join Philotas, who was to take them across the plain of Alea to the river Pyramus. With the infantry and the Royal Squadron of horse he then went to Magarsus, whence, after offering sacrifice to the local Athene, he proceeded to Mallus, where he performed all proper ceremonies in honour of the demi-god Amphilochus. In this latter place he found political troubles in progress, and settled them, remitting the tribute which the town paid to Darius on the ground that Mallus was a colony of Argos and he himself claimed to be descended from the Argive Heracleidae.

He was still at Mallus when a report reached him that Darius and the whole Persian army were at Sochi, a place in Assyrian territory

c

about two days' march from the Assyrian Gates. He at once called a meeting of his staff and told them this important news. They urged unanimously an immediate advance. Alexander thanked them and dismissed the meeting, and on the following day moved forward with the evident intention of attack. Two days later he was past the Gates. He took up a position near Myriandrus, and during the night there was a storm of such violent wind and rain that he was compelled to remain where he was, with no chance of breaking camp.

Meanwhile Darius had no apparent intention of making a move; he had chosen for his position a part of Assyria where the country was flat and open, good for cavalry action, and suitable for manœuvring the vast numbers under his command. Amyntas, son of Antiochus, a deserter from Alexander's army, urged him not to move from such favourable ground, for plenty of space was precisely what the Persian army most needed, its numbers and equipment being what they were. Darius took Amyntas' advice, but later, when there was still no sign of Alexander, who had been held up at Tarsus by his illness, and again at Soli, for nearly as long, by the grand parade and religious ceremonies he held there and, finally, by his expedition against the hill tribes of Cilicia, he began to have his doubts. Moreover, Darius was always ready to believe what he found it most agreeable to believe, and on this occasion flattering courtiers, such as always are, and always will be, the bane of kings, had persuaded him into thinking that Alexander no longer wished to advance further into Asia: in fact, that the news of his own approach was the cause of Alexander's hesitation. First one, then another of them blew up the bladder of his conceit by saying that the Persian cavalry would ride over the Macedonian army and trample it to pieces. Only Amyntas opposed them, persistently affirming that Alexander would seek out Darius in any place where he knew him to be, and urging him not to shift his ground. But the worse counsel prevailed – because it told him what at the moment he liked to hear; more than that, there was surely some supernatural power which led Darius to take up a position where he could get little advantage either from his cavalry or his superiority in numbers of men and weight of missiles – a position where he had no chance of dazzling the enemy with the splendour of his great host, but was doomed to make a present of easy victory to Alexander and the Macedonians. Destiny had decreed that Macedon should wrest the

sovereignty of Asia from Persia, as Persia once had wrested it from
the Medes, and the Medes, in their turn, from the Assyrians.

Darius now moved; he crossed the high ground by what are called
the Amanian Gates – the pass across Mount Amanus – and, making
for Issus, established himself without being perceived in Alexander's
rear. Once in possession of Issus he mutilated and put to death every
Macedonian he found left there as unfit for service, and on the following day moved on to the river Pinarus. Alexander, not trusting
the report that Darius was in his rear, dispatched a party of the
Hetaeri in a galley with orders to sail back to Issus and find out for
themselves whether or not it was true. The coast by Issus is deeply in-
dented, and this fact enabled the party in the galley the more easily to
see what they wished to see – that the Persians were there. So back
they went to Alexander with their news: Darius was indeed at hand.

Alexander now sent for his infantry and cavalry commanders and
all officers in charge of allied troops and appealed to them for confidence and courage in the coming fight. 'Remember', he said, 'that
already danger has often threatened you and you have looked it
triumphantly in the face; this time the struggle will be between a victorious army and an enemy already once vanquished. God himself,
moreover, by suggesting to Darius to leave the open ground and
cram his great army into a confined space, has taken charge of operations in our behalf. We ourselves shall have room enough to deploy
our infantry, while they, no match for us either in bodily strength or
resolution, will find their superiority in numbers of no avail. Our
enemies are Medes and Persians, men who for centuries have lived
soft and luxurious lives; we of Macedon for generations past have
been trained in the hard school of danger and war. Above all, we are
free men, and they are slaves. There are Greek troops, to be sure, in
Persian service – but how different is their cause from ours! They will
be fighting for pay – and not much of it at that; we, on the contrary,
shall fight for Greece, and our hearts will be in it. As for our foreign
troops – Thracians, Paeonians, Illyrians, Agrianes – they are the best
and stoutest soldiers in Europe, and they will find as their opponents
the slackest and softest of the tribes of Asia. And what, finally, of the
two men in supreme command? You have Alexander, they – Darius!'

Having thus enumerated the advantages with which they would
enter the coming struggle, Alexander went on to show that the

rewards of victory would also be great. The victory this time would not
be over mere underlings of the Persian King, or the Persian cavalry
along the banks of Granicus, or the 20,000 foreign mercenaries; it
would be over the fine flower of the Medes and Persians and all the
Asiatic peoples which they ruled. The Great King was there in person
with his army, and once the battle was over, nothing would remain
but to crown their many labours with the sovereignty of Asia. He reminded them, further, of what they had already so brilliantly accomplished together, and mentioned any act of conspicuous individual
courage, naming the man in each case and specifying what he
had done, and alluding also, in such a way as to give least offence,
to the risks to which he had personally exposed himself on the field.
He also, we are told, reminded them of Xenophon and his Ten Thousand, a force which, though not to be compared with their own either
in strength or reputation – a force without the support of cavalry such
as they had themselves, from Thessaly, Boeotia, the Peloponnese, and
elsewhere, with no archers or slingers except a small contingent from
Crete and Rhodes hastily improvised by Xenophon under pressure of
immediate need – nevertheless defeated the King of Persia and his
army at the gates of Babylon and successfully repelled all the native
troops who tried to bar their way as they marched down to the Black
Sea. Nor did Alexander omit any other words of encouragement
such as brave men about to risk their lives might expect from a brave
commander; and in response to his address his officers pressed forward to clasp his hand and with many expressions of appreciation
urged him to lead them to battle without delay.

Alexander's first order was that his men should eat, while at the
same time he sent a small party of mounted men and archers to the
narrow pass by the shore to reconnoitre the road by which he would
have to return; then, as soon as it was dark, he moved off himself with
the whole army to take possession once more of that narrow gateway.
About midnight the passage was secured; for the remainder of the
night he allowed his men to rest where they were, on the rocky
ground, with outposts to keep exact and careful watch, and just before daylight next morning moved forward from the pass along the
coast road. The advance was in column so long as lack of space made it
necessary, but as soon as the country began to open up he gradually
extended his front, bringing up his heavy infantry a battalion at a

time, until he was moving in line with his right on the base of the hills and his left on the sea.

During the advance the mounted troops were kept in the rear, but as soon as open ground was reached Alexander ordered battle stations: the picked infantry battalions and the Longshields, under Parmenio's son Nicanor, were sent to the right wing on the nearby rising ground, with Coenus' battalion on their left in close touch with Perdiccas' men, the whole forming a line from right wing to centre – the position of the heavy infantry. On the extreme left were stationed Amyntas' troops, and in touch with them, and working towards the centre, first Ptolemy's battalion, then Meleager's. Command of the infantry on the left was given to Craterus, of the left wing as a whole to Parmenio, whose orders were on no account to leave a gap between his extreme left and the sea; for if he did, they might well be surrounded, as the numerical superiority of the enemy would certainly enable them to outflank the Macedonians.

When Darius received the report that Alexander was moving forward to the attack, he sent some 30,000 mounted troops and 20,000 light infantry across the river Pinarus, to give himself a chance of getting the main body of his army into position without molestation. His dispositions were as follows: in the van of his heavy infantry were his 30,000 Greek mercenaries, facing the Macedonian infantry, with some 60,000 Persian heavy infantry – known as Kardakes – to support them, half on each of their flanks. These troops were drawn up in line, and the ground would not admit of a greater number. Hard on the rising ground on his left, and facing Alexander's right, was another division about 20,000 strong, some portions of which actually worked round to Alexander's rear; for the hills on their left receded to some distance so as to form a sort of bay, the further shore of which (so to put it) curved round back again, bringing the sections which were posted close under the hill to the rear of Alexander's right wing. In the rear of the Greek mercenaries and the Persians supporting them on either flank was the remainder of Darius' army – a great mass of light and heavy infantry. These were organized according to the countries of their origin and drawn up in greater depth than was likely to prove of much service; mere numbers made this unavoidable – indeed, it is on record that the army as a whole was some 600,000 strong.

As soon as Alexander found the ground in front of him opening

out a little more, he brought his cavalry – the Thessalian and Macedonian divisions, together with the Hetaeri – up from the rear to the
right wing under his own personal command, and at the same time
sent the Peloponnesian troops and other allied divisions round to
Parmenio on the left. Darius, immediately his main infantry force was
in position, recalled by signal the mounted troops which he had sent
across the river to cover the movement, and ordered the greater number of them over to his right, to threaten Parmenio, on the seaward
side, where the ground was rather more suitable for cavalry manœuvre; some, however, he sent to the opposite flank under the hills,
though, as lack of space at that end of the line made them obviously
useless, he soon recalled nearly all of them and ordered them round to
the right flank. Darius himself took the centre, the traditional position
of the Persian Kings. (The general principle of the Persian order of
battle has been explained by Xenophon in his History.)

Nearly all the Persian cavalry had now been transferred to a position on the seaward side facing Alexander's left, and opposing them
he had nothing except the Peloponnesians and other allied cavalry; to
meet this threat he sent his Thessalian cavalry with all speed to their
support, with instructions to conceal their movement from the enemy
by passing in the rear of the massed infantry battalions. At the same
time, at the other end of the line he threw forward his cavalry patrols,
under Protomachus' command, together with the Paeonians under
Ariston, and the archers under Antiochus.

The Agrianes under Attalus, supported by a few units of mounted
troops and archers, were ordered out towards the high ground at an
angle to his main line of advance, thus splitting the right wing of the
army into two separate prongs, one designed to engage Darius and
the main body of the Persians on the further side of the river, the
other the units which had worked round to the hill in the Macedonian
rear. In the van of the infantry on the Macedonian left were the
Cretan archers and the Thracians, under Sitalces, with the cavalry of
the left wing in advance of them; all units had a proportion of foreign
mercenaries assigned to them.

Observing a certain weakness on his right and also the danger of
being outflanked at that end of his line, Alexander withdrew from the
centre two squadrons of the Hetaeri and two others – that, namely,
from Anthemus commanded by Peroedes and the so-called Leugaean

squadron, under Pantordanus, son of Cleander – and ordered them over to the right, with every precaution to conceal their movement; at the same time he further strengthened his right by a contingent of Agrianes and Greek mercenaries which he drew up in line, and so outflanked the Persian left. The Persians on the hills had made no aggressive move; indeed, when Alexander ordered a raid upon them by a small party of the Agrianes and archers, they had been easily dislodged from their position and had sought safety higher up the mountainside, so that Alexander decided that he could use the men originally intended to deal with them to strengthen his main attacking force. Three hundred mounted men were sufficient to keep an eye on the fugitives.

For a while Alexander's advance was slow and deliberate; every now and then he ordered a halt, giving the impression that time was on his side. Darius made no move as yet to attack, but kept his men in their original dispositions on the river bank. In many places the bank was steep, and any sections of it which seemed less easy to defend he had strengthened with a stockade – at once by this precaution making it clear to Alexander's men that his was a craven spirit.

The two armies were now almost within striking distance. Alexander rode from one end of his line to the other with words of encouragement for all, addressing by name, with proper mention of rank and distinctions, not the officers of highest rank only but the captains of squadrons and companies; even the mercenaries were not forgotten, where any distinction or act of courage called for the mention of a name, and from every throat came the answering shout: 'Wait no longer – forward to the assault!'

The Persian army was in full view; still, however, Alexander moved forward in line at a deliberate pace, for a too-rapid advance might have thrown the line out of dressing and caused a break somewhere; but once within range of missiles, Alexander, at the head of his own troops on the right wing, rode at a gallop into the stream. Rapidity was now all in all: a swift attack would shake the enemy, and the sooner they came to grips the less damage would be done by the Persian archers. Alexander's judgement was not at fault: the Persian left collapsed the very moment he was on them – a brilliant local success for the picked troops under his personal command. In the centre, however, things did not go so well: here some of the troops had broken away towards the right and left a gap in the line, and, in contrast with Alexander, who had so swiftly crossed the stream and was already, in close combat, compelling the Persian left to withdraw, the Macedonian centre was much slower off the mark; in a number of places, moreover, the steep banks of the stream prevented them from maintaining a regular and unbroken front, and the result was that Darius' Greek mercenaries attacked precisely at that point in the line where the gap was widest. There was a violent struggle. Darius' Greeks fought to thrust the Macedonians back into the water and save the day for their left wing, already in retreat, while the Macedonians, in their turn, with Alexander's triumph plain before their eyes, were determined to equal his success and not forfeit the proud title of invincible, hitherto universally bestowed upon them. The fight was further embittered by the old racial rivalry of Greek and Macedonian. It was in this phase of the battle that Ptolemy, son of Seleucus, and about 121 Macedonians of distinction met a soldier's death.

Alexander's victorious right wing now swung left towards the centre, hard pressed as it was by Darius' Greeks; they forced them back from the river and then, outflanking the broken enemy left, delivered a flank attack on the mercenaries and were soon cutting them to pieces. The Persian cavalry facing Alexander's Thessalians refused, once the battle had developed, to remain inactive on the further side of the stream, but charged across in a furious onslaught on the Thessalian squadrons. The cavalry action which ensued was desperate enough, and the Persians broke only when they knew that the Greek mercenaries were being cut off and destroyed by the Macedonian infantry, and that Darius himself was in flight. That was the signal for a general rout – open and unconcealed. The horses with their heavily equipped riders suffered severely, and of the thousands of panic-stricken men who struggled in hopeless disorder to escape along the narrow mountain tracks, almost as many were trampled to death by their friends as were cut down by the pursuing enemy. The Thessalians pressed the pursuit without mercy, and the Persian losses in both arms, infantry, and cavalry were equally severe.

The moment the Persian left went to pieces under Alexander's attack and Darius, in his war-chariot, saw that it was cut off, he incontinently fled – indeed, he led the race for safety. Keeping to his chariot as long as there was smooth ground to travel on, he was forced to abandon it when ravines and other obstructions barred his way; then, dropping his shield and stripping off his candys – and even leaving his bow in the war-chariot – he leapt upon a horse and rode for his life. Darkness soon closed in; and that alone saved him from falling into the hands of Alexander, who, while daylight held, relentlessly pressed the pursuit; but when there was no longer light enough to see what he was coming to, he turned back – but not without taking possession of Darius' chariot together with his shield, mantle, and bow. In point of fact his pursuit would have been more rapid had he not turned back at the moment when his line of heavy infantry broke, in the first stage of the battle; he had then waited until he saw that both the Greek mercenaries and the Persian cavalry had been forced back from the river bank.

Among the Persian dead were Arsames, Rheomithres, and Atizyes – all three of whom had served as cavalry officers at the battle on the Granicus; also Sabaces, governor of Egypt, and Bubaces, another person of distinguished rank; of the common soldiers, something like 100,000 were killed, including over 10,000 of the cavalry. Ptolemy, son of Lagus, who was serving with Alexander at this time, says in his account of the battle that the Macedonians in their pursuit of Darius actually crossed a ravine on the bodies of the Persian dead.

Darius' headquarters were stormed and captured; his mother was taken, together with his wife (who was also his sister) and his infant son; in addition to these, two of his daughters fell into Alexander's hands with a few noble Persian ladies who were in attendance upon them. The Persian officers had sent their gear and womenfolk to Damascus, and Darius, too, had sent thither most of his treasure and the various paraphernalia which the luxurious life of a great king seems to require, even on campaign; so that a mere 3,000 talents were found at his headquarters. In point of fact, however, the treasure at Damascus, too, was seized not long afterwards by Parmenio, who was ordered there for the purpose. Such, then, was the result of the battle of Issus, fought in the month of November, during the archonship of Nicocrates at Athens.

Alexander had been hurt by a sword-thrust in the thigh, but this did not prevent him from visiting the wounded on the day after the battle, when he also gave a splendid military funeral to the dead in the presence of the whole army paraded in full war equipment. At the ceremony he spoke in praise of every man who by his own observation or from reliable report he knew had distinguished himself in the fighting, and marked his approval in each case by a suitable reward. He appointed Balacrus, son of Nicanor, a member of the Royal Guard, as governor of Cilicia, promoting Menes, son of Dionysius, to fill the place thus left vacant, and Polysperchon, son of Simmias, was promoted to command the battalion of Ptolemy, son of Seleucus, who had been killed. The people of Soli still owed fifty talents of the fine imposed upon them, but he cancelled the debt and returned their hostages.

His sympathy was extended, moreover, even to Darius' mother, wife, and children. According to some accounts, on the night when he returned from the pursuit he heard upon entering Darius' tent, which had been set aside as his own special portion of the spoils of war, the confused sound of women's voices raised in lamentation somewhere close at hand. He asked who the women were and why they should be in a tent so close to him. 'Sire,' he was told, 'they are Darius' mother and wife and children. They know that you have his bow and his royal mantle and that his shield has been brought back, and they are mourning for his death.' Alexander at once sent Leonnatus, one of the Hetaeri, to tell them that Darius was alive – his mantle and weapons he had left, as he fled for safety, in his war chariot, and these, and nothing else, had fallen into Alexander's hands. Leonnatus entered their tent, gave the message about Darius, and added that Alexander wished them to retain all the marks, ceremonies, and titles of royalty, as he had not fought Darius with any personal bitterness, but had made legitimate war for the sovereignty of Asia. This is the account given by Ptolemy and Aristobulus; there is also another story to the effect that Alexander on the following day entered the tent accompanied only by Hephaestion, and that Darius' mother, in doubt, owing to the similarity of their dress, which of the two was the King, prostrated herself before Hephaestion, because he was taller than his companion. Hephaestion stepped back, and one of the Queen's attendants rectified her mistake by pointing to Alexander; the Queen withdrew in profound embarrassment, but Alexander merely remarked that her error was of no account, for Hephaestion, too, was an Alexander – a 'protector of men'. I record this anecdote not as necessarily true, though it is credible enough. If such were indeed the facts, I cannot but admire Alexander both for treating these women with such compassion and for showing such respect and confidence towards his friend; if the story is apocryphal, it was at least inspired by Alexander's character: thus he would have acted, thus he would have spoken – and on that account I admire him no less.

Meanwhile Darius with a few followers made the best of his escape throughout the night, and with the coming of daylight was joined as he went along by parties of survivors, Persians or mercenaries, until he had in all a body of some 4,000 men; with these he pressed on with all speed towards Thapsacus and the Euphrates with the intention of putting the river between himself and Alexander as soon as he could. Four men who had deserted to Darius – Amyntas son of Antiochus, Thymondas son of Mentor, Aristomedes of Pherae, and Bianor the Acarnanian – fled to the hills with the 8,000 troops under their command and reached Tripolis in Phoenicia; finding hauled ashore there the ships which had brought them from Lesbos, they launched as many as they thought would serve their purpose, burnt the rest as they lay in the yards, to delay pursuit, and sailed first for Cyprus and thence to Egypt – where not long afterwards Amyntas was killed by the Egyptians for meddling in what did not concern him.

All this time Pharnabazus and Autophradates had been hanging about in Chios. Now, after garrisoning the island, they dispatched a part of their fleet to Cos and Halicarnassus, and themselves put to sea with the hundred fastest ships they had; at Siphnos they were met by the Spartan King, Agis, who with a single trireme had come to raise money for the war and to ask that as many ships and men as possible should be sent to him in the Peloponnese. It was at this moment that the news of the battle of Issus came. The effect of it was shattering; Pharnabazus, fearing defeat might lead to trouble in Chios, at once sailed for the island with twelve ships and 1,500 of the mercenaries, while Agis dispatched Hippias to Taenarum to deliver to his brother Agesilaus the ten ships and thirty talents of silver which he had received from Autophradates, adding instructions that he should tell Agesilaus to pay the seamen in full and sail immediately to secure Crete. Agis himself remained for a time in the islands, but subsequently joined Autophradates at Halicarnassus.

Leaving Menon, son of Kerdimmas, as governor of Lowland Syria with the allied cavalry to keep the country under control, Alexander marched for Phoenicia. On the way thither he was met by Straton, the son of Gerostratus, who was the prince of Aradus and its neighbouring peoples; Gerostratus himself had sailed with Autophradates, as had the other petty kings of Phoenicia and Cyprus, so it was left to Straton to present himself before Alexander and to crown him with a gold crown, yielding him the sovereignty of the island of Aradus together with the large and prosperous town of Marathus on the mainland opposite, and Sigon, Mariamne, and everything else under his control.

While Alexander was at Marathus, envoys from Darius came with a request for the release of his mother, wife, and children. They also brought a letter from him, of which the substance was as follows:

Philip and Artaxerxes were on terms of friendship and alliance; but upon the accession of Artaxerxes' son Arses, Philip was guilty of unprovoked aggression against him. Now, since Darius' reign began, Alexander has sent no representative to his court to confirm the former friendship and alliance between the two kingdoms; on the contrary, he has crossed into Asia with his armed forces and done much damage to the Persians. For this reason Darius took the field in defence of his country and of his ancestral throne. The issue of the battle was as some god willed; and now Darius the King asks Alexander the King to restore from captivity his wife, his mother, and his children, and is willing to make friends with him and be his ally. For this cause he urges Alexander to send to him, in company with Meniscus and Arsimes who have brought this request, representatives of his own in order that proper guarantees may be exchanged.

Alexander, having written his reply, ordered Thersippas to accompany Darius' envoys on their return, giving him strict instructions to deliver the letter to Darius but to discuss no question whatever which might arise from it. This was the letter:

Your ancestors invaded Macedonia and Greece and caused havoc in our country, though we had done nothing to provoke them. As supreme commander of all Greece I invaded Asia because I wished to punish Persia for this act – an act which must be laid wholly to your charge. You sent aid to the people of Perinthus in their rebellion against my father; Ochus sent an army into Thrace, which was a part of our dominions; my father was killed by assassins whom, as you openly boasted in your letters, you yourselves hired to commit the crime; having murdered Arses with Bagoas' help, you unjustly and illegally seized the throne, thereby committing a crime against your country; you sent the Greeks false information about me in the hope of making them my enemies; you attempted to supply the Greeks with money – which only the Lacedaemonians were willing to accept; your agents corrupted my friends and tried to wreck the peace which I had established in Greece – then it was that I took the field against you; but it was you who began the quarrel. First I defeated in battle your generals and satraps; now I have defeated yourself and the army you led. By God's help I am master of your country, and I have made myself responsible for the survivors of your army who fled to me for refuge: far from being detained by force, they are serving of their own free will under my command.

Come to me, therefore, as you would come to the lord of the continent of Asia. Should you fear to suffer any indignity at my hands, then send some of your friends and I will give them the proper guarantees. Come, then, and ask me for your mother, your wife, and your children and anything else you please; for you shall have them, and whatever besides you can persuade me to give you.

And in future let any communication you wish to make with me be addressed to the King of all Asia. Do not write to me as to an equal. Everything you possess is now mine; so, if you should want anything, let me know in the proper terms, or I shall take steps to deal with you as a criminal. If, on the other hand, you wish to dispute your throne, stand and fight for it and do not run away. Wherever you may hide yourself, be sure I shall seek you out.

Such were the terms of Alexander's answer.

When he learned that money and other valuables sent by Darius to Damascus in charge of Cophen, son of Artabazus, had been seized and removed together with all the Persians left to guard them, he instructed Parmenio to see that the whole treasure was taken back to Damascus for safe keeping. The envoys from Greece, who had visited Darius before the battle, had also fallen into Parmenio's hands; and these Alexander ordered should be sent to him. They were Euthycles, from Sparta; Thessaliscus, son of Ismenius, and Dionysidorus (the Olympic victor), from Thebes; and Iphicrates, son of the distinguished general of the same name, from Athens. The four men were duly brought before Alexander; Thessaliscus and Dionysidorus, in spite of – or perhaps because of – the fact that they were Thebans, he at once dismissed: he was sorry for Thebes, and could not but feel that, as she had been reduced to slavery by a Macedonian army, her people had done nothing very reprehensible in sending to Darius; after all, they were only looking for what help they could get from Persia for themselves and their country, so he was inclined to take a lenient view of both these men. All the same, he privately declared that he released Thessaliscus out of respect for his family, which was one of the noble families of Thebes, and Dionysidorus because of his success at the Olympic games. Iphicrates, from affection for Athens and the memory of his father's fame, he retained in his personal suite, treating him with every mark of honour, and when he fell ill and died sent his bones to his relatives in Athens. Euthycles, on the contrary, represented a city then bitterly hostile to him; and for that reason, and because he was unable to produce any reasonable claim to clemency, Alexander kept him for the time being under open arrest. Later, however, in the full tide of his success, he let Euthycles go free as well.

Alexander now resumed his advance from Marathus. Byblus and Sidon both surrendered to him – the people of Sidon, who hated Darius and the Persians, actually inviting him to enter the town. He then proceeded in the direction of Tyre, and was met on the way by representatives from the town, who had been sent by its government to say that they had determined to abide by any instructions Alexander might give. The envoys were men of the best families in Tyre and included the son of the Tyrian king, Azemilcus, who himself was at sea with Autophradates; Alexander thanked them for their communication and directed them to return to Tyre and tell their people that he wished to enter the town and offer sacrifice to Heracles.

I must mention in this connexion that there is in Tyre the most ancient temple of Heracles known to man. This is not the Argive Heracles, Alcmena's son; for Heracles was worshipped in Tyre many generations before Cadmus came from Phoenicia to Thebes and became the father of Semele, who bore Dionysus to Zeus. Dionysus would seem to be in the third generation from Cadmus, through Polydorus and Labdacus, while the Argive Heracles was probably in the line of Oedipus, son of Laius. The Egyptians also worship a Heracles, but not the Heracles of Tyre or Greece; according to Herodotus he is regarded by the Egyptians as one of the Twelve Gods. Similarly, the Athenians worship a Dionysus who was the son of Zeus and Kore – and it is to him, not to the Theban Dionysus, that the *Iacchus* hymn is sung during the celebration of the Mysteries. I think that the Heracles who is honoured at Tartessus by the Iberians (where are the so-called Pillars of Heracles) is the Tyrian Heracles, because Tartessus is of Phoenician origin and Heracles' temple there and the ritual of sacrifice performed in it are both in the Phoenician tradition. Moreover, according to the chronicler Hecataeus, Geryones, whose oxen the Argive Heracles was sent by Eurystheus to fetch to Mycenae, had no connexion with Iberia; nor was Heracles sent to some island or other called Erytheia beyond the Straits. It is much more likely that Geryones was a mainland prince somewhere in the region of Ambracia and Amphilochi, and that Heracles' task – and no small one either – was to steal the oxen from there. I know for myself that this region still, today, contains excellent pasture and produces cattle of high quality, and it is likely enough that Eurystheus was not unaware of the reputation of these mainland cattle and of the name of the prince who ruled in those parts; but he would surely not have known the name of the Iberian king right away there in the remotest corner of Europe, or have had any idea whether or not there were good cattle in that distant land. Indeed, to make such an improbable story hang together, one would have to make a myth of it and drag in the goddess Hera, and say that it was she who told Heracles the secret through the mouth of Eurystheus.

It was, then, to this Tyrian Heracles that Alexander expressed a wish to offer sacrifice, and the envoys reported his request to the people of the town. In general, they were willing enough to accede to Alexander's wishes, but there was one thing which they firmly refused to do – and that was to admit any Persian or Macedonian within the walls of the town. This, they felt, was not only the most dignified attitude at the present juncture, but would also be the most likely to ensure their future safety, as the outcome of the war was not yet by any means assured. The decision was duly reported to Alexander, who was very angry; he dismissed the envoys and at once called a meeting of the Hetaeri and other officers of all ranks and addressed them in the following words.

'Friends and fellow soldiers, I do not see how we can safely advance upon Egypt, so long as Persia controls the sea; and to pursue Darius with the neutral city of Tyre in our rear and Egypt and Cyprus still in enemy hands would be a serious risk, especially in view of the situation in Greece. With our army on the track of Darius, far inland in the direction of Babylon, the Persians might well regain control of the coast, and thus be enabled with more power behind them to transfer the war to Greece, where Sparta is already openly hostile to us, and Athens, at the moment, is but an unwilling ally; fear, not friendliness, keeping her on our side. But with Tyre destroyed, all Phoenicia would be ours, and the Phoenician fleet, which both in numbers and quality is the predominant element in the sea-power of Persia, would very likely come over to us. The Phoenician seamen, ships' crews or fighting men, once their towns are in our hands, will hardly endure to face the perils of service at sea for the sake of others. The next step will be Cyprus: it will either join us without trouble on our part, or be easily taken by assault; then, with the accession of Cyprus and the united fleets of Macedon and Phoenicia, our supremacy at sea would be guaranteed, and the expedition to Egypt would thus be a simple matter, and finally, with Egypt in our hands we shall have no further cause for uneasiness about Greece: we shall be able to march on Babylon with security at home, with enhanced prestige, and with Persia excluded not only from the sea, but from the whole continent up to the Euphrates.'

Alexander had no difficulty in persuading his officers that the attempt upon Tyre must be made. He himself had further encouragement by a sign from heaven, for that very night he dreamed that as he was approaching the walls of the town Heracles greeted him and invited him to enter. The dream was interpreted by Aristander as signifying that Tyre would be taken, but with much labour, because labour was characteristic of all that Heracles had himself accomplished.

However – dreams or no dreams – it was obvious enough that the siege of Tyre would be a tremendous undertaking. The town was an island, and surrounded by strong and lofty walls, and, as things then were, with Persia in command of the sea and the Tyrian fleet still strong, any attack by sea would have been unlikely to succeed. In spite of all difficulties, however, Alexander's decision to attack it was accepted.

His plan was to construct a mole across the stretch of shallow water between the shore and the town. In-shore there are patches of mud with little water over them, the deepest part of the channel, about three fathoms, being close to the town. There was an abundant supply of stones, which they used for the foundation of the mole, and plenty of timber, which they packed down on top. It was an easy matter to drive piles into the mud, which itself acted as binding material to keep the stones in place. The men worked with as good a will as their commander, for Alexander was always on the spot giving precise instructions as to how to proceed, with many a word of encouragement and special rewards for conspicuously good work.

Little difficulty was encountered in constructing the in-shore portion of the mole, because the water was shallow and there was no opposition; but as they got out into the deeper water near the town, and within range of missiles from the lofty walls, their troubles began. The men were in working dress and not equipped for battle, and the Tyrians used their superiority at sea to make constant raids on various points along the mole, thus rendering the continuation of the work impossible. To counter these raids, the Macedonians built two towers on the mole (which was now of considerable length) and mounted artillery on them; they faced the towers with skins and hides to prevent damage from incendiary missiles and, at the same time, to afford some protection against arrows for the men working on them, hoping, also, that the Tyrian crews who attempted to harass the men on the mole might be attacked by missiles from the towers and driven off without difficulty.

The Tyrians, however, soon had their answer: they filled a cattle-boat with dry brushwood and various sorts of timber which would burn well, set up twin masts in her bows, and, as far as they could, raised her bulwarks all round in order to make her hold as much inflammable material as possible, including pitch, sulphur, and anything else which would burn fiercely. Across the twin masts they rigged a yard double the usual length, and slung from it cauldrons full of any material which could be poured or flung on the fire to increase its fury, and, finally, heavily ballasted the vessel aft in order to lift her bows as high as possible. Then, having waited for a fair wind, they passed hawsers to a number of triremes and towed her stern-first to the mole. Near the two towers they started the fire, and the crews of the triremes pulled with all their might until they flung the blazing cattle-boat on the edge of the mole. Before she struck the men in her leapt overboard and swam to safety.

The towers were soon caught in a furious blaze; the yards burned through and collapsed, pouring into the fire the contents of the cauldrons which had been designed to increase its intensity. The tiremes lay-to near the mole, their crews shooting continually at the towers so that no one could get near them with anything to extinguish the flames. Then, once the towers were well alight, the Tyrians in the town came swarming out, leapt into boats which they ran upon the mole at various points, and soon succeeded in wrecking the palisade built to protect it, and in setting fire to all the war-engines which had so far escaped the blazing cattle-boat.

The result of all this was that Alexander gave orders for work to start again on the mole from the in-shore end: it was to be made broader, to give space for more towers, and the engineers were to set about the construction of fresh engines. In the meantime he himself with the Longshields and Agrianes moved off for Sidon, in order to assemble there all the warships he possessed; for clearly, so long as the Tyrians were masters of the sea, the siege of Tyre would be no easy matter.

Meanwhile Gerostratus and Enylus, upon receiving a report that Aradus and Byblus were in Alexander's hands, left the fleet which was under Autophradates' command and sailed with their own contingents to join Alexander; the Sidonian warships accompanied them, so that Alexander received a reinforcement of about eighty Phoenician vessels. About the same time he was joined by the patrol ship from Rhodes and nine other vessels, three from Soli and Mallus, ten from Lycia, and a fifty-oared galley from Macedon under the command of Proteus, son of Andronicus. Shortly afterwards the alarming news of Darius' defeat on the Issus, added to the fact that all Phoenicia was in Alexander's hands, induced the Cypriot kings to sail for Sidon with their fleet of some 120 ships.

Alexander was aware that it was by necessity rather than choice that all of them had used their naval strength in support of Persia, and was quite willing, in consequence, to overlook the past.

While the war-engines were still under construction and the fleet was being put into order for active service, Alexander with some squadrons of cavalry, the Longshields, the Agrianes, and the archers made an expedition to Mount Antilibanus in Arabia. Within ten days he made himself master, either by force or agreement, of the country in that neighbourhood, and returned to Sidon, where he found that Cleander, son of Polemocrates, had arrived from the Peloponnese with about 4,000 Greek mercenary troops.

Once the fleet was fully mobilized, he embarked an adequate number of fighting men for the task in hand – on the assumption, that is,
that in the coming engagement close fighting would be the order of
the day rather than naval tactics. The fleet then sailed for Tyre in close
order, with Alexander himself on the right wing to seaward, supported by the Cypriot kings and all the Phoenicians with the exception of Pnytagoras, who, with Craterus, was in command of the left.

It had been the intention of the Tyrians to offer battle if Alexander
attacked by sea; now, however, the situation was very different: here
was a much more powerful fleet than they had expected in their
ignorance of the fact that all the ships of Cyprus and Phoenicia had
joined Alexander; the fleet had lain-to at sea a little way off the town
as a challenge to battle, and now, when the challenge was not answered, it was coming on again in close order and at full speed. In
these circumstances, therefore, the Tyrians decided not to risk an engagement; instead, they blocked their harbour entrances with as many
ships as there was room for, and kept guard there to prevent the
enemy fleet from coming to an anchor in any of them.

On the refusal of the Tyrians to accept his challenge, Alexander
continued his course towards the town. He did not intend to force
an entry into the harbour on the Sidon side of the island, because the
entrance was narrow and blocked by a number of warships lying
bows-on to an approaching enemy; in spite of this, however, the
Phoenicians rammed head-on the three outermost vessels and sank
them, their crews swimming to safety on the friendly shore. After this
incident the fleet brought up in-shore, not far from the mole, where
there seemed to be shelter.

Next day Alexander gave orders for the blockade of the town: the
Cyprian contingent under its commander Andromachus was to take
station off the northern harbour (facing Sidon), and the Phoenicians
off the southern harbour on the other side of the mole, where his own
quarters were.

By this time Alexander had assembled a considerable body of workmen from Cyprus and various parts of Phoenicia, and many war-
engines had been constructed; some were mounted on the mole,
others on the transport vessels which he had brought from Sidon,
others, again, on the slower-sailing triremes. When all was ready,
they were ordered forward into action – not those on the mole only,

but also those from the ships which were lying off the walls of the
town at various points and already beginning the assault.

On the battlements overlooking the mole the Tyrians erected
wooden towers for defensive action, and every threat from Alexander's artillery, wherever it might be, they met with missile weapons,
using fire-arrows against the ships with such effect that their crews
were afraid to approach within range. The walls of the town opposite
the mole were about 120 feet high and proportionately thick, strongly
built of large stone blocks cemented together. There was a further
reason why it was difficult for the Macedonian transports and triremes
to work in close to the town with their artillery, and this was the fact
that blocks of stone in large numbers had been thrown into the water,
and obstructed their advance. Alexander determined to remove them,
but the task proved a difficult one, not only because the men had only
the unsteady ships' decks to work from, but also because the Tyrians
in certain specially-armoured vessels kept driving athwart the bows of
the Macedonian triremes and cutting the anchor cables, so that it was
impossible for them to remain in their station. Alexander, in reply,
filled a number of thirty-oared galleys with similar defensive armour
and moored them broadside-on ahead of the triremes' anchor ropes,
to repel the Tyrian attacks; but the Tyrians, not to be outdone, sent
down divers to cut the cables as before. Then the Macedonians sub-
stituted chain for rope – and against that, at any rate, the divers were
useless. Finally, from the mole, they managed to pass ropes round the
blocks of stone and to haul them out, after which they lifted them
with cranes and dropped them again into deep water, where they
were not likely to cause any further obstruction. Once the water by
the wall was clear of obstacles, the ships could lie there, close in, without much difficulty.

The Tyrians, now in serious trouble, decided to attack the Cyprian
contingent which was blockading the northern harbour. Some time
previously they had rigged sails across the harbour entrance to act
as a screen behind which they could man their vessels unobserved;
and now, about midday, when the crews of the Greek ships were
dispersed upon whatever job they happened to have in hand, and
Alexander had just left the fleet on the other side of the town to withdraw to his quarters, they completed their preparations. Having
manned three quinqueremes, three quadriremes, and seven triremes

with picked crews – their smartest men, their best-armed marines, specially selected for their courage in naval warfare – they slipped quietly out of harbour in single file. No one called the time to the men at the oars; they rowed in silence until just before they turned to come within sight of the Cyprians, when with a hearty shout and cheers of mutual encouragement they laid to their oars and bore down upon the enemy at their best speed.

It so happened that though Alexander had retired to his quarters that day, he had not taken his customary rest, but had almost immediately returned to the fleet. The Tyrian surprise proved successful: some of the blockading squadron they found without a single man aboard; others were being manned under difficulties with whoever was available at the last moment, with the enemies' battle-shout in their ears and the attack imminent; and the result was that Pnytagoras' quinquireme was rammed and sunk at the first encounter. The ships commanded by Androcles of Amathus and Pasicrates of Thurieus suffered the same fate. The rest of the squadron was driven ashore and broken up.

As soon as it was reported to Alexander that the Tyrian triremes had been out, he ordered most of the ships on the south side of the town, the instant that each could be got ready for action, to lay-to off the south harbour entrance, in order to prevent another sortie; then with his quinquiremes and the five or six triremes which had been smartest in getting their crews aboard, he sailed round to the north side of the town in search of the Tyrian squadron which had made the attack. When the Tyrians on the battlements saw what was happening and that Alexander in person was with the enemy squadron, they shouted a warning to the men in their own ships to get back into harbour, and, when the din and clatter of action made their shouts inaudible, tried signals of various sorts to indicate the necessity of withdrawing to shelter. The Tyrian crews saw Alexander's ships coming; they put about and made for the harbour – but too late: a few managed to get in in time, but most of them were rammed; some were put out of action and one quinquireme and one quadrireme were captured right at the harbour entrance. Loss of life was not severe; the men on board, once they knew their ships were done for, swam off into the harbour and escaped without difficulty.

All hope of protection by the fleet was now gone, and this was the moment when the Macedonians began to bring their artillery into action. From the mole the siege engines could make little impression because in that sector the city wall was too strong. Another attempt was made on the north side, where a number of ships with artillery aboard were brought into action; but their success was no greater. Alexander, accordingly, turned his attention to the southern sector of the defences, feeling methodically for a weak spot, and it was here that he had his first success. A considerable length of the wall began to give under the assault, and an actual breach was made, though not a large one. Alexander then made a tentative attack – a probing movement, not much more, in point of fact, than the throwing of a bridge across the breach. The movement was easily repulsed.

Three days later, when Alexander had the weather he wanted, he addressed some words of encouragement to his officers and ordered the ship-borne artillery into action. Great damage was done to the defences, and as soon as he thought that a breach of sufficient breadth had been made, he withdrew the artillery carriers and ordered up two other vessels equipped with gangways which he proposed to throw across the breach. One of these vessels, commanded by Admetus, was taken over by a battalion of the Longshields, and the other by Coenus' battalion, the Foot Guards. Alexander himself was with the Longshields, ready to mount the breach wherever it was practicable. Some of his triremes he ordered round to the two harbours, on the chance that they might succeed in forcing an entrance while the enemy's attention was engaged in trying to repel the assault elsewhere; other vessels which had archers on board or carried ammunition for the artillery were instructed to cruise round the island and, wherever they could, close in with the wall, lying off but within range if it so happened that to get close in was impossible, so that the defenders might be threatened from every point and caught, as it were, in a ring of fire.

No sooner were Alexander's ships in under the city wall and the gangways lowered, than the men of the Longshields sprang upon them and pressed powerfully forward into the breach. In the ensuing action Admetus played a soldier's part, and Alexander himself was in the thick of it, fighting like the rest, and ever on the watch for any act of conspicuous courage in the face of danger among his men. The section of the defences where Alexander had chosen to take personal command was, in fact, the first to fall; the attacking force were no longer faced by a sheer and precipitous ascent but had, for the first time, firm ground under their feet, and succeeded, in consequence, in driving the defenders from their position without difficulty. Admetus, leading the assault and calling to his men to follow, was killed by a spear-thrust while still upon the shattered wall, but Alexander, hot on his heels, seized the breach and, having established control of some of the towers together with the sections of wall connecting them, passed on through the battlements towards the royal quarters, this way appearing to offer the most practicable descent into the town.

Meanwhile the operations of the fleet had been no less successful: the Phoenicians who were lying off the southern harbour smashed a way in through the defensive booms and made short work of the shipping inside, ramming some vessels where they lay afloat and driving others ashore; and the northern harbour, which was not even protected by booms, presented no difficulty to the Cyprians. They sailed straight in and quickly gained control of that portion of the town.

The main body of the Tyrian defenders abandoned the wall once they saw it was in the enemy's hands, and withdrew to the shrine of Agenor, where they turned to face the Macedonians. Alexander and the Longshields were soon upon them; some fell fighting, others fled, with Alexander in pursuit. The troops from the harbour were masters of the town; Coenus' battalion was already in; the slaughter was terrible – for the Macedonians, sick as they were of the length of the siege, went to work with savage ferocity. There was another reason, too, which roused them to rage; the Tyrians had taken some prisoners on their way from Sidon; these men they had subsequently dragged up on to the battlements, cut their throats in full view of the Macedonian army, and flung the bodies into the sea.

The Tyrian losses were about 8,000; the Macedonians, in the actual assault, lost Admetus, who was the first to mount the breach, and died as a soldier should, and twenty men of the Longshields who were with him. In the siege as a whole they lost about 400.

Azemilcus, the King of Tyre, together with the dignitaries of the town and certain visitors from Carthage who had come to the mother city to pay honour to Heracles according to an ancient custom, had fled for refuge to Heracles' temple: to all of these Alexander granted a free pardon; everyone else was sold into slavery. In all, including native Tyrians and foreigners taken in the town, some 30,000 were sold.

After the victory Alexander offered sacrifice to Heracles and held a ceremonial parade of his troops in full battle equipment; the fleet also took part in the review in the god's honour, and there were athletic contests in the Temple enclosure and a torch-race. The piece of siege-artillery which had made the breach was dedicated in the Temple, and the Tyrian ship sacred to Heracles, which had been captured in the naval action, was also solemnly presented to the god. There was an inscription on the vessel, composed either by Alexander himself or someone else. In any case it is not worth remembering, so I have not thought fit to record it here. In this way, then, Tyre was taken; the year was that of the archonship at Athens of Anicetus, and the month August.

While Alexander was still occupied with the siege, he was visited by envoys from Darius, who in the King's name offered a sum of 10,000 talents in exchange for his mother, wife, and children; they further proposed that all the territory west of the Euphrates right to the Aegean Sea should belong to Alexander, who should seal his bond of friendship and alliance with Persia by marrying Darius' daughter. These proposals were made known at a meeting of Alexander's personal advisers, and Parmenio, according to all reports, declared that were he Alexander he would be happy to end the war on such terms and be done with any further adventures. 'That,' replied Alexander, 'is what I should do were I Parmenio; but since I am Alexander, I shall send Darius a different answer.' And send it he did. He had no need, he wrote, of Darius' money, nor was there any call upon him to accept a part of the continent in place of the whole. All Asia, including its treasure, was already his property, and if he wished to marry Darius' daughter he would do so, whether Darius liked it or not. If, moreover, Darius wanted kindliness and consideration at his hands, he must come to ask for it in person. Upon receiving this reply, Darius abandoned all thought of coming to terms and began once more to prepare for war.

Alexander's next objective was Egypt. All of what is known as Syrian Palestine except the town of Gaza had already accepted Alexander's control. The master of this stronghold, however, a eunuch of the name of Batis, refused to join him. He had raised a force of mercenary Arab troops, and for some time past had been laying in stores sufficient for a protracted siege, and that, added to his confident belief that the town was too strongly defended ever to be taken by assault, induced him to refuse Alexander admission.

Gaza is about two and a half miles from the sea; the approach to it from the coast is over deep sand, and the sea off-shore is all encumbered with shoals. It was a large town, standing high on an eminence, and encircled by a strongly-built wall – the last town, on the edge of the desert, as one travels south from Phoenicia to Egypt.

Once within striking distance, Alexander took up a position opposite that section of the defences which seemed most open to assault, and ordered the assembly of his siege engines. His engineers expressed the opinion that the mound, or artificial eminence, on which the town stood was so high that it would not be possible to carry it by assault; Alexander, however, was firm in his belief that the greater the difficulty, the more necessary it was to take it; for a success so far beyond reason and probability would be a serious blow to the morale of the enemy, while failure, once Darius and the Greeks got to know of it, would be an equally serious blow to his own prestige.

The plan of campaign was to enable the siege engines to be brought to bear upon the defences by ringing the town with a raised earthwork up to the level of their base, and mounting the engines upon it; the work was concentrated chiefly upon the southern sector, where the wall appeared more vulnerable than elsewhere, and when a sufficient height had been reached the engines were mounted and prepared for action. At this moment Alexander, the ceremonial wreath upon his head, was on the point of offering, according to precedent, the first victim of the sacrifice, when a bird of prey flew over the altar and dropped upon his head a stone which it was carrying in its talons, and when Alexander asked Aristander what the omen might mean, 'Sire,' the seer replied, 'you will capture the town, but today you must take care for your own safety.'

Alexander, accordingly, kept out of range for a while, close to where his artillery was posted; before long, however, the defenders of the town made a sortie in strength; the Arab troops endeavoured to set fire to the siege engines, and heavy attacks with missile weapons delivered from their commanding position almost succeeded in thrusting the Macedonians back down the earthwork they had raised. At the sight of this reverse, Alexander forgot the seer's prophetic warning. Maybe he deliberately ignored it – perhaps the excitement of action put it out of his mind: in any case, at the head of his Long-shields he hurried to the support of the Macedonians at the very point where they were hardest pressed. For them, at any rate, his help was just in time: he saved them from being driven ignominiously from their position on the earthwork; but in the action a missile from a catapult pierced his shield and corselet and penetrated his shoulder. Aristander, then, had been right – he had foreseen the wound. Alexander was delighted, for he believed that the other prophecy would also be fulfilled, and that the town would fall. Meanwhile the wound was serious and did not easily yield to treatment.

The artillery which had been instrumental in the capture of Tyre had already been sent for, and now arrived by sea. Alexander gave orders for the raised earthwork, two furlongs broad and fifty-five feet high, to be carried right round the town. The artillery was assembled, mounted on the earthwork, and brought into action. Long stretches of the wall suffered heavy damage; saps were dug at various points, the earth being removed unobserved by the enemy, until in many places the wall, having nothing to support it, collapsed and fell. Pouring in volleys of missile weapons, the Macedonians were soon in control of a wide sector, thrusting the defenders back from the towers. Three assaults the men of Gaza bravely resisted, in spite of heavy casualties in dead and wounded; but at the fourth Alexander brought into action the main body of his heavy infantry on all sides of the town, the wall, already undermined, was battered down or widely breached where the artillery had already done its work, so that it was now an easy matter to get ladders on to the shattered defences, and thus force an entry. Once the ladders were in position, every Macedonian soldier who had any claim to courage vied with his fellows to be the first man up. The honour fell to Neoptolemus, one of the Hetaeri and an Aeacid by blood; hot on his heels came battalion after battalion, led by their officers, and no sooner had the leading sections penetrated the defences than they smashed down all the gates they could find and cleared an entrance for the whole army.

The defenders, though the town was taken, still stood shoulder to shoulder and fought to the last. Every one of them was killed at his post. Their women and children were sold as slaves. People from neighbouring tribes were settled in the town and Alexander used it as a block-house for possible future operations.

BOOK THREE

ALEXANDER now made for Egypt, which was the original object
of his southerly march, and a week after leaving Gaza arrived at
Pelusium, where the fleet which had accompanied him, sailing coast-
wise from Phoenicia, was already at anchor. Mazaces, the Persian
governor of Egypt under Darius, had no native troops under his
command, and this, added to the report of the battle of Issus and of
Darius' ignominious scramble for safety, and the fact that Phoenicia,
Syria, and most of Arabia were already in Macedonian hands, induced
him to receive Alexander with a show of friendship and to offer no
obstacle to his free entry into Egypt and its cities.

Alexander garrisoned Pelusium and, after giving orders to the fleet
to proceed up the Nile to Memphis, set out southward along the east
bank of the river, and, crossing the desert, arrived at Heliopolis. All
the country along his route he secured without any native opposition.
From Heliopolis he crossed the river to Memphis, where, among the
other gods, he offered a special sacrifice to Apis and held Games with
both athletic and literary contests. The most famous performers in
Greece came over to take part. From Memphis he sailed down the
river again with his Longshields and archers, the Agrianes, and the
Royal Cavalry Squadron of the Hetaeri, to Canobus, when he proceeded round Lake Mareotis and finally came ashore at the spot where
Alexandria, the city which bears his name, now stands. He was at once
struck by the excellence of the site, and convinced that if a city were
built upon it, it would prosper. Such was his enthusiasm that he could
not wait to begin the work; he himself designed the general layout of
the new town, indicating the position of the market square, the number of temples to be built, and what gods they should serve – the gods
of Greece and the Egyptian Isis – and the precise limits of its outer
defences. He offered sacrifice for a blessing on the work; and the
sacrifice proved favourable.

A story is told – and I do not see why one should disbelieve it – that
Alexander wished to leave his workmen the plan of the city's outer
defences, but there were no available means of marking out the

ground. One of the men, however, had the happy idea of collecting
the meal from the soldiers' packs and sprinkling it on the ground behind the King as he led the way; and it was by this means that Alexander's design for the outer wall was actually transferred to the
ground. The soothsayers pondered the significance of this – especially,
of course, Aristander of Telmissus, who had the reputation of having
already proved a true prophet to Alexander on many occasions – and
their conclusion was that the new town would prosper and that,
among its blessings, the chief would be the fruits of the earth.

Meanwhile Hegelochus arrived in Egypt by sea with the news that
Tenedos, which had been forcibly annexed by Persia, had now revolted and come over to Macedon. Chios, too, in spite of the puppet
government introduced by Autophradates and Pharnabazus, had invited the Macedonians in; Pharnabazus had been captured in the
island together with Aristonicus, the master of Methymna: the latter
had entered the harbour at Chios with five pirate chasers, not being
aware that it was already in Macedonian hands and misled by the
statement of the men in charge of the defences that the vessels inside
were Pharnabazus' fleet. All the pirate crews had been killed then and
there, but he was bringing Aristonicus to Alexander, together with
Apollonides, Phisinus, Megareus, and everyone else who had taken
part in the original revolt of the island and had unlawfully seized control of its affairs. He further reported that he had taken the control of
Mitylene from Chares and that the other Lesbian towns had consented
to support him; Amphoterus had been dispatched with sixty ships to
Cos, at the invitation of its people – indeed, he had himself visited Cos
and found it already in Amphoterus' hands. All the other prisoners he
brought with him, with the exception of Pharnabazus, who had given
his guards the slip in Cos and escaped.

Alexander sent the political bosses back to the towns in which they
had exercised their power, to be dealt with by the people on the spot
as the fancy took them; the Chians with Apollonides he sent to
Elephantine in Egypt under regular guard.

After these events Alexander suddenly found himself passionately
eager to visit the shrine of Ammon in Libya. One reason was his wish
to consult the oracle there, as it had a reputation for infallibility, and
also because Perseus and Heracles were supposed to have consulted it,
the former when he was sent by Polydectes to slay the Gorgon, the

latter during his journeys in Libya and Egypt in search of Antaeus and
Busiris. But there was also another reason: Alexander longed to equal
the fame of Perseus and Heracles; the blood of both flowed in his
veins, and just as legend traced their descent from Zeus, so he, too,
had a feeling that in some way he was descended from Ammon. In
any case, he undertook this expedition with the deliberate purpose of
obtaining more precise information on this subject – or at any rate to
say that he had obtained it.

He began his journey, according to Aristobulus' account, by marching 200 miles along the coast to Paraetonium. The country through
which he passed was uninhabited but not waterless. At Paraetonium
he turned south towards the interior, where the oracle of Ammon
was situated. The way to it is across the desert, most of it sandy and
waterless. Fortunately for Alexander there was much rain – the god's
own gift, as he supposed. Now it happens that a southerly wind in
those parts buries the track deep in sand so that it is impossible to see
it; travellers lose their bearings like sailors at sea; there are no marks
along the track, no hill, no tree, no eminence of solid earth thrusting
up through the sand, to enable the wayfarer to set his course, as seamen do by the stars. In fact, the guides were lost and Alexander's army
was going astray. In this dangerous situation, however, the god had
another gift to give: according to Ptolemy, son of Lagus, two snakes
led the army, hissing as they went, and Alexander told his guides to
trust in providence and follow them. This they did, and the snakes led
the way both to the oracle and back again. There is a commoner version of the story recorded by Aristobulus: according to this, Alexander's guides were two crows which flew along in front of the army;
in any case I have no doubt whatever that he had divine assistance of
some kind – for what could be more likely? But precisely what form
it took we shall never know because of the disparity in the various
records.

The shrine of Ammon is surrounded on all sides by a waterless
desert of sand; but in the midst of this waste there is a small plot of
ground, five miles wide at its broadest point, and thickly planted with
fruit trees – olives and date-palms. This, the actual site of the temple,
is the only spot in the surrounding desert which has any moisture.
Dew falls, and there is a spring, quite unlike other springs elsewhere:
its water at midday is cold to the taste and still more so to the touch –

nothing could be colder; but as the sun goes down and evening draws in, it gets warmer, and continues to rise in temperature until midnight, when it reaches its peak. After midnight it cools again, and by dawn it is already cold, though coldest, as I have said, at noon. The same changes in temperature are repeated every day in a regular cycle. Natural salt is also mined in this region; some of it is taken to Egypt by priests of the Temple, who before they begin their journey pack it in palm-leaf baskets and then carry it as a present, sometimes to the king. The salt is in large grains, some of which have been found to be more than three fingers broad, and it is as clear as crystal. The Egyptians and other people who are particular about religious observance use it for their sacrifices in preference to sea salt, because of its greater purity.

It was with deep admiration that Alexander surveyed the Temple and its site. He put his question to the oracle and received (or so he said) the answer which his heart desired. Then he began his return journey to Egypt, following, according to Aristobulus, the same route as before. Ptolemy, son of Lagus, states that he took a different route and went direct to Memphis.

At Memphis he was visited by a number of deputations from Greece, and not a man of them did he send away without a favourable answer to his requests. He was joined here by a force of 400 Greek mercenaries sent by Antipater under the command of Menidas, son of Hegesander, and 500 Thracian cavalry commanded by Asclepiodorus, son of Eunicus. Here, too, he offered sacrifice to Zeus the King and held a ceremonial parade of his troops in battle order, followed by games with athletic and literary contests. He reorganized the country politically, appointing Doloaspis and Petisis, both Egyptians, as provincial governors, each to control one half of the country; but as Petisis declined the appointment, the whole was taken over by Doloaspis. To command the garrisons at Memphis and Pelusium he posted, respectively, Pantaleon of Pydna and Polemon of Pella, son of Megacles; Lycides, a Greek from Aetolia, was given the charge of the mercenaries. Other appointments were that of Eugnostus, son of Xenophantes, a member of the Hetaeri, to be Secretary of foreign troops, and of Aeschylus and Ephippus of Chalcis to superintend the work of the two latter men. The governorship of the neighbouring county of Libya was given to Apollonius, son of Charinus, and of

Arabia by Heröopolis to Cleomenes of Naucratis; the latter was instructed to permit the existing nomarchs, or district governors, to carry on as before except for the collection of tribute, which they, in their turn, were ordered to pay him. Peucestes son of Macartatus and Balacrus son of Amyntas were posted to the command of the troops to be left in Egypt, and Polemon son of Theramenes to the command of the fleet. Leonnatus son of Onasus was taken into the King's personal bodyguard in place of Arrhybas, who had died. Antiochus, the commander of the archers, had also died, and a Cretan named Ombrion was appointed to succeed him. Calanus took over the allied infantry in place of Balacrus, who was to remain in Egypt.

Alexander was deeply impressed by Egypt, and it is generally supposed that the potential strength of the country, which was greater than he expected, induced him to divide the control of it among a number of officers, as he judged it to be unsafe to put it all into the hands of one man. No doubt the Romans took a leaf from Alexander's book when they decided to keep Egypt under strict surveillance, and never to send a senator there as proconsul, but always a man from the class of Equites, or Knights.

At the first sign of spring Alexander left Memphis, crossing the Nile by a bridge which had been built for him over the river and all its canals, and marched for Phoenicia. At Tyre he found the fleet awaiting him, and here, once again, he did honour to Heracles by religious celebrations and games. While he was in Tyre, the Athenian State Galley arrived with Diophantus and Achilles on board – and indeed her entire crew, being all free citizens, were members of the deputation. Approaching Alexander, these men achieved all the objects of their mission, the most important of which was the return of the Athenian prisoners of war taken at the battle of the Granicus. News now came that things were on the move in the Peloponnese, and Amphoterus was sent with instructions to support all the Greek communities in that part of the country, which had sound views on the Persian war and did not take their orders from Sparta. Phoenicia and Cyprus were to furnish 100 ships for the Peloponnese, in addition to the fleet which was being dispatched with Amphoterus.

The time had now come to be on the march again – inland, for Thapsacus and the Euphrates. Before starting, he entrusted Coeranus of Beroea with the collection of tribute in Phoenicia, and Philoxenus in Asia west of Taurus; both these men had been in charge of the money actually with Alexander on campaign, and their office was now taken over by Harpalus, son of Machatas, who had recently been recalled from exile. Harpalus had twice fled the country: the first time was when Philip was still on the throne of Macedon, and he was then driven into exile for his loyalty to Alexander. Ptolemy son of Lagus, Nearchus son of Androtimus, Erigyus son of Larichus, and his brother Laomedon all shared the same fate for the same reason; for the fact was that at that period Philip's marriage with Eurydice, in open contempt of Alexander's mother Olympias, had given rise to certain suspicions in the young Prince's mind. These men were recalled from exile after Philip's death, and raised by Alexander to important offices: Ptolemy was enrolled in the King's bodyguard; Harpalus, whose health was not good enough for active service, was given control of the treasury, Erigyus the command of the allied cavalry, and his brother Laomedon, who happened to be as fluent in the Persian language as in Greek, was put in charge of prisoners of war. Nearchus was appointed Governor of Lycia and the neighbouring territory as far as Mount Taurus. However, shortly before the battle of Issus, Harpalus was persuaded by a scoundrel named Tauriscus to desert – which they both did: Tauriscus made his way to Alexander of Epirus in Italy, where he died; and Harpalus took refuge in the Megarid. In spite of this conduct Alexander urged him to return, assuring him that he would in no way suffer for his desertion. Nor, indeed, did he; on the contrary, Alexander restored him to the control of the treasury.

Finally, Alexander sent Menander, one of the Hetaeri, as governor to Lydia, appointing Clearchus to succeed to his command of the mercenaries; the governorship of Syria was given to Asclepiodorus, son of Eunicus, in place of Arimmas, who, in Alexander's opinion, had scamped his work of supplying and equipping the troops for their march into the interior.

Alexander reached Thapsacus in August, during the archonship of Aristophanes in Athens. Two bridges were already across the river. For some time previously Mazaeus, under orders from the Persian King, had been guarding the approaches to the river with a force of 3,000 mounted troops, two-thirds of them Greek mercenaries; and for this reason the Macedonians had not carried their bridge right to the further bank, lest the enemy should attack it at their end. Mazaeus, however, no sooner got wind of Alexander's approach than he made off at his best speed with all his men, whereupon the two bridges were promptly completed, and Alexander was able to use them to get his army across.

Thence he proceeded north and east, keeping the Euphrates and the Armenian mountains on his left, through Mesopotamia; for once across the river he preferred not to follow the direct route to Babylon, as by this other route supplies of all sorts, including fodder for the horses, would be more readily available; other needs for man and beast could be supplied by the country through which they passed, and, furthermore, the heat would be less intense.

During the march some prisoners were taken – men from Darius' army who had gone off on reconnaissance. They reported that Darius had taken up a position on the Tigris and intended to resist any attempt by Alexander to cross it. The force under his command greatly exceeded in numbers what he had had at the battle of Issus. Alexander's reply to this news was to push on for the Tigris at all speed. However, upon reaching it he found neither Darius nor the guard he had left there; so he crossed without opposition – except from the current, which was swift and made the operation a difficult one. Once over the river, he gave his men a rest.

While the troops were resting, there was an almost total eclipse of the moon, and Alexander offered sacrifice to Moon, Sun, and Earth, the three deities supposed to be concerned in this phenomenon. The opinion of Aristander, the seer, was that the moon's failure was propitious for Alexander and the Macedonians, and that the coming battle would be fought before the month was out; he concluded, moreover, that the sacrifices portended victory.

Alexander now continued his advance through Aturia, keeping the Tigris on his right and the mountains of Gordya on his left. Four days after the crossing of the river a report came in from his scouts that enemy cavalry had been sighted in open ground, but their numbers could not be accurately estimated; Alexander accordingly, before advancing further, made the necessary dispositions for an engagement, and immediately afterwards more scouts rode in; these had had a better view of the enemy force, and declared their belief that it was not above 1,000 strong, whereupon Alexander rode for it at the gallop

D

with the Royal Squadron, one squadron of Hetaeri, and the Paeonian
rangers. The main body of the army was ordered to follow at its
own pace. The sight of Alexander's rapid approach was too much for
the Persian cavalry, who incontinently fled, with Alexander in hot
pursuit; most of them got away, but a few, whose horses could not
stand the pace, were killed, and a few others were taken alive, horses
and all. From these prisoners they learned that Darius was not far off,
with a powerful force.

Darius' army had been reinforced by the Sogdians, the Bactrians,
and the Indian tribes on the Bactrian border – all under the command
of Bessus, satrap of Bactria; their lead had been followed by certain
contingents of the Sacae (a branch of the Asiatic Scythians) who,
though they owed no allegiance to Bessus, were in military alliance
with Persia. These troops were mounted archers, and were commanded by Manaces. The Arachotians and the Indian hillmen were
commanded by Barsaentes, satrap of Arachotia; the Areians by their
satrap, Satibarzanes; the Parthians, Hyrcanians, and Tapurians, all
mounted troops, by Phrataphernes; the Medes, to whom were attached the Cadusians, Albanians, and Sacesinians, by Atropates; all
contingents from the neighbourhood of the Persian Gulf by Ocondo-
bates, Ariobarzanes, and Orxines; the Uxians and Susiani by Oxathres,
son of Abulites; the Babylonians, to whom were attached the Sitacenians and Carians, by Bupares (these Carians had previously been re-
settled after a mass transference of population); the Armenians by
Orontes and Mithraustes; the Cappadocians by Ariaces; the lowland
and Mesopotamian Syrians by Mazaeus. Darius' total force was estimated at 40,000 cavalry, 1,000,000 infantry, 200 scythe-chariots, and
a few elephants – the Indian troops from the hither side of the Indus
had about fifteen of them.

This was the army which had taken up a position under Darius at
Gaugamela, near the river Bumodus, about seventy-five miles from
Arbela. The country where it lay was level and open, all places where
a broken surface might obstruct the movement of cavalry having
been worked on some time previously by the Persian troops, so that
all of it was now good going for both chariots and cavalry. The reason
for this precaution was the fact that it had been urged upon Darius that
much of his trouble at the battle of Issus had been due to lack of space to
manœuvre in – an explanation which Darius was very ready to accept.

On receiving this information from the Persian prisoners, Alexander stayed where he was for four days, to rest his men after their march. He fortified his camp with a ditch and palisade, as he proposed to leave the pack-animals there together with all troops unfit for service, while he himself led to battle the remainder burdened with nothing but their weapons. The order to fall in was given, and at night, about the second watch, the advance began – so timed as to engage the enemy at dawn. The report that Alexander was on the move soon reached Darius, and he, too, ordered his men to battle stations. Meanwhile Alexander was drawing nearer, his troops ready to engage – but the opposing armies were still seven miles apart and had not yet seen each other, as each was screened by a ridge of high ground.

Past the crest of the ridge, just as he was beginning the descent, Alexander had his first sight of the enemy, about four miles away. He gave the order to halt, and sent for his officers – his personal staff, generals, squadron commanders, and officers of the allied and mercenary contingents – to consult upon the plan of action. The alternatives were either to advance at once with the main corps of infantry, as the majority urged him to do, or to accept the advice of Parmenio and stay where they were long enough to enable a careful reconnaissance of the ground to be made; for there might well be reasons for caution – hidden obstructions, concealed trenches or stakes – and, in addition to that, it would be wise to get a more accurate knowledge of the enemy's dispositions. Parmenio's proposal appeared the better of the two; so for the moment there was no further forward move, the troops all remaining in the order in which they were to engage.

Alexander meanwhile carried out a wide reconnaissance with his light infantry and the mounted Hetaeri, minutely examining the whole terrain where the battle would be fought; he then returned and called a second meeting of his officers. There was no need, he said, for any words from him to encourage them to do their duty; there was inspiration enough in the courage they had themselves shown in previous battles, and in the many deeds of heroism they had already performed. All he asked was that every officer of whatever rank, whether he commended a company, a squadron, a brigade, or an infantry battalion, should urge to their utmost efforts the men entrusted to his command; for they were about to fight, not, as before, for Syria or

Phoenicia or Egypt, but this time the issue at stake was the sovereignty of the whole Asian continent. What need, then, was there for many words to rouse his officers to valour, when that valour was already in their own breasts? Let him but remind them each for himself to preserve discipline in the hour of danger – to advance, when called upon to do so, in utter silence; to watch the time for a hearty cheer, and, when the moment came, to roar out their battle-cry and put the fear of God into the enemy's hearts. All must obey orders promptly and pass them on without hesitation to their men; and, finally, every one of them must remember that upon the conduct of each depended the fate of all: if each man attended to his duty, success was assured; if one man neglected it, the whole army would be in peril.

With some such brief words of exhortation Alexander addressed his officers, and in reply they begged him to have every confidence in them. Orders were then given for the troops to rest and eat.

Some authorities state that Parmenio went to Alexander's tent and advised a night attack, because the enemy would not be expecting it, and it would naturally cause alarm and confusion. Alexander and Parmenio were not alone in the tent; others were listening, and that, perhaps, was one reason for Alexander's reply: 'I will not,' he said, 'demean myself by stealing victory like a thief. Alexander must defeat his enemies openly and honestly.' However, these lofty words probably indicated confidence in danger rather than vanity, and in my own opinion they were based upon perfectly sound sense: night-fighting is a tricky business; unexpected things happen to both sides – to those who have carefully planned the attack as much as to those who are taken off their guard – and often enough the better men get the worst of it, while victory, contrary to everybody's expectation, goes to the weaker side. More often than not Alexander took risks in his battles; but on this occasion he felt the chances of a night attack to be too unpredictable; moreover, the mere fact that it was delivered stealthily and under cover of darkness would save Darius, were he again defeated, the necessity of admitting inferiority, either in himself or in his men; while if they themselves suffered an unexpected reverse, they would be a defeated army in an unfamiliar country among enemies thoroughly at home and surrounded by friends – and of those enemies not a few would be the prisoners of war, who might well attack them at night even after an indecisive victory, not to mention a defeat.

These arguments were sound enough, and I therefore commend Alexander's decision, and approve no less his resounding claim to act openly.

During the night Darius' army kept the same dispositions as on the previous day, the reason for maintaining battle stations being their fear of a night attack, added to the fact that their position had no regular defence works. One thing, at this critical moment, told against the Persians more than anything else: their protracted stand under arms, and the consequent fear, natural enough when lives are at stake, but on this occasion rendered less bearable by the fact that it did not come, as it were, in a flash from the moment's crisis, but had been brooded on hour after hour until their spirit was sapped.

We are informed by Aristobulus that Darius' written orders for the disposition of his troops came into Greek hands after the battle; we know, consequently, what his order of battle was. On his left was the Bactrian cavalry supported by the Daae and Arachotians; in touch with them were mixed Persian cavalry and infantry, followed by Susian, and then by Cadusian contingents. These units composed the left wing of the army as far as the centre. On the right were the contingents from Lowland Syria and Mesopotamia, and the Medes; then, in touch with these, were the Parthians and the Sacae; then the Tapurian and Hyrcanian contingents; lastly, next to the centre, the Albanians and Sacesinians. In the centre, with Darius himself and his kinsmen, were the royal Persian bodyguard with the golden apples on their spear-butts, the Indians, the so-called 'stateless' Carians, and the Mardian archers. Uxians, Babylonians, troops from the Persian Gulf, and Sitacenians were drawn up in depth behind them. In advance of the left wing, facing Alexander's right, were the Scythian cavalry, about 1,000 Bactrians and 100 scythe-chariots – the elephants and fifty war-chariots were posted in close support of the Royal Squadron of the King's cavalry. In advance of the Persian right were fifty scythe-chariots and the Armenian and Cappadocian cavalry; the Greek mercenaries – the only troops likely to be a match for the Macedonian infantry – were drawn up facing them in two sections, one on each side of Darius and his Persian guard.

On the right wing of Alexander's army was the mounted brigade of the Hetaeri, led by the Royal Squadron under the command of Cleitus, son of Dropides; in touch with them, and working towards the centre, were the squadrons under the following officers and in the following order: Glaucias, Ariston, Sopolis son of Hermodorus, Heracleides son of Antiochus, Demetrius son of Althaemenes, and Meleager; finally there was the royal squadron commanded by Hegelochus son of Hippostratus. Parmenio's son Philotas was general officer in command of the mounted Hetaeri. Of the infantry, the shock troops of the Longshields were posted in closest touch with the cavalry, and were supported on their own left by the other Long-shields units under the command of Nicanor, son of Parmenio; next to them was the brigade of Coenus son of Polemocrates, followed (working towards the left) by the units commanded respectively by Perdiccas son of Orontes, Meleager son of Neoptolemus, Polysper-chon son of Simmias, and Amyntas son of Andromenes – the last being commanded by Simmias, as Amyntas had been sent to Mace-donia to recruit.

The left of the Macedonian infantry line consisted of the brigade of Craterus son of Alexander – who commanded all the infantry in that sector; in touch with him were the allied cavalry units under Erigyus son of Larichus, supported by the Thessalian cavalry commanded by Philippus son of Menelaus. The Thessalian cavalry extended to the left wing of the army, the whole of which was under the general command of Parmenio son of Philotas. Close about this officer were grouped the mounted troops of Pharsalia, the finest and most power-ful unit of the Thessalian cavalry.

Such was the disposition of Alexander's front line, in addition to which he posted reserve formations in order to have a solid core of infantry to meet a possible attack from the rear; the officers of the re-serve had orders, in the event of an encircling movement by the enemy, to face about and so meet the threatened attack. One half of the Agrianes, commanded by Attalus and in touch with the Royal Squadron on the right wing, were, together with the Macedonian archers under Briso, thrown forward at an oblique angle, in case it should suddenly prove necessary to extend or close up the front line of infantry, and in support of the archers was the so-called 'Old Guard' of mercenaries under Cleander. In advance of the Agrianes and archers were the mounted skirmishers and the Paeonians, com-manded by Aretes and Ariston; the mercenary cavalry commanded by Menidas were posted right in the van. The position in advance of

the Royal Squadron and other units of the Hetaeri was occupied by
the other half of the Agriane contingent and of the archers, supported
by Balacrus' spearmen who stood facing the Persian scythe-chariots.
Menidas had orders to wheel and attack the enemy in the flank, should
they attempt an out-flanking movement.

So much for Alexander's right; on his left, forming an angle with
the main body, were the Thracians under Sitalces supported, first, by
the allied cavalry under Coeranus and, secondly, by the Odrysian
cavalry under Agathon son of Tyrimmes. Right in the van of this
sector was the foreign mercenary cavalry commanded by Andromachus son of Hiero. The Thracian infantry had orders to stand guard
over the pack-animals. The total strength of Alexander's army was
7,000 cavalry and about 40,000 foot.

The two armies were now close together. Darius and his picked
troops were in full view. There stood the Persian Royal Guard, the
golden apples on their spear-butts, the Indians and Albanians, the
Carians and the Mardian bowmen – the cream of the Persian force,
full in face of Alexander as he moved with his Royal Squadron to the
attack. Alexander, however, inclined slightly to his right, a move
which the Persians at once countered, their left outflanking the Macedonians by a considerable distance. Meanwhile in spite of the fact that
Darius' Scythian cavalry, moving along the Macedonian front, had
already made contact with their forward units, Alexander continued
his advance towards the right until he was almost clear of the area
which the Persians had levelled during the previous days. Darius
knew that once the Macedonians reached rough ground his chariots
would be useless, so he ordered the mounted troops in advance of his
left to encircle the Macedonian right under Alexander and thus check
any further extension in that direction. Alexander promptly ordered
Menidas and his mercenary cavalry to attack them. A counter-attack
by the Scythian cavalry and their supporting Bactrians drove them
back by weight of numbers, whereupon Alexander sent in against the
Scythians Ariston's Paeonian contingent and the mercenaries. This
stroke had its effect, and the enemy gave ground; but the remaining
Bactrian units came to the support of the Paeonians and foreign
troops and succeeded in rallying the fugitives. A close cavalry action
ensued, in which the Macedonians suffered the more severely, outnumbered as they were and less adequately provided with defensive

armour than the Scythians were – both horses and men. None the less the Macedonians held their attacks, and by repeated counter-charges, squadron by squadron, succeeded in breaking the enemy formation.

Meanwhile as Alexander moved forward the Persians sent their scythe-chariots into action against him, in the hope of throwing his line into confusion. But in this they were disappointed; for the chariots were no sooner off the mark than they were met by the missile weapons of the Agrianes and Balacrus' javelin-throwers, who were stationed in advance of the mounted Hetaeri; again, they seized the reins and dragged the drivers to the ground, then surrounded the horses and cut them down. Some few of the vehicles succeeded in passing through, but to no purpose, for the Greeks had orders, where-ever they attacked, to break formation and let them through deliber-ately: this they did, with the result that neither they, the objects of the attack, nor the vehicles themselves suffered any damage whatever. Such as got through were, however, subsequently dealt with by the Royal Guard and the army grooms.

Darius now brought into action the main body of his infantry, and an order was sent to Aretes to attack the Persian cavalry which was trying to outflank and surround the Greek right. For a time Alexander continued to advance in column; presently, however, the movement of the Persian cavalry, sent to the support of their comrades who were attempting to encircle the Macedonian right, left a gap in the Persian front – and this was Alexander's opportunity. He promptly made for the gap, and, with his mounted Hetaeri and all the heavy infantry in this sector of the line, drove in his wedge and raising the battle-cry pressed forward at the double straight for the point where Darius stood. A close struggle ensued, but it was soon over; for when the Macedonian horse, with Alexander himself at the head of them, vigor-ously pressed the assault, fighting hand to hand and thrusting at the Persians' faces with their spears, and the infantry phalanx in close order and bristling with pikes added its irresistible weight, Darius, who had been on edge since the battle began and now saw nothing but terrors all around him, was the first to turn tail and ride for safety. The outflanking party on the Macedonian right was also broken up by the powerful assault of Aretes and his men.

On this part of the field the Persian rout was complete, and the Macedonians pressed the pursuit, cutting down the fugitives as they rode. But the formation under Simmias and his staff, unable to link up with Alexander to join in the pursuit, was forced to stand its ground and continue the struggle on the spot, a report having come in that the Macedonian left was in trouble. At this point the Greek line was broken, and some of the Indian and Persian cavalry burst through the gap and penetrated right to the rear where the Macedonian pack-animals were. There was some hard fighting; the Persians set about it with spirit, most of their adversaries being unarmed men who had never expected a break-through – at any rate here, where the phalanx was of double strength; moreover, the prisoners joined in the attack. However, the officers in command of the reserves on this sector, the moment the situation was clear, faced about according to orders and appeared in the Persian rear. Many of the Persians, as they swarmed round the baggage-trains, were killed; others did not stay to fight, but made off.

Meanwhile the Persian right, not yet knowing that Darius had fled, made a move to envelop Alexander's left and delivered a flank attack on Parmenio. The Macedonians being caught, as it were, between two fires, Parmenio sent an urgent message to Alexander that his position was serious and that he needed help. Alexander at once broke off the pursuit, wheeled about with his mounted Hetaeri and charged the Persian right at the gallop. Coming first into contact with those of the enemy cavalry who were trying to get away, he was soon heavily engaged with the Parthians, some of the Indians, and the strongest and finest cavalry units of Persia. The ensuing struggle was the fiercest of the whole action; one after another the Persian squadrons wheeled in file to the charge; breast to breast they hurled themselves on the enemy. Conventional cavalry tactics – manoeuvring, javelin-throwing – were forgotten; it was every man for himself, struggling to break through as if in that alone lay his hope of life. Desperately and without quarter, blows were given and received, each man fighting for mere survival without any further thought of victory or defeat. About sixty of Alexander's companions – picked troops of the Hetaeri – were killed; among the wounded were Coenus, Menidas, and Hephaestion himself.

In this struggle Alexander was once again victorious. Such Persians as managed to fight their way through galloped off the field to save their skins.

Alexander was now on the point of engaging the Persian right; but his help was not needed, as in this sector the Thessalian cavalry had fought hardly less magnificently than Alexander himself. The Persians were already in retreat by the time he made contact with them, so he turned back and started once more in pursuit of Darius, continuing as long as daylight served. Parmenio, in chase of his own quarry, was not far behind him. Once across the Lycus, Alexander halted for a brief rest for men and horses, and Parmenio went on to take possession of the Persian camp and all its contents; baggage, elephants, and camels.

Allowing his troops to rest till midnight, Alexander then pressed on to Arbela in the hope that he might catch Darius there and seize his treasure and all the other stuff with which a King of Persia takes the field. But though he reached this place on the following day, after a chase since the battle of some seventy-five miles, he failed to find Darius, who in his efforts to escape had kept going without a single break; his treasure, however, and all his valuables fell into Alexander's hands, including his chariot, shield, and bow – all captured for the second time.

Alexander's losses in this battle amounted to about 100 men killed; over 1,000 horses – nearly half of them belonging to the Hetaeri – perished either from wounds or from exhaustion in the pursuit. The Persian losses were reckoned at about 300,000 dead, a figure greatly exceeded by the number of prisoners. The elephants and such war-chariots as escaped destruction were also captured. Such was the end of the battle of Gaugamela, fought in the month of October during the archonship at Athens of Aristophanes. Aristander had foretold that before the month which saw the moon's eclipse was over, the battle would be fought and Alexander would win it. He was a true prophet.

Upon leaving the field, Darius made straight for Media by way of the Armenian mountains; with him was the Bactrian cavalry, which had been posted at his side during the fight, and certain Persians – his kinsmen and a small number of the Royal Guard. He was joined on the way by about 2,000 foreign mercenary troops under the command of Paron of Phocis and Glaucus of Aetolia. The reason why he made for Media was his belief that Alexander, once the battle was over, would take the road to Susa and Babylon, which was a fairly easy one for his transport; moreover, all that part of the country was inhabited, and, which was more important, Babylon and Susa were obvious prizes for a victorious army. The route to Media, on the other hand, was an awkward one for a large force.

Darius' guess was right, for Alexander did, in point of fact, make straight from Arbela to Babylon. Not far from the city, which he took the precaution of approaching in battle order, he was met by the people of the place who with their priests and magistrates came flocking out to bring him various gifts and to offer to put the city, with the citadel and all its treasures, into his hands. He marched in accordingly, and instructed the people to restore the temples which had been destroyed by Xerxes, in particular the temple of Bel, the god held by the Babylonians in the greatest awe. He appointed Mazaeus to the governorship of the city, Apollodorus of Amphipolis was put in command of the troops to be left there, and Asclepiodorus, son of Philo, was entrusted with the collection of tribute. Mithrines, the man who had surrendered to Alexander the inner defences of Sardis, was sent as governor to Armenia.

It was here in Babylon that Alexander came into contact with the Chaldaeans; in all matters of religious ceremonial he took their advice, offering sacrifice to Bel in particular, according to their instructions.

His next objective was Susa. He was met on the way there by the governor's son and a messenger with a letter from Philoxenus, whom he had sent to Susa immediately after the battle; the letter stated that the people of Susa had opened their gates and that all the treasure was secured. The march from Babylon took twenty days, and the treasure which Alexander took over upon entering the city amounted to 50,000 talents of silver in addition to other valuables formerly in possession of the King; nor was this by any means all that Susa yielded, for there also fell into Alexander's hands all the treasures which Xerxes had brought there from Greece, among them bronze statues of Harmodius and Aristogeiton. These statues Alexander sent back to Athens, where they now stand in the Cerameicus, on the way to the Acropolis, opposite the Metroön and not far from the altar of the Eudanemi. This altar stands on the level ground, as everyone knows who has been initiated into the mysteries of the Two Goddesses at Eleusis.

Here in Susa, Alexander offered the traditional sacrifices and celebrated games and a torch race; before leaving, he appointed a Persian
named Abulites as governor of the province, made Mazarus, one of
the Hetaeri, garrison commandant of the city, and promoted Archelaus, son of Theodorus, general of the forces. Before setting out for the
province of Persia, he sent Menes to the coast as governor of Syria,
Phoenicia, and Cilicia, giving him 3,000 talents of silver with instructions to pay over to Antipater as much of that sum as he should need
for the expenses of the Lacedaemonian war. Here too he was joined
by Amyntas, son of Andromenes, with the fresh troops from Macedonia, both horse and foot; the former he attached to the cavalry of
the Hetaeri, and distributed the latter according to nationality among
the various infantry units. He also – this was an innovation – formed
two companies in each cavalry squadron and put them under the
command of such officers of the Hetaeri who had distinguished themselves.

He then set out for the province of Persia, and after crossing the
Pasitigris entered the territory of the Uxians, a part of whom – those,
namely, who occupied the plains and owed allegiance to the Persian
satrap – surrendered to Alexander. The hill tribes, on the contrary,
who had never recognized Persian dominion, sent a message to Alexander to the effect that they would not allow him or his army to pass
through into Persia unless they first received what they always used
to receive from the Persian King, whenever he chanced to come that
way. Alexander dismissed the messengers with an invitation to meet
him at the pass, the control of which also gave them – or so they supposed – the control of the route into Persia. At the pass, he declared,
he would give them what they asked for. Then with a force consisting
of his personal guard, the Longshields, and about 8,000 other troops,
and with a party of guides from Susa, he set out under cover of darkness by a route no one would be likely to expect him to take; the
going was rough and difficult, and within a single day he swooped
down on the villages, carried off a great deal of plunder, and killed a
number of the villagers before they could rise from their beds – the
rest escaped to the hills. He then hurried on to the pass, where the
Uxians counted upon meeting him with all the force they could
muster, to receive payment of the customary dues. Craterus, meanwhile, had been sent in advance to seize the high ground to which the

Uxians would in all probability try to make their escape, when they found themselves hard pressed.

Alexander's advance was rapid and unhesitating; he seized the pass before the natives could reach it, and from this commanding position began, in battle order, to move down to the attack. So swiftly had he acted that the Uxians were taken hopelessly by surprise; robbed of the position in which their chief advantage lay, they made no attempt at resistance, but incontinently fled. Some were killed as they tried to get away, and many more on the rough and precipitous mountain track; most of them, however, managed to reach the hills, where they perished at the hands of Craterus and his men. Such were the 'dues' paid by Alexander to the Uxians; they had hard work, moreover, in persuading him to allow them to keep possession of their territory upon payment of an annual tribute. Ptolemy, son of Lagus, states that Darius' mother begged Alexander on their behalf to let them remain in their old homes. The tribute was assessed at 100 horses a year, 500 mules, and 30,000 sheep – the Uxians possessed no money and no arable land, being for the most part herdsmen.

After this Parmenio was given orders to proceed by the main road into Persia with the Thessalian cavalry, the allied and mercenary contingents, all the other more heavily armed units, and the baggage-trains; Alexander himself, at the head of a force consisting of the Macedonian infantry, the mounted Hetaeri, the Agrianes, archers, and mounted skirmishers, set off with all speed through the hills. At the Persian Gates he encountered Ariobarzanes, the satrap of the province, who had already built defences across the pass and with a force of about 40,000 foot and 700 horse had taken up a position there to prevent Alexander from getting through. Alexander checked his advance, but on the following day moved to the assault of the pass. It proved a hard task, as the enemy were in a commanding position and the ground was far from favourable to an attacker; they suffered severely from missiles hurled or catapulted from above, and Alexander was compelled to make a temporary withdrawal to his original position. His prisoners, however, undertook to show him another way round by which he could reach the further side of the pass; the track he was to follow was, he understood, a rough and narrow one, so he instructed Craterus to remain behind with his own and Meleager's brigade, a few archers, and about 500 mounted troops, and to attack the defences of the pass as soon as he was sure that the advanced party were safely round to the further side and were actually approaching the Persian position. The timing of this movement would cause no difficulty, as he would get a signal from the trumpeters.

Alexander moved off under cover of darkness and after a march of some twelve miles detached a force consisting of the Longshields, Perdiccas' brigade, the most lightly armed of the archers, the Agrianes, the Royal Squadron of the Hetaeri, and one double squadron of cavalry; with these troops he then made a turning movement and, still guided by the prisoners, went straight for the pass. Amyntas, Philotas, and Coenus had orders meanwhile to take the remainder of the troops down the hills and to bridge the river which would have to be crossed before entering the province of Persia. The track Alexander had to follow was still a rough and difficult one; however, he lost no time, taking most of it at the double. He was on top of the first enemy outpost before daylight, overwhelmed it and most of the second as well; nearly all the men in the third got away – not, however, back to the army, which they made no attempt to rejoin, but in panic flight to the hills – so that Alexander was enabled just before dawn to make a surprise attack on Ariobarzanes' main position. As he fell upon the trench, the trumpets sounded, and Craterus, accordingly, immediately moved to the assault of the outer defences on the other side. The enemy were properly caught; making no attempt at resistance, they would have fled for their lives had it been possible, but the Greeks were all round them, on one side Alexander pressing his attack, on the other Craterus and his men rapidly thrusting forward, so that most of them had no option but to turn back to the inner defences in the hope of saving themselves there. But these defences too were already in Macedonian hands, for Alexander, having foreseen how things would go, had left Ptolemy there with 3,000 infantrymen, who in some close fighting cut the greater part of the enemy to pieces. A few escaped, but in their desperate efforts to avoid destruction leapt to their death over the edge of the cliffs. Ariobarzanes and a few mounted men got clear away into the hills.

Alexander now pressed on with all speed to the river. It was already bridged and the army crossed without difficulty. Thence he marched to Persepolis with such rapidity that the garrison had no time to plunder the city's treasure before his arrival. He also captured the treasure of Cyrus the First at Pasargadae. He appointed Phrasaortes son of Rheomithras, to the governorship of Persepolis. He burnt the palace of the Persian kings, though this act was against the advice of Parmenio, who urged him to spare it for various reasons, chiefly because it was hardly wise to destroy what was now his own property, and because the Asians would, in his opinion, be less willing to support him if he seemed bent merely upon passing through their country as a conqueror rather than upon ruling it securely as a king. Alexander's answer was that he wished to punish the Persians for their invasion of Greece; his present act was retribution for the destruction of Athens, the burning of the temples, and all the other crimes they had committed against the Greeks. My own view is that this was bad policy; moreover it could hardly be considered as punishment for Persians long since dead and gone.

Having learned that Darius was in Media, Alexander made that country his next objective. Darius had decided, in the event of Alexander's stopping in the neighbourhood of Susa and Babylon, to remain in Media and to watch for any new move which he might make; if, on the other hand, Alexander advanced directly to attack him, he proposed to withdraw up-country to Parthia and Hyrcania and on to Bactra, scorching the earth as he went in order to impede any further advance by his enemy. His women and covered waggons and such other gear as he still had with him he sent to the pass known as the Caspian Gates, while he himself held on in Ecbatana with such troops as he had managed, in the circumstances, to get together. It was the report of this which induced Alexander to start for Media without delay. On the way he invaded and subdued the Paraetacae and left as governor there Oxathres son of Abulites, the former governor of Susa; then, a report reaching him that Darius who had been reinforced by troops from Scythia and Cadusia had determined upon risking another encounter, he proceeded in full battle order with the main body of his army, leaving the baggage-trains to follow on with their guards and all the rest of the stores.

Within twelve days he was in Media, where he learned that no Scythian or Cadusian reinforcements had reached Darius; his army was too weak to risk a battle, and he had determined upon a further withdrawal. Alexander, accordingly, increased the speed of his advance. About three days' march from Ecbatana he was met by

Bistanes son of Ochus, Darius' predecessor on the throne, and was informed by him that Darius had already been in retreat for five days; he was taking with him his treasure from Media amounting to 7,000 talents, and had a force of 3,000 cavalry and about 6,000 infantry.

At Ecbatana Alexander dismissed his Thessalian cavalry and the other allied contingents and ordered them back to the Aegean. The agreed amount of pay was settled in full, with a sum of 2,000 talents added by Alexander as gratuity. Any man who wished on his own account to continue his service as a paid soldier was to have his name entered on the pay-roll, and a considerable number thus voluntarily enlisted; the remainder were put under the command of Epocillus son of Polyeides with orders to march back to the Aegean. They were given a mounted guard, as the Thessalians had sold their horses. Instructions were added that when they reached the coast, Menes should attend to their transport by sea to Euboea. Parmenio was ordered to transfer the captured Persian treasure to the citadel in Ecbatana and hand it over for safe keeping to Harpalus, who had been left in charge of it with a guard of 6,000 Macedonians, a few light troops, and some cavalry. Parmenio was then to proceed through Cadusia to Hyrcania with the mercenaries, the Thracians, and all cavalry units except those of the Hetaeri; Cleitus, the commander of the Royal Squadron, who had been left behind on the sick-list in Susa, was ordered, as soon as he should arrive in Ecbatana, to start for Parthia with the Macedonian troops which had been left to guard the treasure. Alexander himself also proposed to make for Parthia.

Without delay Alexander's march began, its objective Darius. His force consisted of the mounted Hetaeri, the mounted skirmishers, the mercenary cavalry under Erigyus' command, the Macedonian heavy infantry (all of it except those sections detailed to guard the treasure), the archers, and the Agrianes. So rapid was the march that many of the men, unable to stand the pace, dropped out, and a number of horses were worked to death; but Alexander pressed on regardless of loss, and in eleven days reached Rhagae, a day's march – at this speed – from the Caspian Gates. Darius, however, had already passed through.

Many of Darius' men had deserted during the course of his retreat and dispersed to their homes, and a considerable number had surrendered to Alexander, who now, abandoning hope of overtaking Darius, halted for a five days' rest. He appointed to the governorship

of Media a Persian named Oxodates, a man who had been arrested by
Darius and confined in Susa – a circumstance which induced Alexander to trust him. Then he moved on towards Parthia. At the end of
the first day's march he halted close to the Caspian Gates; on the
second day he passed through, and advanced to the limit of cultivated
land; then, on a report that the country beyond was uninhabited, he
dispatched Coenus with a party of mounted troops and a few infantrymen to forage for supplies.

At this juncture two important persons in Darius' army, Bagistanes, a Babylonian nobleman, and Antibelus, one of Mazaeus' sons,
sought an interview with Alexander. Admitted to his presence, they
reported that Darius had been forcibly seized and put under arrest by
Nabarzanes, commander of the cavalry which had accompanied his
retreat, Bessus, satrap of Bactria, and Barsaentes, satrap of Arachotia
and Drangia. Instantly Alexander was on the march again, with
greater rapidity than ever; he did not even wait for Coenus' foraging
party, and the only troops he took with him were the Hetaeri, the
mounted skirmishers, and a picked body of the toughest of his light
infantry. His other men he put under Craterus' command, with orders to follow on at their own pace. His own force carried nothing
but their weapons and two days' rations. Marching all night and half
the following day, he stopped at noon for a brief rest; then he was off
again and, after a second all-night march, reached at daybreak the
camp where Bagistanes had been before his visit. It was empty – the
enemy had gone. He learned, however, that the story of Darius' arrest
was true: he was being taken off in a covered wagon and Bessus had
assumed power in his place. Bessus had received the royal salute from
the Bactrian cavalry and all the Persians who had been with Darius on
his retreat, except Artabazus and his sons – and the Greek mercenaries
– who remained loyal. These, unable to prevent what had taken place,
had left the main road and made for the hills on their own, refusing to
take any part in the action of Bessus and his supporters. Darius' captors had determined to hand him over if they heard that Alexander
was after them, and thus get favourable terms for themselves; if, on
the other hand, there should be no pursuit, they proposed to muster as
large a force as they could and unite in preserving their power. For the
time being Bessus was in command, as he was related to Darius, and
also because it was in his province that this daring act had taken place.

The news made it plain to Alexander that he must continue to press his pursuit without a moment's delay. His men and horses were both pretty well exhausted already by their unremitting exertions, but Alexander drove them forward none the less, and after covering a great deal of ground during the night and the following morning reached about noon a village where Darius and his captors had stopped the previous day. Learning that they had resolved to continue their journey by night, he asked the natives of the place if they knew a short cut by which he could catch up with them. They said they did – but the way was through uninhabited country and there was no water – but no matter: Alexander at once ordered them to act as guides.

He knew that the pace would be too much for his infantry, so he dismounted about 500 cavalrymen and mounted in their place the toughest and fittest officers of his infantry and other units, ordering them to keep their own arms and equipment; Nicanor and Attalus, who commanded, respectively, the Longshields and Agrianes, were instructed to take the remainder of the force by the way already followed by Bessus and his party; they were to proceed as lightly equipped as was possible, and the rest of the infantry were to follow in their regular formation. Alexander himself then started off again at dusk with all the speed he could make, and covering some fifty miles in the course of the night, came up with the Persians just as dawn was breaking. They were straggling along unarmed; only a few made any offer of resistance; most of them incontinently fled the moment they saw it was Alexander himself who was upon them. Those who attempted to fight also made off after losing a few men. Bessus and his friends did not at once abandon the attempt to get Darius away in the wagon, but when Alexander was close upon them, Nabarzanes and Barsaentes struck him down and left him and made their escape with 600 horsemen. The wound proved fatal, and Darius died shortly afterwards, before Alexander could see him.

Alexander sent Darius' body to Persepolis to be buried in the royal tombs, like the kings before him. He appointed a Parthian named Amminaspes as Governor of Parthia and Hyrcania – he was one of Mazacus' party who had surrendered Egypt to Alexander. Tlepolemus, son of Pythophanes, was given a post to assist him in keeping an eye on things in the two provinces.

Such was the end of Darius; he died in July, during the archonship of Aristophon in Athens. In military matters he was the feeblest and most incompetent of men; in other spheres his conduct appears to have been moderate and decent – though the truth may well be that, as his accession to the throne coincided with the declaration of war by Macedon and Greece, he had no opportunity to play the tyrant. In the circumstances, being himself in greater peril than his subjects, he could hardly have treated them with the usual cruelty of an Oriental despot, even had he wished to do so. His life was an unbroken series of disasters from the moment of his accession to the throne. He was immediately faced by the defeat of his satraps and their mounted troops on the Granicus; the loss of Ionia and Aeolis swiftly followed, with the two Phrygias, Lydia, and all Caria except Halicarnassus; soon afterwards Halicarnassus, too, was gone, and the whole coast as far as Cilicia; then came his own defeat at Issus, and the bitter sight of his mother, wife, and children as prisoners in enemy hands. The loss of Phoenicia and Egypt was followed by the *débâcle* at Arbela, his own shameful flight from the field, and the destruction of the mightiest army of the whole East; then, a homeless fugitive in the land he once ruled, ruthlessly betrayed by his own guards, a monarch in chains contemptuously smuggled away from the scene of his former glory, he was finally murdered by the treachery of those most bound in duty to serve him. Such was the unhappy life of Darius; dead, he was more fortunate; for he was buried in the royal tomb, his children were given by Alexander the same upbringing and education they would have had if he had still been king – and his daughter became Alexander's wife. He was about fifty when he died.

The troops left behind during the pursuit of Darius now rejoined, and Alexander advanced into Hyrcania, a country which lies on the left of the road to Bactria. One side of it is bounded by high wooded hills; on the other the plains extend to the Caspian Sea. He chose this route because of a report that it was the way taken by Darius' mercenaries in their escape to the mountains of Tapuria, and also because he intended to subdue the Tapurian people. Dividing his force into three, he took charge of the largest and most lightly-armed section himself, and proceeded by the shortest but most difficult road; Craterus was sent against the Tapurians with his own and Amyntas' contingent, some of the archers, and a small group of mounted men, while Erigyus had orders to take the mercenaries and the rest of the cavalry by the better, though longer, route, accompanied by the baggage-wagons and non-combatant units.

Alexander halted after crossing the first range of hills, and then went on with the Longshields, some of the archers, and the most mobile of the Macedonian infantry. The going was rough and difficult; as he proceeded, he left parties of men to guard the tracks at dangerous points, to prevent the possibility of his own troops, who were coming along behind, being set upon by the enemy who held the hills. Once through the pass with his archers, he halted on level ground by a small river.

While he was there, Nabarzanes, commander of Darius' cavalry, Phrataphernes, satrap of Hyrcania and Parthia, and other high-ranking Persian officers, came and gave themselves up. Alexander stayed four days in camp at this spot; by that time all the men left behind on the march had rejoined: most of them came through safely, though the Agrianes, who formed the rearguard, had been attacked by the hill-tribes. However, their long-range fighting was too good for the enemy, who had the worst of it and withdrew.

On the march again, Alexander now advanced to Zadracarta, a town in Hyrcania, where he was rejoined by Craterus' division; they had not encountered Darius' mercenaries, but had managed to take over all the territory through which they had marched, either by force or surrender. Erigyus also rejoined at this point with the baggage-wagons and gear. Shortly afterwards Artabazus came over to Alexander with three of his sons – Cophen, Ariobarzanes, and Arsames; with them were delegates from the mercenary troops who had served under Darius, and Autophradates, the satrap of Tapuria. Autophradates was permitted to retain his satrapy, and Artabazus and his sons, not only because of their rank but especially because of their loyalty to Darius, were kept in close attendance upon his person and treated with every mark of respect. The Greek delegates asked for terms for all Greek mercenaries now prisoners of war; this, however, Alexander categorically refused: Greek soldiers, he maintained, who fought for Persia against their own country were little better than criminals and all proper Greek feeling was against them. Far from agreeing upon terms, he gave orders that they should all put them-

selves into his hands to be dealt with as he saw fit – or, if they preferred, to take what measures they could for their own safety. They
chose the former alternative, and at the same time asked for an officer,
to give the prisoners safe conduct. The number of prisoners was
reckoned to be about 1,500. Alexander sent them Artabazus and
Andronicus, son of Agerrhus.

He now marched for Mardia, his force consisting of the Longshields, the archers, the Agrianes, the brigades of Coenus and Amyntas, half the mounted Hetaeri, and the mounted javelins, a brigade of
which had by now been formed. He overran the greater part of
Mardia, and the people of the province suffered severely: many were
killed either attempting to escape or, in some cases, offering resistance,
and many prisoners were taken. Mardia is a rugged and difficult
country; its people, although poor, are sturdy fighters, and it was
many years since an invader had set foot upon their soil; they had
not the least apprehension of an attack by Alexander, especially as he
already appeared to have by-passed their territory, so for these reasons
they were caught off their guard even more than they would otherwise have been. Many of them did succeed in escaping to the mountains, which are very lofty and precipitous in this part of the world,
confident that there, at least, Alexander would not come after them;
however, he did; so they had nothing for it but unconditional surrender. The spokesmen who brought the offer of surrender were
allowed by Alexander to return to their people, and Autophradates
was made governor of the province, as well as of Tapuria.

Returning to the spot whence he had started upon his expedition to
Mardia, Alexander found the Greek mercenaries awaiting him.
Dropides the Athenian, and the Spartans Callicratidas, Pausippus,
Monimus, and Onomas – envoys from Greece on their way to Darius'
court – had also arrived. They were all arrested. The envoys from
Sinope were dismissed, as Sinope did not really belong to Greece
proper, and the fact that, as Persian subjects, they were sending a delegation to the Persian King seemed to Alexander reasonable enough.
The delegates from all other Greek states which had sent troops to
Persia before the conclusion of the Macedonian alliance were also dismissed, as was Heracleides, the delegate from Calchedon; the remainder were ordered to serve under Alexander at the same rate of
pay. Andronicus was made their commander: it was he who had

brought them to Alexander, and he had made it clear that he considered the safety of his men a matter of the first importance.

This business completed, Alexander went on to Zadracarta, the
chief town of Hyrcania and site of the royal palace. He remained
there fifteen days, sacrificed to the gods in accordance with custom,
celebrated Games, and then moved on by way of Parthia to the frontiers of Aria. At Susia, a town in this province, he was visited by the
satrap, Satibarzanes, whose office he confirmed, sending Anaxippus,
one of the Hetaeri, to accompany him on his return with about forty
mounted javelins. This force was to enable him to set guards to save
the people of Aria from molestation at the hands of the troops passing
through.

About this time some Persians came with a report that Bessus was
proclaiming himself King of Asia: he was wearing the royal mantle
and the cap with the point erect, in royal fashion, and had changed his
name to Artaxerxes. He already had with him the Persian troops who
had escaped into Bactria, besides a considerable number of the Bactrians themselves, and was expecting reinforcements from Scythia.
Alexander marched at once for Bactria with his whole force, which
had now reassembled, and was met there by Philip, son of Menelaus,
who had come from Media with the mercenary cavalry under his own
command, the Thessalian volunteers, and Andromachus' contingent
of foreign troops. Parmenio's son Nicanor, the commander of the
Longshields, had already died of sickness.

On the way to Bactria news came in that Satibarzanes, satrap of
Aria, had murdered Anaxippus and the forty men with him; he was
arming the Arians and concentrating them at Artacoana (where the
palace was), and had resolved, as soon as he should learn that Alexander had put sufficient space between them, to join Bessus with the
force at his disposal and assist him in attacking the Macedonians
wherever an opportunity should present itself. Alexander changed his
plans accordingly: leaving Craterus in command on the spot, he took
the mounted Hetaeri, the mounted Javelins, the archers, the Agrianes,
and Amyntas' and Coenus' brigades, and marched with all speed
against Satibarzanes and the Arians, reaching Artacoana after covering
some seventy-five miles in two days.

The rapidity of the march took Satibarzanes completely by surprise, and he fled as soon as he heard that Alexander was coming. A

few horsemen got away with him, but the majority of his men, once they, too, knew that Alexander was approaching, had deserted immediately the attempt to escape began. All who had had any hand in the revolt or had left their villages at the time of its occurrence were rapidly hunted down and rounded up in various places. Some were killed, others sold into slavery. Arsames, a Persian, was appointed to the governorship of Aria.

The troops left in charge of Craterus now rejoined Alexander, and, marching for Zarangia, he arrived at the town where the palace was situated. This region was then under the control of Barsaentes, one of the conspirators who had fatally wounded Darius during the attempt to get him away; and when he learned of Alexander's approach, he fled for refuge to the Indians west of the Indus. But they arrested him and sent him back to Alexander, who had him executed for his treachery to Darius.

It was here, too, that Alexander learned of Philotas' plot against his life. According to Ptolemy and Aristobulus, information of what was going on had come to his ears before, while he was in Egypt, but he had refused to believe it; for Philotas had long been his friend, he had trusted him, and had also bestowed the highest honours upon his father, Parmenio. Ptolemy's account of what now occurred is this: Philotas was brought before the Macedonians to stand his trial; Alexander made his accusation in no uncertain terms, and Philotas answered the charge. Then the persons who had reported the affair came forward, with various irrefutable proofs of his own guilt and that of his fellow-conspirators, of which the most damning was that he admitted knowledge of a plot against Alexander but had said nothing about it, in spite of the fact that he was in the habit of visiting Alexander's tent twice a day. Thereupon he was shot by the Macedonians, and the others who were concerned in the conspiracy shared the same fate. Parmenio was executed as well: Polydamas, one of the Hetaeri, was sent to him with a letter from Alexander addressed to Cleander, Sitalces, and Menidas, three generals in Media who had been posted to the army which Parmenio commanded. It was they who put him to death.

The reason for Parmenio's execution may have been that Alexander could not believe that he had no share in his son's conspiracy; on the other hand, even granting his innocence, his living on after his son's

execution was already in fact a danger; for he was a man of immense
prestige: he had great influence not only with Alexander himself but
also with the army – and not alone with the Macedonian units, but
also with the mercenary soldiers, whom so often by Alexander's orders and with Alexander's approbation he had led on special missions
or in the ordinary course of duty.

It is said that Amyntas, son of Andromenes, and his brothers,
Polemon, Attalus, and Simmias, were brought to trial at the same
time for complicity in the plot against Alexander, on the grounds of
the closeness of their association with Philotas. Most people were the
more inclined to believe in their guilt because Polemon deserted to the
enemy when Philotas was arrested. In any case, Amyntas stood his
trial with his other two brothers, and after making a vigorous defence
was acquitted, whereupon he immediately asked permission of the
Court to go and find his brother and bring him back. Permission was
granted, and he started out the same day, returning later with Polemon. This was a strong additional proof of Amyntas' innocence.
Soon after, however, during the siege of some village or other, he
died of a wound from an arrow, so that all the benefit he got from his
acquittal was death without dishonour.

In view of these events Alexander split the Hetaeri into two separate
divisions and appointed, respectively, Hephaestion son of Amyntor
and Cleitus son of Dropides to command them. The reason for this
step was that he did not think it advisable that one man – even a personal friend – should have control of so large a body of cavalry – especially as the Hetaeri were the most famous and formidable of all his
mounted troops. This done, he proceeded to the territory of the Aria-
spians (this, by the way, was their original name: later they came to
be known as the Benefactors, in recognition of the help they gave
Cyrus, son of Cambyses, in his expedition to Scythia). These people
Alexander treated with every courtesy; he honoured them for the service rendered to Cyrus in the old days and also for the fact, which he
observed for himself, that their political institutions were different
from those of other tribes in that part of the world: like the best of the
Greeks, they claimed to know the distinction between right and
wrong. He accordingly allowed them to retain their freedom, and
offered to give them as much of their neighbours' territory as they
wanted – and they asked only for a small slice.

There Alexander sacrificed to Apollo – and arrested one of his personal guards named Demetrius on suspicion of complicity in Philotas' plot. Ptolemy, son of Lagus, was appointed in his place.

These difficulties settled, Alexander advanced against Bessus in Bactria. On the way to Bactria he subdued the Drangae, the Gadrosians, and the Arachosians, appointing Menon as governor of Arachosia. In fact, he got as far as the neighbouring Indian tribes. The march was all the way through deep snow, and his men suffered severely from exhaustion and lack of supplies.

A report came in that, Satibarzanes having entered Aria with a force of 2,000 cavalry which he had received from Bessus, the Arians had again revolted; Alexander accordingly sent the Persian officer Artabazus there, accompanied by Erigyus and Caranus, two of the Hetaeri, with further orders to Phrataphernes, the satrap of Parthia, to assist them in dealing with the Arians. The troops of Erigyus and Caranus fought a brisk engagement with Satibarzanes, the Persians holding their ground until Satibarzanes in hand-to-hand fight with Erigyus was struck in the face with a spear and killed; then they broke, and fled in confusion.

Alexander's route now led him to the Indian Caucasus. Here he founded a city and named it Alexandria; then, after the traditional religious observances, he crossed the Caucasus range. A Persian called Proexes was made governor of the district, and Neiloxenus, one of the Hetaeri and son of Satyrus, was appointed overseer, and left there with a body of troops at his disposal.

According to the testimony of Aristobulus, the Caucasus range is as lofty as any in Asia, and most of it, at any rate on its hither side, is barren. It extends for a very great distance – so far, indeed, that the Taurus range, which forms the boundary of Cilicia and Pamphylia, is supposed to be a part of it, as are other great mountains distinguished from it by various names according to the countries in which they are situated. Here – that is, in the Indian Caucasus – nothing grows (to quote Aristobulus once more) except silphium and terebinth; nevertheless the region was by no means sparsely inhabited; large numbers of sheep and other cattle grazed there, for sheep like silphium, and if they smell the plant in the distance make straight for it and bite off the flower, and even grub up and eat the root. For this reason the people of Cyrene keep their flocks as far away as they can from the places where silphium grows; sometimes they fence the ground to keep the sheep out should they approach, so valuable is this plant to them.

Bessus did his utmost to prevent Alexander from advancing further: he had with him, besides the Persians who had taken part in the arrest of Darius, about 7,000 Bactrians and the Daae from the hither side of the Tanais, and with these troops he proceeded to lay waste the country round the foothills of the Caucasus, in the hope that if all crops and everything edible between Alexander and himself were destroyed, Alexander would be halted by sheer lack of supplies. The hope, however, was vain; Alexander, in spite of everything, continued to advance. Snow and privation made it a laborious task – but they could not stop him.

When the report reached Bessus that Alexander was already close at hand, he crossed the Oxus in boats, which he then burned, and withdrew to Nautaka in Sogdiana; he was accompanied by the troops of Spitamenes and Oxyartes, together with the mounted troops of Sogdiana and the Daae from the Tanais. The Bactrian cavalry dispersed to their homes as soon as they knew that Bessus had made up his mind to avoid a conflict.

At Drapsaka, Alexander halted to rest his men, and then went on to Aornos and Bactra, the two chief towns of Bactria; both of them were surrendered without resistance. He left a garrison in Aornos under the command of Archaelaus son of Androcles, one of the Hetaeri. From the rest of Bactria he met with little opposition, and appointed the Persian officer Artabazus as governor of the district. His next objective was the river Oxus.

The source of the Oxus is in the Indian Caucasus; it is greater than any other Asian river reached by Alexander's army, except the rivers of India, which are the greatest in the world. It empties itself into the Caspian Sea in Hyrcania. At Alexander's first attempt to cross it, it seemed an impossible task: it was about six furlongs wide and much deeper than its breadth would lead one to expect; the combination of a rapid current and a sandy bottom made it impossible to drive piles securely into its bed: they could get no grip on the soft sand and were quickly loosened by the force of the stream. Moreover, timber was scarce, and it seemed a great waste of time to go far afield in search of enough to construct a bridge. Accordingly Alexander had all the hides

collected which served the men for tents, and gave instructions that
they should be filled with chips and other dry rubbish, and then tied
up and carefully sewn to make them water-tight. When they were
filled and sewn, there were enough of them to get the men across in
five days.

Before the crossing, Alexander sent home all Macedonians whose
age rendered them no longer fit for service, and also the Thessalian
volunteers who had remained with the army. He sent Stasanor, one
of the Hetaeri, to Aria with orders to put Arsames, the satrap, under
arrest for suspected treason and to take over the governorship in his
place.

Once over the river, he pressed on with all speed to where Bessus
and his army were reported to be. Meanwhile a message arrived from
Spitamenes and Dataphernes to the effect that if a body of troops – not
necessarily a large one – under command of an officer were sent them,
they would arrest Bessus and hand him over to Alexander. In fact,
they already had him under open arrest. On receipt of this message
Alexander slackened the speed of his advance, halting frequently, and
ordered Ptolemy, son of Lagus, to go on ahead with forced marches
and make contact with Spitamenes and Dataphernes with the least
possible delay: he was to take with him a force consisting of three
units of the mounted Hetaeri, all the mounted Javelins, Philotas' infantry brigade, one regiment of the Longshields, all the Agrianes, and
half the archers. With these troops Ptolemy covered in four days a
distance which would normally take ten, and reached the spot where
Spitamenes' men had bivouacked on the preceding day. There he
learned that Dataphernes and Spitamenes were in two minds about
the surrender of Bessus, so leaving his infantry with instructions to
follow in marching order, he rode off with his cavalry to a village not
far away where Bessus and a few soldiers were. Spitamenes had already left the place, he and his men feeling the actual betrayal of
Bessus to be too much for their conscience.

The little settlement was fortified more or less, having an outer wall
with gates in it. Ptolemy cordoned it off with his mounted troops and
announced to the Persians inside that if they gave Bessus up they
would be allowed to go without molestation; he was accordingly admitted, whereupon he seized Bessus and again withdrew, sending off
a messenger to ask Alexander how he wished Bessus to be brought

into his presence. Alexander replied that he must be stripped of his
clothes and led in a dog-collar and made to stand on the right of the
road along which he and his army would pass. The order was obeyed,
and when Alexander saw him there, he stopped his chariot and asked
him why he had treated Darius, his king, kinsman, and benefactor, so
shamefully, first seizing him, then hurrying him off in chains, and
finally murdering him. Bessus answered that the decision to do what
he had done was not his alone: everyone close to Darius at that time
had shared in it, and their object was to win Alexander's favour and so
save their lives. At this Alexander ordered him to be scourged; and at
every lash a crier was to repeat the words of reproach he had himself
used as he asked the reason for his treachery. After this humiliating
punishment he was sent away to Bactra to be executed.

The foregoing account of the fate of Bessus is Ptolemy's; Aristobulus states that he was brought along, on Ptolemy's behalf, and
handed over to Alexander by the friends of Spitamenes and Dataphernes. He confirms the details of the stripping and the dog-collar.

Many of Alexander's horses had died of exhaustion in the long
climb over the Caucasus and during the marches to and from the
Oxus; he therefore brought his cavalry units up to strength with
fresh horses taken from the neighbouring country, and then marched
for Marakanda, the royal city of Sogdiana, moving on thence to the
Tanais. Like the Oxus, this river, too (according to Aristobulus the
natives call it the Jaxartes) rises in the Indian Caucasus and flows into
the Caspian Sea; it can hardly be the Tanais which the historian Herodotus describes as the eighth of the Scythian rivers, having its source
in a great lake and flowing into a greater, called Maeotis: this other
Tanais is regarded by some as the boundary between Asia and Europe,
on the supposition that from this corner of the Black Sea Lake
Maeotis and the river flowing into it actually divide Asia from Europe
in the same way as the straits between Gadeira and the nomad Libyans
divide Libya from Europe – and in the same way, presumably, as
Libya is divided from the rest of Asia by the Nile.

It was on this river (call it Tanais, or Jaxartes) that a party of Macedonians foraging for supplies was cut up by natives. After their attack
the tribesmen, who were some 30,000 in number, withdrew to a
position in the hills, where the ground was not only excessively
broken but as steep as a cliff on every side. None the less Alexander,

with his lightest troops, moved to the assault. Again and again the Macedonians struggled for a foothold on the precipitous ascent, but without success: the missiles of the natives drove them back. Many were wounded, including Alexander himself, who was shot through the leg with an arrow and had the fibula broken. But despite every obstacle he at length took the place; some of the enemy were killed by his troops, and many others leapt to death over the edge of the cliffs. Of their 30,000 not more than 8,000 escaped with their lives.

BOOK FOUR

A FEW days after the events previously recorded Alexander was
visited by a deputation from the tribe known as the Abian
Scythians – Homer, by the way, mentioned these people with approval, calling them 'the most righteous of mankind'. They are
Asiatics and have kept their independence, thanks, as much as anything, to their poverty and fair dealing. Another deputation came
from the European Scythians, the most numerous of all the European peoples. Alexander instructed certain officers of the Hetaeri to
return with the delegates ostensibly to conclude formally a pact of
friendship with their country, though his actual purpose was rather
to gather information about Scythia – its geographical peculiarities,
the customs of its people, their numbers, and military equipment.

It was his intention to found a city on the Tanais and to name it
after himself. The site, he considered, was a good one; a settlement
there would be likely to increase in size and importance, and would
also serve both as an excellent base for a possible future invasion of
Scythia and as a defensive position against raiding tribes from across
the river. Without doubt both its numbers and the splendour of its
name would one day turn the new settlement into a great city.

Meanwhile, however, the native tribes along the Tanais took the
offensive: they seized and killed the Macedonian garrisons in their
towns and began to look to their safety by strengthening their own
defences. They were joined in this hostile move by most of the people
of Sogdiana, who were incited to it by the party which had arrested
Bessus, and these, in their turn, drew into the movement some of the
Bactrians as well. The reason for it may have been simply fear of
Alexander; on the other hand, they may have justified the movement
by the fact that Alexander had issued an order for the leading men of
that country to meet for a conference at Sariaspa, the capital – an
order which might well conceal some sinister purpose.

The report of the revolt led to immediate counter-measures: each
section of infantry was ordered to prepare a definite number of scaling-ladders, and Alexander himself at once moved forward to Gaza,

the nearest of the native settlements to his own position – there were, according to report, seven of these towns in which the natives had shut themselves up. At the same time he sent Craterus to Cyropolis, the largest of the seven and now occupied by the greatest number of natives. His instructions were to take up a position close to the town, surround it with a ditch and stockade, and then assemble such siege engines as might suit his purpose, in order to concentrate the defenders' attention upon himself and his troops, and thus prevent them from sending assistance to their friends elsewhere.

Arrived at Gaza, Alexander ordered an immediate assault with scaling-ladders on every side of the town's defences, which consisted of an earthen wall of no great height; as the infantry moved forward, the slingers, archers, and javelin-throwers poured their missiles into the defenders on the wall and at the same time the catapults went into action. Under the storm of missiles the wall was soon cleared; the ladders were fixed and the Macedonians were up in a moment. All males in the town were killed, by Alexander's orders; the women and children were treated as prizes of war, and carried off with anything else of value. Then, without delay, Alexander proceeded to the next settlement, took it the same day and in the same manner, and dealt with the inhabitants with the same severity. Thence he went on to the third, and on the day following took this, too, at the first assault.

While the infantry was engaged in these operations, the cavalry was dispatched to the next two towns with orders to take strict measures to prevent any of the people there from getting away; for it was likely enough that, when they learned of the fall of the neighbouring towns and of Alexander's impending approach, they would scatter in flight and pursuit might be impossible. Alexander's guess was right, and the dispatch of the cavalry came in the nick of time; for the men in the two settlements which had not yet fallen, as soon as they saw the smoke rising from the settlement nearest to them and got direct news of its capture from a few survivors, in a confused and desperate attempt to get out in time, ran straight into the cordon of mounted troops and were nearly all killed.

Five of the seven towns were thus taken in two days, and their women and children sold into slavery. Alexander then moved on to the largest of the seven, Cyropolis. This place had been founded by

Cyrus, and it was defended by a loftier wall than the other towns; moreover the natives who had shut themselves up in it were more numerous, and the best fighters of the district, so its capture presented the Macedonians with a much tougher problem. Alexander's first move was to order up the siege engines, intending to batter the defences and force an entrance through the breaches, as and wherever they were made; but he soon observed something which induced him to change his tactics. A stream ran through the town, but there was water in it only in winter; now it was dry, and in each of its several channels, at the points where they emerged, its bed was below the base of the surrounding wall, leaving just room enough for men to crawl through and so get into the town. Alexander, therefore, while the enemy's attention was engaged by the siege engines and the attempted assault within their sector, ordered the Longshields, the archers, the Agrianes, and his personal guard to hold themselves in readiness, and himself, with a few men only, crept unobserved by the dried-up water-course, under the wall, into the town. Once inside he broke open the nearest gates and admitted the rest of the troops without difficulty.

The enemy saw that the town was already taken; none the less they turned to fight and fell furiously upon Alexander's men. Alexander himself received a violent blow from a stone upon his head and neck; Craterus was wounded by an arrow, and many other officers were hurt. But in spite of strong opposition they cleared the centre of the town, while at the same time the assault on the outer defences was equally successful: the defenders were all driven off and the wall was taken without further resistance.

The enemy force in this town amounted to about 15,000 fighting men; of these, in the first phase of the operations about 8,000 were killed. The rest took refuge in the central fortress. Alexander stationed troops all round the fortress, and kept a close watch on the fugitives. After one day they surrendered for lack of water.

The seventh town was taken without trouble. In this case, however, accounts differ: Ptolemy says they surrendered; Aristobulus that the place was stormed and everyone in it massacred. Ptolemy also states that Alexander distributed the prisoners among the various units of his army with orders that they should be kept bound and under constant supervision all the time he should remain in that part of the country; not one, in fact, who had taken part in the revolt was to be allowed his liberty.

About this time a force of Asian Scythians arrived at the Tanais. Most of them had heard that some of the tribes beyond the river had declared their hostility to Alexander and intended to join in an attack upon the Macedonians in the event of a serious rising. A report also came in that Spitamenes was blockading the troops which had been in the fortress of Maracanda. To meet this situation, Andromachus, Menedemus, and Caranus were dispatched with a force consisting of sixty mounted Hetaeri, 800 of Caranus' mercenaries, and some 15,000 mercenary infantry. Pharnuches the interpreter was attached to the troops: he was a Lycian, thoroughly familiar with the language of this part of the country, and had often shown a skilful touch in dealing with the natives.

Alexander spent twenty days on the work of fortifying the site of his proposed new town and arranging for the settlement there of any Greek mercenaries and neighbouring tribesmen who expressed a wish to avail themselves of the opportunity, and also of a number of Macedonians no longer fit for active service. To mark the occasion, after his customary religious observances he held games, with athletic and equestrian contests.

Meanwhile the Scythians made no move to leave the Tanais. The river was not broad at that point; they could be seen shooting arrows into the water, and heard calling out, in their barbarous way, insulting remarks to Alexander and boasting that he would never dare to lay a finger upon men like them – or, if he did, that he would soon find out the difference between Scythians and Asiatic savages. To Alexander such an exhibition was most annoying, so he proposed to cross the river and deal with them as they deserved. The skin floats were being prepared for the crossing when he found that the omens, at the preliminary sacrifice, were against him. In spite of his vexation, he nevertheless made the best of it and abandoned the enterprise. The Scythians, however, continuing their insufferable behaviour, he sacrificed again; but this time, too, Aristander the seer declared that the omens portended danger. Thereupon Alexander replied that it was better to face the worst of perils than for the conqueror of nearly all Asia to make himself ridiculous to a pack of Scythians – as Darius, the father of Xerxes, had done long ago. None the less, Aristander refused

E

to misinterpret the divine prediction merely because Alexander wished it otherwise.

When all the skin floats were ready and the army in full equipment drawn up on the river-bank, the catapults, at the word of command, opened up on the Scythians who were riding along the edge of the water on the further side. Some of them were hit; one was pierced through both shield and breastplate and fell dead from his horse. The Scythians were taken completely aback by the long range of the cata-pults, and that, together with the loss of a good man, induced them to withdraw a short distance from the river, whereupon Alexander, see-ing their consternation, ordered the trumpets to sound and himself led the way over the water, followed by his men. First to be put ashore were the archers and slingers, who were then ordered to open up on the enemy to prevent them from closing on the main infantry units before the mounted troops were all safely over; then, as soon as every man was across and the army massed on the river-bank, a squadron of mercenaries and four companies of pikemen were ordered forward to lead the attack. The Scythians met the challenge; their numbers were for the moment superior; they made circles round the small attacking force, shooting as they rode, and then galloped off to a safe distance. At this Alexander ordered an advance by a mixed force consisting of the cavalry together with the archers, the Agrianes, and the other light troops, and, when they were almost within striking distance, gave gave the word for three regiments of the Hetaeri and all the mounted Javelins to charge, while he himself at the head of the remaining cavalry came on in column at the gallop.

This effectually put a stop to the enemy's circling movements; the Macedonian cavalry, with the light troops mixed with it in close sup-port, was now right on top of them, and it was no longer possible for them to repeat their former manœuvre without the certainty of des-truction. Indeed, from this moment they were well and truly beaten; in their attempt to get away, about 1,000 were killed, includ-ing Satraces one of their commanders, and some 150 were made prisoner.

The rapid pursuit, in the great heat, was exhausting; every man suffered acutely from thirst, and Alexander himself, as he rode, was forced to drink whatever water he could find. Unfortunately it was not pure, and gave him a severe attack of diarrhoea. This proved the salvation of some, at any rate, of the Scythians; for had not Alexander had this trouble, I do not think a single one of them would have escaped with his life.

Alexander did, in fact, become very seriously ill, and was carried back to camp – so Aristander was a true prophet after all.

Not long after this Alexander was visited by an embassy from the Scythian King. Its purpose was to offer an explanation of what had occurred and to make it clear that the recent incident was merely a casual raid by a pack of brigands and in no sense the deliberate policy of the Scythian State. The King, moreover, was willing to carry out such instructions as Alexander might give him. Alexander returned a polite answer, for the situation was an awkward one: clearly it was his duty to continue the campaign if he distrusted the protestations of the King; but, at the same time, the moment was not propitious for doing so.

The Macedonian garrison, beset in the fortress at Marakanda, in reply to an attempted assault by Spitamenes made a successful sortie, killing a number of the enemy without loss to themselves; they then resumed their position in the fortress. Then, when it was reported to Spitamenes that the troops which Alexander had dispatched to the town were already near, he abandoned his siege and withdrew to the capital of the district. Pharnuches and the officers with him, pressing on with all speed with the intention of getting him right out of the country, followed his withdrawal towards the frontier of Sogdiana, and in the course of the pursuit came to blows with the Nomad Scythians. This wholly unpremeditated action had serious consequences: for Spitamenes, having now an accession to his force of some 600 Scythian mounted men, was emboldened by this unexpected assistance to stand and take the offensive. He took up a position on level ground near the Scythian desert, then, at the approach of the Macedonians, with whom he had no intention of risking a close engagement, he dispatched his cavalry to gallop round the Macedonian infantry formations, discharging their arrows as they rode. Pharnuches' men attempted to charge, but to no purpose; the enemy, on their swifter horses, were out of range in a moment. Their horses, moreover, were fresh, while those of Andromachus' men were in poor condition from long, forced marches and inadequate feeding. The Macedonians tried now to stand their ground, now to withdraw;

but all to no effect: in either case the weight of the Scythian cavalry
was too much for them. Many were wounded, some killed, until
finally the officers formed the men into a square and withdrew to the
river Polytimetus. Near the river there was a little wood, which
would give some cover against the enemy's arrows and at the same
time enable them to make better use of their own infantry.

Caranus, who was in command of the cavalry, without a word to
Andromachus of his intention, attempted to cross the river to get his
men and horses into safety; the infantry without orders promptly followed suit, scrambling down the steep bank into the water in a panic-
stricken and disorderly rabble. The Scythians soon turned this fatal
error to their own advantage: galloping up from all directions, they
plunged into the stream; some rode hard on the heels of the Greeks
already across and trying to get away; others confronted the fugitives in mid-stream and dragged them down; or flung themselves
upon those not yet in the water, while all the time from the flanks
showers of arrows were poured in. The Macedonians were helpless,
and all who survived took refuge on a small island in the river; but
this did not save them, for Spitamenes' cavalry and the Scythians surrounded the island and shot them down to a man. The few prisoners
taken were promptly butchered.

Aristobulus' account of this disaster is somewhat different: according to him, most of the Macedonian force was caught and destroyed
by an ambush. The Scythians had concealed themselves in a park, and
fell unexpectedly on the Macedonians when they were already engaged. This happened to be the moment when Pharnuches was offering to surrender his command to the Macedonian officers who had
been sent with him on the expedition – on the ground that he was
ignorant of military tactics and had been sent by Alexander not to
command troops in battle, but to establish relations with the natives,
while the others, unlike him, were true-born Macedonians and Companions of the King. But Andromachus, Caranus, and Menedemus
refused to accept the command, partly to avoid the responsibility of
a personal decision not covered by Alexander's explicit orders, and
partly because, in the present dangerous situation, they did not wish
to incur individual blame in the event of defeat, much less to expose
themselves to the general charge of inferior leadership. It was in this
situation, when everything was at sixes and sevens, that the Scythian

attack occurred – with results so disastrous that only about forty of
the cavalry and 300 infantrymen escaped with their lives.

News of the *débâcle* caused Alexander great distress, and he determined to march with all speed against Spitamenes. Accordingly, with
half the mounted troops of the Hetaeri, all the Longshields, the
Agrianes, the archers, and the most lightly armed infantry units, he
proceeded towards Marakanda, whither he knew that Spitamenes had
returned and was again besieging the garrison in the fortress. In three
days he covered about 185 miles, and at dawn on the fourth was close
to the town. At the report of his approach Spitamenes and his men
abandoned the town and fled; Alexander followed in close pursuit,
passing the scene of the battle, where he paused to give such burial to
the dead as circumstances permitted. At the edge of the desert he
turned back and began the work of systematic destruction; a number
of natives had fled for refuge to the forts, and on a report that they
had joined in the attack on the Macedonians, he had them all butchered. He covered in this way the whole region watered by the
Polytimetus.

The country is desert beyond the spot where the Polytimetus dis-
appears – for disappear it does, in spite of the fact that it is a river of
some size. It vanishes into the sand. The same phenomenon can be observed with other rivers in this part of the world – rivers, too, of considerable volume, not mere streamlets such as dry up in the summer:
the Epardus, for instance, which flows through Mardia, and the
Areius, from which the country of Aria takes its name, and the Ety-
mandrus, which runs through the country of the Energetae. All these
are larger than the Peneus in Thessaly, which reaches the sea through
the pass of Tempe. The Polytimetus is much larger than the Peneus.

Having brought these operations to an end, Alexander went to
Zariaspa, where he stayed for the worst of the winter. He was visited
there by Phrataphernes, satrap of Parthia, and Stasanor, the officer
who had been sent to Aria to arrest Arsames; they brought Arsames
with them under close guard, and also Barzanes, who had been appointed to the satrapy of Parthia by Bessus, and a number of other
prisoners, all men who had assisted Bessus in his movement to depose
Darius. At about the same time Epocillus, Melamnidas, and Ptole-
maeus, general of the Thracians, returned from their mission of escort-
ing to the coast the allies and the treasure sent with Menes. Alexander

was also joined in Zariaspa by Asander and Nearchus with a force of Greek mercenaries, and by further reinforcements from the coast in charge of the satrap of Syria (also named Bessus) and of Asclepiodorus, the provincial governor.

Alexander had Bessus brought before a full meeting of his officers and accused him of treachery to Darius. He then gave orders that his nose and the tips of his ears should be cut off, and that thus mutilated he should be taken to Ecbatana to suffer public execution before his own countrymen, the Medes and Persians.

I do not myself approve the excessive severity of this punishment; for mutilation of that sort is, I think, a barbarous custom. I admit, moreover, that Alexander came to allow himself to emulate Eastern extravagance and splendour, and the fashion of barbaric kings of treating their subjects like dirt; regrettable, too, was the assumption by a descendant of Heracles of Median dress in place of what Macedonians have worn from time immemorial, and the unblushing exchange of his familiar head-gear, so long victoriously worn, for the pointed bonnet of the vanquished Persians. I have no praise for such conduct; but in my opinion, at least, the splendid achievements of Alexander are the clearest possible proof that neither strength of body, nor noble blood, nor success in war even greater than Alexander's own – not even the realization of his dream of circumnavigating Libya and Asia and adding them both to his empire, together with Europe too: that none of these things, I say, can make a man happy, unless he can win one more victory in addition to those the world thinks so great – the victory over himself.

In connexion with this I may as well relate here an incident which actually took place a little later: I mean the death of Cleitus, son of Dropides, and its effect upon Alexander. The Macedonians used to celebrate a festival in honour of Dionysus, and it was Alexander's custom to offer sacrifice each year on the sacred day. The story is that on this particular occasion Alexander, for some reason best known to himself, sacrificed not to Dionysus but to Castor and Polydeuces, the Dioscuri. There had been some pretty heavy drinking (another innovation – in drink, too, he now tended to barbaric excess), and in the course of talk the subject of the Dioscuri came up, together with the common attribution of their parentage to Zeus instead of to Tyndareus. Some of the company – the sort of people whose sycophantic tongues always have been and always will be the bane of kings – declared with gross flattery that, in their opinion, Polydeuces and Castor were not to be compared with Alexander and his achievements; others, being thoroughly drunk, extended the invidious comparison to Heracles himself: it was only envy, they maintained, which deprived the living of due honour from their friends.

Now Cleitus for some time past had quite obviously deprecated the change in Alexander: he liked neither his move towards the manners of the East, nor the sycophantic expressions of his courtiers. When, therefore, he heard what was said on this occasion (he, too, had been drinking heavily), he angrily intervened; it was intolerable, he declared, to offer such an insult to divine beings, and he would allow no one to pay Alexander a compliment at the expense of the mighty ones of long ago – such a compliment was not for his honour but for his shame. In any case, he continued, they grossly exaggerated the marvellous nature of Alexander's achievements, none of which were mere personal triumphs of his own; on the contrary, most of them were the work of the Macedonians as a whole.

Alexander was deeply hurt – and I, for my part, feel that Cleitus' words were ill-judged; in view of the fact that most of the party were drunk, he could, in my opinion, have quite well avoided the grossness of joining in the general flattery simply by keeping his thoughts to himself. But there was more to come: for others of the company, hoping, in their turn, to curry favour with Alexander, brought up the subject of Philip, and suggested, absurdly enough, that what he had done was, after all, quite ordinary and commonplace. At this Cleitus could control himself no longer; he began to magnify Philip's achievements and belittle Alexander's; his words came pouring out – he was, by now, very drunk indeed – and, among much else, he taunted Alexander with the reminder that he had saved his life, when they fought the Persian cavalry on the Granicus.

'This is the hand,' he cried, holding it out with a flourish, 'that saved you, Alexander, on that day.'

Alexander could stand no more drunken abuse from his friend. Angrily he leapt from his seat as if to strike him, but the others held him back. Cleitus continued to pour out his insulting remarks, and Alexander called for the Guard. No one answered.

'What?' he cried, 'have I nothing left of royalty but the name?

Am I to be like Darius, dragged in chains by Bessus and his cronies?'

Now nobody could hold him; springing to his feet, he snatched a spear from one of the attendants and struck Cleitus dead.

Accounts of this incident differ. Some authorities say it was not a spear but a pike; Aristobulus does not mention the occasion of the drinking bout: according to him, Cleitus need not have been killed but for his own action; for when Alexander sprang up in rage to kill him, Ptolemy, son of Lagus, a member of the King's personal guard, hurried him out of the door and over the wall and ditch of the fortress. But, unable to control himself, he went back to the banquet room and met Alexander just at the moment when he was calling his name.

'Here I am, Alexander!' he cried, and, as he spoke, the blow fell.

Personally, I strongly deprecate Cleitus' unseemly behaviour to his sovereign; and for Alexander I feel pity, in that he showed himself on this occasion the slave of anger and drunkenness, two vices to neither of which a self-respecting man should ever yield. But when the deed was done, Alexander immediately felt its horror; and for that I admire him. Some have said that he fixed the butt of the pike against the wall, meaning to fall upon it himself, because a man who murdered his friend when his wits were fuddled with wine was not fit to live. Most writers, however, say nothing of this; they tell us that Alexander lay on his bed in tears, calling the name of Cleitus and of his sister Lanice, who had been his nurse. 'Ah,' he cried, 'a good return I have made you for your care, now I am a man! You have lived to see your sons die fighting for me, and now with my own hand I have killed your brother.' Again and again he called himself the murderer of his friends, and for three days lay without food or drink, careless of all personal comfort.

One result of these painful events was that soothsayers began to suggest that the god Dionysus was angry because Alexander had failed to offer him sacrifice; and when at last he was with difficulty persuaded by his friends to take food and attend in some measure to his bodily needs, he did offer the neglected sacrifice. Doubtless he was not unwilling that what had happened should be attributed rather to the wrath of God than to his own wickedness. Here again, I have nothing but admiration for him: he made no attempt to justify his

crime; he never added to his guilt by becoming champion and advo-
cate in his own defence; he quite simply admitted that, being no more
than human, he had done wrong.

There is a story that Alexander sent for the sophist Anaxarchus, in
the hope he might give him comfort, and was still on his bed, bewail-
ing his fate, when he came in.

Anaxarchus laughed. 'Don't you know,' he said, 'why the wise
men of old made Justice to sit by the side of Zeus? It was to show that
whatever Zeus may do is justly done. In the same way all the acts of
a great king should be considered just, first by himself, then by the
rest of us.'

This was some consolation, at any rate for a time – though in my
opinion he did Alexander a wrong more grievous than his grief, if he
seriously, as a philosopher, put forward the view that a king need not
act justly, or labour, to the best of his ability, to distinguish between
right and wrong – if he really meant that whatever a king does, by
whatever means, should be considered right.

In this connexion it is widely believed that Alexander wished people
to prostrate themselves in his presence. This was due partly to the
notion that his father was not Philip but Ammon, and partly to his
growing admiration, expressed also by the change in his dress and
other personal adornments, of Median and Persian extravagance.
There were plenty of people, moreover, who, to flatter him, submitted to this servile behaviour: Anaxarchus the sophist was one of
the worst – and the Argive poet Agis.

There was one man, however, who did not approve of these inno-
vations. This was Callisthenes of Olynthus, a pupil of Aristotle. Thus
far I agree with Callisthenes; but he was a somewhat tactless man, and
his remark (if it has been rightly reported) that, without the history
he proposed to write, Alexander and his work would be forgotten,
was, I feel, most unfortunate. He used to declare that he had come not
in the hope of honour for himself, but merely to spread Alexander's
fame throughout the world; adding that if Alexander was destined to
have a share of divinity, it would not be owing to Olympias' absurd
stories about his birth, but to the account of him which he would
himself publish in his history. According to another anecdote, Callisthenes was once asked by Philotas who he thought was held in the
greatest honour by the Athenian people.

'Harmodius and Aristogeiton,' Callisthenes replied, 'because they killed one of the tyrants and abolished irresponsible government.'

'And do you think,' Philotas went on, 'that a tyrannicide could find asylum in any Greek community he liked to choose?'

'Even if no one else would have him,' said Callisthenes, 'he would be safe in Athens; for the Athenians once fought for the children of Heracles even against Eurystheus, who was at that time absolute master of Greece.'

I will now relate a widely accepted story about Callisthenes' opposition to Alexander in this matter of prostration. Alexander had arranged with the sophists and the Persian and Median noblemen at his Court that the subject should be brought up one day at a party. The discussion was begun by Anaxarchus, who declared that Alexander had a better claim upon them to be considered divine than Dionysus or Heracles. The reason for this was not merely his brilliant and successful career, but also the fact that neither Dionysus nor Heracles was connected with Macedon: Dionysus belonged to Thebes, and Heracles to Argos – the latter's only connexion with Macedon was through Alexander, who had his blood in his veins. This being so, there would be greater propriety in the Macedonians paying divine honours to their own King. In any case there was no doubt that they would honour him as a god after he had left this world; would it not, therefore, be in every way better to offer him this tribute now, while he was alive, and not wait till he was dead and could get no good of it?

Those who were, so to put it, 'in the know' expressed their approval of what Anaxarchus said, and were only too willing to begin prostrating themselves forthwith; but the Macedonians – or most of them – who were present, strongly dissented, and said nothing. Suddenly Callisthenes intervened. 'For my part,' he said, 'I hold Alexander fit for any mark of honour that a man may earn; but do not forget that there is a difference between honouring a man and worshipping a god. The distinction between the two has been marked in many ways: for instance, by the building of temples, the erection of statues; the dedication of sacred ground – all these are for gods; again, for gods sacrifice is offered and libations are poured; hymns are composed for the worship of gods, while panegyrics are written for the praise of men. Yet of all these things not one is so important as this very custom of prostration. Men greet each other with a kiss; but a god, far above us on his mysterious throne, it is not lawful for us to touch – and that is why we proffer him the homage of bowing to the earth before him.

'Again, for the worship of gods we perform the ceremonial dance and sing the song of praise. There is nothing surprising in this, for even the gods are worshipped by varying forms of ceremonial; and heroes and demi-gods, remember, have, again, their own peculiar, and quite different, rites.

'It is wrong, therefore, to ignore these distinctions; we ought not to make a man look bigger than he is by paying him excessive and extravagant honour, or, at the same time, impiously to degrade the gods (if such a thing were possible) by putting them in this matter on the same level as men. Suppose some fellow or other, by some quite unjustified vote or show of hands, were brought to enjoy royal honours: would Alexander tolerate it? Of course he would not. By the same reasoning there are much better grounds for the gods' resentment against men who invest themselves with divine honours, or allow other people to do it for them.

'Now Alexander deserves his reputation of being incomparably the bravest of the brave, the most kingly of kings, the worthiest to command of all commanders. And you, Anaxarchus – you who are admitted to Alexander's presence for the express purpose of instructing him in the truth – you, above all people, should have been the first to speak as I am speaking; you should have stopped the mouth of anyone who dared argue on the other side. To take the lead in the way you did was a disgraceful thing: you ought to have remembered that you are not the attendant and adviser of Cambyses or Xerxes, but of Philip's son, a man with the blood of Heracles and Aeacus in his veins, a man whose forefathers came from Argos to Macedonia, where they long ruled not by force, but by law.

'Again, not even Heracles was accorded divine honours by the Greeks while he was alive – nor when he was dead either, until the command to do so was given by an oracle of Apollo at Delphi. Well, here we are in a foreign land; and if for that reason we must think foreign thoughts, yet I beg you, Alexander, to remember Greece; it was for her sake alone, that you might add Asia to her empire, that you undertook this campaign. Consider this too: when you are home again, do you really propose to force the Greeks, who love their

liberty more than anyone else in the world, to prostrate themselves
before you? Or will you let the Greeks off and impose this shameful
duty only on the Macedonians? Or will you make a broad and general
distinction in the matter, and ordain that barbarians only should keep
their barbarous manners, while Greeks and Macedonians honour you
honourably as a man, according to the traditions of Greece?

'It is said that Cyrus, son of Cambyses, was the first man to receive
the homage of prostration, and that this humiliating custom there-
after became an accepted thing in Persia. So be it; none the less you
must remember that the great Cyrus was cured of his pride by a tribe
of Scythians – poor men but free; that Darius was humbled by
Scythians too, as Xerxes was by Athens and Sparta, and Artaxerxes
by the Ten Thousand of Clearchus and Xenophon. And now Alexander has robbed another Darius of his pride – though no man has yet
bowed to the earth before him.'

This speech vexed Alexander profoundly, but not the Macedonians, who found what he said very much to their mind. Alexander
was aware of this, and told the Macedonians accordingly to forget
the matter: the need to prostrate themselves would not in future
arise.

For a moment there was silence; then the senior Persian officials
rose from their seats and one by one grovelled on the floor before the
King. Leonnatus, a member of the Hetaeri, thought one of them
bungled his bow, and burst out laughing at his attitude, which was,
indeed, hardly dignified. Alexander was angry – but his anger passed
and he was afterwards willing to make friends again.

One more story on this subject is on record. Alexander sent round
a golden loving-cup, passing it first to those with whom the agreement about the act of prostration had been made. The first to drink
rose from his seat, prostrated himself, and then received a kiss from
Alexander. The rest followed suit; but Callisthenes, when his turn
came, first drank, then rose to his feet, and then, without prostrating
himself, walked up to Alexander and offered to kiss him. Alexander,
at the moment, was talking to Hephaestion, and did not trouble to
observe whether or not Callisthenes had properly performed the act
of obeisance, but one of the Hetaeri – Demetrius, son of Pythonax –
mentioned the fact that he had omitted to do so before going up for
his kiss. Thereupon Alexander refused to allow him to kiss him.

'Well then,' Callisthenes exclaimed, 'I must go back to my place one kiss the poorer.'

In my opinion all these stories are deplorable in so far as they reflect upon Alexander's growing arrogance and Callisthenes' bad manners. It is enough, I think, once a man has consented to enter a king's service, that he should exalt his master as much as he can, while at the same time preserving a decent modesty in his own behaviour; and for that reason I feel that Alexander was not unjustified in being angry with Callisthenes both for his absurd conceit and for letting his tongue run away with him. And this, I imagine, is why credit was so readily given to the story that Callisthenes had a hand in the plot which was laid against Alexander by his young attendants – or indeed that he was actually the prime mover of it.

It was Alexander's father, Philip, who first instituted the custom of making the adolescent sons of Macedonian nobles personal attendants upon the king. These boys were entrusted with the general care of his person and also with the duty of guarding him when he was asleep; when he went riding, they would receive the horses from the grooms, lead them up and assist him to mount in the Persian manner, and share with him the friendly rivalry of the hunt.

One of these boys was named Hermolaus; he was the son of Sopolis, and was supposed to be interested in philosophy, an interest which brought him into close touch with Callisthenes. Now the story is that during a hunt Alexander was charged by a boar and, before he could strike, was forestalled by Hermolaus, who himself struck the boar and killed it. Alexander was furious at missing his chance, and ordered Hermolaus to be whipped in front of the other boys, and then took his horse from him.

Bitterly hurt by this high-handed treatment, Hermolaus told Sostratus, son of Amyntas and his bosom friend, that life would not be worth living till he had had his revenge for this brutal insult, and Sostratus, who adored him, was easily persuaded to take a hand in planning it. The two boys then obtained the support of Antipater, son of Asclepiodorus, a former governor of Syria, and of three others: Epimenes son of Arseus, Anticles son of Theocritus, and Philotas son of a Thracian named Carsis. It was agreed between them that, when Antipater's turn of night duty came round, they should murder Alexander in his sleep.

It so happened that on the night in question Alexander sat up drinking until dawn. This may have been pure chance, though Aristobulus has a different explanation. According to him, there was a certain Syrian woman with the gift of second sight, who kept following Alexander about. He and his friends used to laugh at her; but, as time went on and everything she foretold in her trances turned out to be true, Alexander began to feel differently. He no longer found her a figure of fun, but let her come to him whenever she wished, by day or night, and on many occasions allowed her to watch over him while he slept.

This woman, in one of her prophetic trances, met him as he was coming away from his potations. She begged him to go back and drink the night out, and Alexander, convinced that there was something more than human in the warning, took her advice. So the boys' plot fell through.

Epimenes, one of the guilty ones, also, like Hermolaus, had a bosom friend, Charicles, son of Menander; and to him, on the following day, he told the whole story. Charicles told Epimenes' brother, Eurylochus, who went to Alexander's tent and passed everything on to Ptolemy son of Lagus, of the King's Guard, who, in his turn, told Alexander. Alexander ordered the arrest of all the boys whose names were given him by Eurylochus. Questioned under torture, they admitted their guilt, and at the same time implicated certain others as well.

Aristobulus declares – and Ptolemy supports him – that the boys said that Callisthenes had urged them to commit the crime. Most authorities, however, have no mention of this; they merely suggest that Alexander was ready enough to believe the worst about Callisthenes, first, because he already disliked him, and, secondly, because of his close association with Hermolaus.

In some writers, moreover, we find the story that Hermolaus, when he was brought to stand his trial, openly confessed his guilt, declaring that it was no longer possible for an honourable man to endure Alexander's inhuman arrogance; and then went on to give a list of his crimes – the lawless killing of Philotas, the still more arbitrary execution of his father Parmenio and the other officers who were put to death on the same occasion, the murder in his cups of Cleitus, his assumption of Persian dress, the duty of prostration he had planned, and was still planning, to impose, his heavy drinking and his drunken sleeps: what he desired was to free himself and the Macedonians from evils such as these, which were no longer to be borne. Hermolaus and the other boys arrested with him were then stoned to death on the spot.

Callisthenes' fate is variously reported: Aristobulus writes that he was dragged about in chains wherever the army went, till his health broke and he died. According to Ptolemy he was just tortured and then hanged. So we see that even the most trustworthy writers, men who were actually with Alexander at the time, have given conflicting accounts of notorious events with which they must have been perfectly familiar. Many other details of this affair have been handled by other writers, too, in a most confusing and contradictory manner – so I can do no better than leave the story as I have told it. I have, indeed, anticipated events a little; but I do feel that, for the purposes of my narrative, the story of Hermolaus is closely connected with the story of Alexander and Cleitus; so for that reason I have related it here, as an immediate sequel.

Alexander was now for the second time visited by envoys from the European Scythians, who arrived in company with the envoys he had himself sent to Scythia. The reigning King of Scythia at the time of their dispatch had died; he had been succeeded by his brother, and the purpose of the present embassy was to express the willingness of Scythia to accede in every point to Alexander's instructions; they brought as presents from the King such things as are reckoned most valuable in their country, and communicated to Alexander their King's desire to cement the friendship and alliance between their countries by giving him his daughter in marriage. Should Alexander be unwilling to marry the Scythian Princess, the King was none the less anxious to do the next best thing and to give as brides to his most trusted officers the daughters of the governors and other personages of rank in Scythian territory. He would, moreover, visit Alexander in person, if he were called upon to do so, and thus be enabled to take his instructions from Alexander's own lips.

About the same time the King of the Chorasmians, Pharasmanes, arrived at the Court with 1,500 mounted troops. He told Alexander that his territory had common frontiers with the Colchians and the Amazon women, and that if Alexander should ever contemplate an invasion of those countries with the object of reducing the various peoples in that part of the world as far as the Black Sea, he was willing to act as his guide and to provide all the necessary supplies for his army.

To the envoys from Scythia, Alexander gave a polite and suitable reply: he had no need, he said, of a Scythian marriage. He thanked Pharasmanes for his offer and concluded a pact of friendship with him, adding that an expedition to the Black Sea was not at the moment convenient; and, before dismissing him, he put him in touch with Artabazus, the Persian, to whom he had given charge of affairs in Bactria, and also with the various governors of the neighbouring provinces. His own thoughts were at present occupied with India, and he pointed out that once India was his he would be master of all Asia, after which his intention was to return to Greece and to make from thence an expedition to the Black Sea region by way of the Hellespont and the Propontis with all his land and sea forces combined. Pharasmanes, therefore, would oblige him if he deferred the fulfilment of his offer until that occasion should arise.

Alexander now returned to the Oxus. His intention was to proceed to Sogdiana, as a report had come in that many of the people there were refusing to obey the governor he had appointed and had shut themselves up in the forts. While he was in camp on the Oxus, a spring of water and another of oil quite near it came up from the ground close to his tent. Ptolemy, son of Lagus, was informed of this remarkable event, and Ptolemy told Alexander, who, to mark his sense of its miraculous nature, offered sacrifice according to the form prescribed by his soothsayers. Aristander declared that the spring of oil was a sign of difficulties to come and of eventual victory.

Four officers – Polysperchon, Attalus, Gorgias, and Meleager – were left in Bactria with instructions to destroy all natives who had refused submission and to keep a sharp look-out for any further trouble; and Alexander himself, after crossing into Sogdiana, divided his remaining strength into five, one division to be commanded by Hephaestion, another by Ptolemy, son of Lagus, a third by Perdiccas, a fourth by Coenus and Artabazus. The fifth he took over himself and proceeded with it in the direction of Marakanda, while the other four commanders carried out offensive operations as opportunity offered, storming the forts where some of the native tribesmen were trying to hold out, or receiving the voluntary surrender of others.

The greater part of Sogdiana was covered by these operations, and when the whole force was reunited at Marakanda, Alexander sent Hephaestion to plant settlements in the various towns, and at the same time dispatched Coenus and Artabazus to Scythia, where Spitamenes, according to report, had taken refuge. Meanwhile Alexander with the remainder of his force marched against those parts of Sogdiana which were still in rebel hands, and had no difficulty in subduing them.

Spitamenes, while all this was going on, had made his way with a number of fugitives from Sogdiana to that branch of the Scythian people known as the Massagetae; there they got together 600 native horsemen and presented themselves at one of the forts in Bactria. Neither the garrison nor its commander had expected any hostile move; Spitamenes took them by surprise, killed the men, and captured their officer, whom he kept under guard. This success emboldened him a few days later to approach Zariaspa. They did not venture an assault upon the town, though they rounded up a lot of livestock and carried it off as booty.

A few men of the mounted Hetaeri had been left behind sick in Zariaspa, and among them were Sosicles' son, Peithon, who had charge of all arrangements for the King's personal comfort in that town, and the harp-player, Aristonicus. These two had sufficiently recovered to ride and bear arms when the Scythian raid occurred; so as soon as they knew of it, they got together about eighty mounted men – mercenaries, left to garrison the town – and with them and a few of the King's boy squires rode out to the attack. The Scythians were taken by surprise, and the first charge was successful: they recovered all the stolen cattle and killed a number of the men who were driving them off; but as they were straggling back to the town, in a more or less go-as-you-please fashion, Spitamenes and his Scythians caught them in an ambush. Seven of the Hetaeri were lost and sixty mercenaries. Aristonicus, too, was killed – having fought, however, not like a harpist but like a man; and Peithon was wounded and taken prisoner.

As soon as he got the news of this action, Craterus lost no time in marching against the Massagetae, who withdrew hastily towards the desert when they observed his approach. Craterus followed them up, and not far from the edge of the desert made contact with them and another force of their mounted troops, over 1,000 strong. A sharp engagement ensued, in which the Macedonians were victorious. The Scythians lost 150 mounted men; the rest of them got safely away into the desert, Craterus finding it impracticable to continue his pursuit.

About this time Artabazus asked to be relieved of the governorship of Bactria on account of his age. Alexander granted his request and appointed Amyntas, son of Nicolaus, in his place. He left Coenus in that part of the country with a force consisting of his own and Meleager's divisions, about 400 mounted Hetaeri, all the Javelins, and such troops from Bactria and Sogdiana as were attached to Amyntas. His instructions were that they should all take their orders from Coenus and winter in Sogdiana, partly as a precautionary measure, and partly on the chance that they might succeed in laying a trap for Spitamenes, should he be riding around in the neighbourhood in the course of the winter.

When Spitamenes found that the whole country was held by Macedonian garrisons and that there was little likelihood of escape for himself or his men, he determined to make a move against Coenus, in the hope of making a better fight of it in that part of the country. At Bagae, a stronghold of Sogdiana on the Massagetaean frontier, they had no difficulty in inducing a force of some 3,000 Scythian mounted troops to join them in a raid on Sogdiana. These Scythians are always ready at a word to take part in any fighting which may be going on: their extreme poverty might be reason enough; but, in addition to that, they have no towns, no settled homes, and consequently no cause to fear the loss of what is dearest to them.

Learning of the approach of Spitamenes' cavalry, Coenus went out to meet them. There was a vigorous engagement, in which the Macedonians were successful; over 800 enemy horsemen were killed, while Coenus' losses amounted to about twenty-five mounted men and twelve infantrymen. While Spitamenes was trying to make his escape, he was deserted by most of the Bactrians and such troops from Sogdiana as were still with him. All these surrendered to Coenus. The Massagetae marked their defeat by plundering the baggage-trains of their late companions in battle, and then made with Spitamenes for the desert; but no sooner had they learned that Alexander, too, was on the move towards the desert than they cut off Spitamenes' head and sent it to him, in the hope that by this friendly act they might keep him from molesting them.

Meanwhile Alexander was rejoined at Nautaca by Coenus and Stasanor, satrap of Aria, and also by the troops under the command of Craterus and Phrataphernes, satrap of Parthia. These officers had successfully carried out all Alexander's instructions. As it was now mid-winter, Alexander rested his men at Nautaca, and dispatched Phrataphernes to fetch Autophradates, the satrap of Mardia and Tapuria, who on a number of previous occasions had ignored Alexander's orders to come and report himself. He sent Stasanor to take over the governorship of the Drangae, and Atropates to replace Oxodates in Media, as the latter appeared to be unreliable. Mazaeus, the governor of Babylon, being reported dead, Stamenes was sent to succeed him. Sopolis, Epocillus, and Menidas were ordered home to Macedonia to fetch reinforcements.

News had come in that a large number of the natives had taken refuge on the Rock of Sogdiana, and among them the wife and daughters of Oxyartes the Bactrian, who had himself refused to submit to Alexander and had chosen this refuge for his family in the belief that the Rock was impregnable. It was the last stronghold of Sogdiana: should it fall, there would be nothing left for those who still hoped to offer resistance. To the Rock, therefore, Alexander advanced, at the beginning of spring.

He found, on a near approach, that it rose sheer on every side against attack. The natives had provisioned it for a long siege, and deep snow on its summit caused the double disadvantage of making the ascent more awkward for the Macedonians and of ensuring the defenders an unlimited supply of water. None the less, Alexander determined on assault.

In point of fact the reason for his determination was something the natives had said, an offensive bit of bragging which made him angry and put him on his mettle. He had called on them to discuss terms, and offered to allow them to return unmolested to their homes on condition of surrendering the stronghold; but their answer to the offer was a shout of laughter. Then in their barbaric lingo they told Alexander to find soldiers with wings to capture the Rock for him, as no other sort of person could cause them the least anxiety. As a result of this, Alexander proclaimed that he would give a prize of twelve talents to the first man up, and of eleven to the second, and ten to the third, and so on to the twelfth, who would receive 300 gold darics. The men were keen enough already, but this proclamation was an added spur.

There were some 300 men who in previous sieges had had experience in rock-climbing. These now assembled. They had provided themselves with small iron tent-pegs, which they proposed to drive into the snow, where it was frozen hard, or into any bit of bare earth they might come across, and they had attached to the pegs strong flaxen lines. The party set off under cover of darkness to the steepest part of the rock-face, which they knew was least likely to be guarded; then, driving their pegs either into bare ground or into such patches of snow as seemed most likely to hold under the strain, they hauled themselves up, wherever each could find a way. About thirty lost their lives during the ascent – falling in various places in the snow, their bodies were never recovered for burial – but the rest reached the top as dawn was breaking, and the summit of the Rock was theirs. Then, in accordance with Alexander's orders, they signalled their success to the troops below by waving bits of linen, and Alexander sent a crier to shout the news to the enemy's advanced posts that they might now surrender without further delay, as the men with wings had been found and were already in possession of the summit. And, as the crier gave them this information, Alexander pointed to his men, where they stood on top of the Rock.

The unexpectedness of the sight was a severe shock to the natives; indeed, they were so much alarmed by the handful of Macedonian troops they could actually see, that, imagining a larger force, and fully armed at that, must be in possession, they surrendered. Many women and children were among the prisoners – notably the wife and daughters of Oxyartes.

One of these daughters was named Roxane. She was a girl of marriageable age, and men who took part in the campaign used to say she was the loveliest woman they had seen in Asia, with the one exception of Darius' wife. Alexander fell in love with her at sight; but, captive though she was, he refused, for all his passion, to force her to his will, and condescended to marry her. For this act I have, on the whole, more praise than blame.

As for Darius' wife, said to be the most beautiful woman in Asia, either he felt for her no desire, or, if he did, he controlled it, in spite of the fact that he was both young and on top of the world – a combination of circumstances which leads most men to all sorts of excess. But he respected her and let her alone. In this he showed great restraint – and also, no doubt, a quite natural anxiety to be well spoken of.

There is a story about Darius that shortly after the battle of Issus the eunuch who had charge of his wife succeeded in making his way to him. Darius' first question was whether his mother, wife, and children were still alive, and hearing that they not only were, but were also addressed by the title of princess and treated with as much ceremony as when he was on the throne, he proceeded to inquire if his wife still preserved her chastity.

'She does,' replied the eunuch.

'And has Alexander offered her no violence – no insult?'

'My lord,' exclaimed the eunuch with an oath, 'your wife is as you left her, and Alexander is the best of men and the least ready to yield to temptation.'

Darius raised his hands to heaven in prayer. 'My lord Zeus,' he cried, 'to whom it is given to order the affairs of kings in this world, keep safe for me now the empire over the Medes and Persians, even as once you gave it me; but, if it is no longer your will that I be King of Asia, then entrust my throne, I pray, to no man but Alexander – so deeply does he care to act with honour even towards his enemies.'

When Oxyartes learned that his daughters were prisoners, the further intelligence that Alexander was interested in Roxane emboldened him to present himself, and Alexander, as was only proper in these happy circumstances, treated him with all respect.

With the capture of the Rock, the operations in Sogdiana were successfully concluded, and Alexander's next move was to the territory of the Pareitacae, where a large force of natives were said to be holding another rock fortress, the Rock of Chorienes. Chorienes himself, with many others of eminence in the country, had taken refuge there. This rock, some 4,000 feet high and about seven miles in circumference, rose sheer on every side; there was only one way up, by a narrow and difficult track hewn out of the rock-face and consequently awkward to ascend even in single file and without opposition. The fortress was further defended all round by a deep ravine, so that any attempt to assault it would have had to be preceded by the labour of filling this up, to enable the attack to be launched from level ground. However, the reckless courage engendered by success had by this time brought Alexander to believe that there was no place where he might not set his foot and no fortress which could hold out against him; so, despite the difficulties, he set to work. Felling some of the lofty pine-trees, which grew in large numbers round the base of the hill, he had ladders constructed to enable his men to descend into the ravine, which would have been impracticable by other means. Alexander personally superintended the work during the day, half his men being on duty; at night the other half came on, divided into three shifts, under the respective command of his Guards, Perdiccas, Leonnatus, and Ptolemy, son of Lagus. It was such an awkward spot to work in, and the work itself so hard, that about thirty feet was all they could manage in a daylight shift, and rather less at night, though the entire army was employed. The method they used was to climb right down to the narrowest part of the ravine and drive in stakes properly spaced to carry the load to be laid on them, which consisted of wattles (as in bridge-building) bound firmly together, with a layer of soil on top. In this way the troops would be enabled to get to the base of the rock across level ground.

In its early stages the enemy contemptuously ignored the whole thing as a hopeless undertaking; but as the work proceeded arrows began to find their mark; all attempts to dislodge the Macedonians by missile attacks from above proved abortive, and the work continued in perfect security under the protection of screens. Faced by this unexpected situation, Chorienes lost his nerve, and sent a messenger to Alexander with a request that Oxyartes should be allowed to come to him. Alexander agreed, and Oxyartes urged Chorienes to give up the stronghold and surrender to Alexander. Against Alexander and his men no place in the world, he declared, was impregnable; on the other hand, should the question of a loyal and friendly agreement arise, he had nothing but praise for Alexander's sense of honour and justice. Of this there were many examples, if proof were wanted, and not least the treatment he had himself received. Chorienes allowed himself to be persuaded; he came to Alexander together with some of his kinsmen and friends, and received from him a kindly assurance of friendship. Alexander kept him at his side, and told him to send back to the fortress with a demand for its surrender certain of the men he had brought down with him. The troops holding out there duly surrendered it, and Alexander himself subsequently ascended the rock, out of curiosity to see it, with a party of some 500 Longshields. Chorienes he treated with the utmost consideration, actually putting the control of the rock into his hands and letting him continue to administer the same territory as before.

The winter had brought Alexander's men considerable distress, as much snow had fallen during the course of the siege, and supplies were short. Chorienes, however, offered a gift of two months' rations for the whole army; from his stores on the rock he distributed grain, wine, and dried meat – so much for each tent, or mess – and declared that, even so, he had not used a tenth part of what had been laid in for the siege. Alexander's respect for him was much increased by this, for it clearly indicated that the surrender had been a matter not of necessity but of deliberate policy.

Alexander's next move was for Bactria. Craterus, with a force consisting of 600 mounted Hetaeri, his own and Alcetas' infantry brigades, and the unit commanded by Polysperchon and Attalus, was ordered to march against Catanes and Austanes, the last two in the territory of the Pareitacae to be still refusing submission. There was a sharp clash, in which Craterus was victorious; Catanes was killed in action, and Austanes was taken prisoner and brought to Alexander. Of the native forces under their command, about 120 cavalrymen were killed and 1,500 infantry. After this success Craterus proceeded with his men to join Alexander in Bactria. It was in Bactria that Alexander had his unpleasant experience with Callisthenes and the boys.

Towards the end of spring Alexander began his march for India, leaving Amyntas in Bactria with a force of 3,500 mounted troops and 10,000 infantry. He crossed the Indian Caucasus, and in ten days reached Alexandria, the town he had founded in the territory of the Parapamisidae during his first expedition into Bactria. The governor, whom he had appointed on that occasion, he dismissed for incompetence, and increased the population of the settlement by the addition of families from the neighbourhood and such of his own men as were unfit for service. Nicanor, one of the Hetaeri, was put in control of the actual settlement, and Turiaspes was made governor of the territory of the Parapamisidae and of the rest of the country as far as the

river Cophen. Then, by way of Nicaea, where he offered sacrifice to
Athene, Alexander marched for the Cophen, having first sent instructions to Taxiles and the Indians west of the Indus to meet him at
whatever time each might find it convenient. Taxiles and the other
chiefs obeyed the summons, bringing with them the sort of presents
which are most valued in their country, and offering to give Alexander the twenty-five elephants they had with them.

Alexander now divided his force. Hephaestion and Perdiccas, with
the brigades of Gorgias, Cleitus, and Meleager, half the mounted
Hetaeri and all the mercenary cavalry, were ordered forward to
Peucelaotis, in the direction of the Indus. Their instructions were to
take over either by force or agreement all places on their march, and
on reaching the Indus to make suitable preparations for crossing.
Taxiles and the other Indian chiefs were sent with them, and Alexander's orders were duly carried out when the force arrived at the river.

Astes, the governor of Peucelaotis, caused some trouble, but lost his
life in the process and involved in his own ruin the town in which he
had attempted to hold out. It was taken by Hephaestion after a thirty
days' siege. After Astes' death, Sangaeus was put in control of the
town – he had deserted Astes some time previously and joined Taxiles,
a circumstance which enabled Alexander to trust him.

Alexander's next objective was the territory of the Aspasians,
Guraeans, and Assacenians. The force he took with him consisted of
the Longshields, all the mounted Hetaeri not at the moment serving
under Hephaestion, the so-called Foot Guards, the archers, the
Agrianes, and the mounted Javelins. The route, which followed the
river Choes, was rough and mountainous, and the crossing of the
river was no easy task. Once over, he ordered the main body of the
infantry to follow at their own pace and himself with the mounted
troops and about 800 Macedonian foot, whom he also mounted still
carrying their infantrymen's shields, pressed on with all speed, following a report that the natives thereabouts had taken up defensive positions either in the hills or in such towns as were strong enough to offer
a chance of resistance. Attacking the first of these towns which lay on
his route, he had no trouble in driving in the force which was
stationed outside, and compelling the men to take refuge within the
defences; but during the operation he was wounded in the shoulder
by a missile which pierced his corselet. The wound was not serious, as

the corselet prevented the missile from going right through his shoulder. Ptolemy, son of Lagus, and Leonnatus were also hurt. Alexander
then took up a position opposite the section of the town's defences
which appeared most promising for an assault, and moved forward at
dawn the following day. There was a double ring of defence-works
round the town, and the outer one, which was carelessly constructed,
was forced by the Macedonians without trouble; at the second the
enemy maintained a brief resistance, but once the ladders were in position and the defenders began to suffer losses from the missile weapons
concentrated upon them, they abandoned the town and made a dash
for the hills. Some were killed as they were trying to get away, and
all prisoners were butchered by the Macedonians in revenge for the
wound they had given Alexander; the greater number, however,
escaped to the hills, which were not far off. Alexander razed the town,
and moved on to another – Andaca – which was surrendered to him.
Craterus and the other infantry commanders were left in the district
to organize affairs as the situation demanded, and to reduce any other
towns which refused submission, while Alexander himself continued
his advance with the Longshields, the archers, the Agrianes, Coenus'
and Attalus' brigade, the picked cavalry and some four regiments of
the other mounted Hetaeri, and half the mounted Archers. His route
lay towards the river Euaspla, and after a long march he reached on
the second day the town where the governor of the Aspasians was.
The natives were no sooner aware of his approach than they fired the
town and made their escape to the hills, with Alexander's men in hot
pursuit all the way. Many were cut down before the rough hill-
country enabled them to shake off their pursuers.

During the pursuit, Ptolemy, son of Lagus, actually spotted the
chief of the Indians of this district: he had already reached a hill and
was trying to get away with some of his guards. Ptolemy, though he
had a much inferior force, nevertheless rode for him; but it was too
steep and too rough going for his horse, so he dismounted, gave it to
a man to lead, and continued to chase the Indian on foot. Seeing him
coming, the Indian and his guards turned to face him. They met; and
the chief struck Ptolemy in the breast with his long spear, which
pierced his corselet but did not penetrate his body. With a blow clean
through the Indian's thigh, Ptolemy laid him flat, and began to strip
him, whereupon his guards, seeing that their chief was down, turned

and fled. Other Indians, however, on the neighbouring hills, grieved
at the sight of their leader's body being carried off by the enemy, came
hurrying down, and a fierce struggle ensued over the corpse. By then
Alexander and his cavalrymen, now dismounted, were not far from
the hill; they joined in the *mêlée* and finally succeeded in driving the
Indians into the hills and getting possession of the body.

Having crossed the range, Alexander came down at a settlement
called Erigaeum. He took the place, though it had been burnt and deserted by the inhabitants. He was rejoined there by Craterus and his
troops, all his instructions having been successfully carried out. It occurred to him that the site of Erigaeum had much to recommend it,
so he ordered Craterus to fortify the place and settle in it any of the
natives in the vicinity who were willing to go there, and such of his
own men as were unfit for service. That done, he moved on towards
the region where report had it that most of the native forces had concentrated, with an eye to their own defence, and came to a halt at the
foothills of a range of mountains.

While he was encamped at this spot, Ptolemy, who had been sent
foraging and had gone ahead of the army with a small party to reconnoitre, reported that he had seen the enemy camp-fires, and that they
were more numerous than their own. Alexander received this report
with some scepticism, convinced as he was that the number of camp-
fires was a ruse; he determined, therefore, to advance. Part of his force
he left where they were at the foot of the mountains, and himself
moved forward with a body of troops which he thought sufficient to
meet the situation according to the report he had received. As soon as
they got a close view of the fires, he split his force into three, putting
one section, consisting of the brigade of Attalus and Balacrus, under
Leonnatus, a member of his personal guard, another, consisting of one
third of the Longshields, the brigade of Philip and Philotas, two regiments of archers, the Agrianes, and half the cavalry, under Ptolemy,
son of Lagus, while the third section he took charge of in person and
advanced with it to where the natives appeared to be concentrated in
the greatest numbers.

The Indians were rendered confident both by their numbers and by
their position, which was a commanding one; so when they saw the
Macedonians coming, contemptuous of their apparently inadequate
strength they began to leave the high ground and advanced to meet

them. A fierce battle followed, the result of which, however, was not long in dispute where Alexander's section was concerned. Ptolemy's section did not wait to be attacked on the level ground; the natives held a hill, and Ptolemy pressed forward in column to what appeared the best point for assault; he then surrounded the hill, leaving a gap in his line for the enemy to get through, should they wish to make their escape. Here, too, there was a hard struggle – for the Indians' position itself presented a tough problem, and they happened to be much the best and most courageous fighters of all the tribes in that part of the country. None the less, they, too, were driven from their hill, while the third section, under Leonnatus, was equally successful. According to Ptolemy's account, the total number of prisoners was over 40,000, and more than 230,000 oxen were taken. Alexander picked out the finest of them, as they seemed to be of uncommon size and beauty, and expressed a wish to send them to Macedonia to work on the land.

From there he marched to the territory of the Assacenians, who were reported to be prepared for resistance with 2,000 cavalry, over 30,000 infantry, and thirty elephants at their disposal. His force consisted of the mounted Hetaeri, the mounted Javelins, the brigade of Coenus and Polysperchon, the thousand Agrianes, and the archers, while Craterus, who by now had completed the fortification of the town the settlement of which he had been left to organize, brought along for him the more heavily armed units and the siege engines, in case of need. Alexander's route lay through the country of the Guraeans. The river which gives the district its name proved difficult to cross, being both deep and rapid; and the large round stones with which its bed is strewn gave a treacherous foothold. None the less, the native troops, when they saw Alexander coming, had no heart to stand massed to meet him, but broke up and straggled away in groups to their various towns, where they proposed to defend themselves, and to save their homes – if they could.

Alexander's first move was against Massaga, the largest town in this neighbourhood. On his approach to the walls, the natives were so confident in the effectiveness of some 7,000 mercenary troops from the interior of India, whom they had in their pay, that they advanced at the double as soon as they saw the Macedonian army begin to take up its position. It was clear to Alexander that the fight would take place close to the town; he determined, therefore, to draw the enemy on, in order to ensure that, if they were repulsed – as he was certain they would be – they would not have a short and easy way of retreat within the protection of their walls. Accordingly, the moment he saw them come pouring out of the town, he gave the order for withdrawal to a piece of high ground rather less than a mile from the position he had originally intended to take up. This apparent sign of defeat put fresh fire into the enemy; and in a disorderly rabble they came charging on. But as soon as his men were within range of their arrows, Alexander gave the signal to face about and brought the phalanx at the double to meet them. The first to go into action were the mounted Javelins, the Agrianes, and the archers, and, while they were engaged, Alexander steadily advanced at the head of his infantry. The Indians were badly shaken by this unexpected reversal, and in the close fighting which ensued they broke and withdrew to the town. About 200 of them were killed, and the rest shut themselves up within their defences.

Alexander advanced his infantry close under the walls, and an arrow, shot from them, wounded him slightly in the ankle.

The following day he brought his machines into action and had no difficulty in making a breach. The Macedonians tried to force their way through, but, as the Indians offered stout resistance, the assault was temporarily called off. The day after that, the attack had more power behind it: a wooden tower was brought up; from it the archers shot with greater effect, and that, added to the weight of missiles from the catapults, did much to keep the defenders within bounds. Even so, the Macedonians were unable to force their way in.

On the third day Alexander once more brought his infantry into action, and from one of the siege engines threw a bridge across the breach in the wall. Over this he led his Longshields, the unit which, by the same tactics, had helped him to the capture of Tyre. The men, their blood being up, pressed forward in great numbers, but their weight was too much for the bridge, which broke under them and let them down. At this the enemy with a shout of triumph poured in a hail of missiles – stones from the wall, arrows, or anything else they had or could lay their hands on – while others rushed out through the little gates between the towers and rained blows upon the Macedonians before they could recover themselves.

At this juncture Alexander sent Alcetas with his brigade to pick up the wounded and to recall the men who were still engaged. On the fourth day of the battle the procedure was repeated – another engine was brought into action, and another bridge laid.

So long as their chief survived, the Indians fought with great courage; but when he was killed by a missile from a catapult, what with their own losses in the four days' continuous siege and the large numbers of men wounded or put out of action, they sent to Alexander to ask for a truce. For him it was a pleasure to save the lives of such brave men, and he agreed with the Indian mercenaries that they should serve under himself, as a part of his own army. These troops, accordingly, marched with their arms out of the town and went into camp by themselves on a hill facing the Macedonian position. Their intention was not what Alexander expected; for, having no desire to fight against other Indians, they meant to desert under cover of night and disperse to their homes. Their purpose, however, was reported to Alexander, and that same night he stationed his whole force in a ring round the hill, caught the Indians in a trap, and butchered them. He then seized the town, now undefended. Assacenus' mother and daughter were among the prisoners. During the operation as a whole Alexander's losses amounted to about twenty-five men.

From Massaga, Alexander sent Coenus to Bazira, on the supposition that the people of that town, when they learned of the fate of Massaga, would surrender to him. At the same time Attalus, Alcetas, and Demetrius, the cavalry commander, were dispatched to Ora, with instructions to blockade it with a ring-wall pending his own arrival. The Indians in Ora made a sally against Alcetas' troops, but were repulsed without difficulty and forced to withdraw within the wall again. At Bazira, meanwhile, Coenus was unsuccessful; the natives there were encouraged to resist by the natural strength of the town's position – it stood very high and was well fortified on every side – and showed no sign of surrender.

Alexander started for Bazira as soon as he learned of this check; he was diverted, however, by a further report that some of the Indians of the neighbourhood, upon instructions from Abisarus, were preparing to make their way secretly into Ora. So he made Ora his first objective, sending an order to Coenus to construct a blockhouse outside Bazira, garrison it sufficiently to prevent the people of the town from making free use of the surrounding country, and then join him with the remainder of his troops.

When the Indians in Bazira saw the greater part of Coenus' forces moving off, they were not unnaturally contemptuous: the Macedonians – evidently – were no match for them. So out they all came, and a brisk engagement ensued. During the course of it about 500 of the Indians were killed and more than seventy captured; the remainder withdrew within the town. After this incident the garrison of the blockhouse took still stronger measures to bar access to the surrounding country.

The siege of Ora gave Alexander very little trouble; in fact, he took the place at the first assault – including the elephants which had been left there.

The news from Ora soon persuaded the Indians at Bazira that their position was hopeless. At midnight they abandoned the town. The other Indians of the district all followed their example: without exception they left their towns and fled for refuge to what was known as the Rock of Aornos. This rock is a really tremendous thing; and the story goes that Heracles himself, the son of Zeus, was unable to capture it. Personally, of course, I should not like to state categorically that the Theban, or the Tyrian, or the Egyptian Heracles did, in fact, go to India. I incline to fancy that he did not; for it seems to me that people like to make difficulties look much more difficult than they really are, and to this end start a legend about Heracles' failure to overcome them. That, at any rate, is my opinion about this rock: the name of Heracles was introduced simply to make the story more impressive. The circumference of Aornos is said to be about 25 miles, and its height, not including the peaks, nearly 8,000 feet. There is only one way up it, a difficult path, hewn from the rock. On the summit there is an abundant supply of pure water from a spring – it comes streaming out – and also woodland and enough good arable land to keep 1,000 men busy.

The description of this remarkable place awakened in Alexander a passionate desire to capture it, and the story about Heracles was not the least of his incentives.

Ora and Massaga he converted into blockhouses for keeping order in the neighbourhood. Bazira was fully fortified. Hephaestion and Perdiccas, having fortified and garrisoned another town, called

Drobatis, started for the Indus, where they set about the construction of the bridge according to Alexander's orders. Nicanor, one of the Hetaeri, was appointed governor of the territory west of the Indus.

On his march to Aornos, Alexander started in the direction of the Indus; the town of Pencelaotis, which stood not far from the river, he took over by surrender and garrisoned with Macedonian troops under the command of Philip. A number of other small places on the river also fell into his hands. He was accompanied on his march by the chiefs of the district, Cophaeus and Assagetes. Arrived at Embolima, a town close to Aornos, he detached a portion of his forces, under the command of Craterus, with orders to lay in supplies of all kinds in sufficient quantity for a long period of time, as his intention was to use the town as a base from which he could, by a protracted siege, little by little break the resistance of the Indians on Aornos, should it prove impossible to take the Rock by assault. Then, with the archers, the Agrianes, Coenus' brigade, the best-armed and most lightly equipped of the other infantry units, 200 mounted Hetaeri and 100 mounted archers, he moved on towards the Rock.

Before the day was over he halted in what he judged to be a convenient spot, and on the morrow advanced a little further; then halted again. While he waited there, some natives sought an interview with him. They put themselves into his hands, and then declared that they would guide him to the most vulnerable point of the Rock and from there he would be able to secure a valuable offensive position without difficulty. Alexander accepted the offer and ordered Ptolemy, son of Lagus, of his personal Guard, with the Agrianes, the other light-armed units, and a picked company of Longshields, to go with the guides, seize the position they mentioned, make sure to secure it strongly, and inform him by signal in the event of his success.

The rough track made difficult going, but Ptolemy, unperceived by the enemy, reached the position and occupied it. He at once proceeded to secure it by a ditch and stockade, and raised a fire-signal on an eminence where Alexander would be sure to see it. Alexander did see it, instantly, and on the following day began his own advance, but, meeting resistance from the enemy and great difficulty from the broken ground, achieved, for the time being, nothing. The Indians no sooner perceived that Alexander's offensive was getting nowhere than they turned their attention to Ptolemy. They moved to the attack, and there was a fierce struggle, the Indians doing all they could to tear down the stockade, while Ptolemy fought to maintain his hold. The weight of the Macedonian missiles overpowered the Indians, who at nightfall were forced to withdraw.

Wishing to get a message through to Ptolemy, Alexander chose as his messenger one of the Indian deserters, a trustworthy fellow with the further recommendation of an intimate knowledge of the locality. Under cover of darkness he sent this man with a letter containing instructions to Ptolemy, not to rest content with holding the position he had occupied, but to take the offensive: his attack, moreover, should be simultaneous with his own, so that the Indians would be caught between two fires. Next day at dawn Alexander moved; he marched for the track by which Ptolemy had made his secret ascent, in the belief that if once he could get through and join Ptolemy, what remained to do would be comparatively easy. All went according to plan: there was a hard struggle lasting until noon, the Macedonians trying to force their way up and the Indians doing what they could to stop them by all the missiles they could muster. Company by company the Macedonians pressed relentlessly up the slope, the leading files pausing till their companions below could join them, and at last, just as the light was going, they managed to get through and made contact with Ptolemy. The whole force, now united, then moved forward to the assault of the actual Rock. The assault, however, proved abortive, and for what remained of the day nothing else was accomplished.

The following dawn Alexander issued an order for every man to cut a hundred stakes. This was done, and he then began the construction of an extensive earthwork, to reach from his present position on the crest of the hill across to Aornos itself. From the top of this he judged that the defenders of the Rock would be within range both of arrows and of catapults. Every man set to and took a hand, while Alexander himself kept an eye upon things and was as quick to punish shoddy work as to praise what was well and truly done.

During the first day the earthwork was carried forward about 800 yards; by the second, slingers and catapults operating from the portion already completed were able to check enemy raids on the men still working; within three days the entire space was filled. Then, on the fourth day, a small party of Macedonians stormed and secured another height, of no great extent, the summit of which was level with the Rock, and Alexander promptly began to extend the earth-work in this direction, in order to make it run without a break right up to this new position.

The seizure of this second height was an act of daring wholly beyond the Indians' experience; they were badly shaken, and when they saw the earthwork completed and continuous, they abandoned any further hope of resistance, and sent an offer to Alexander to surrender the Rock upon terms. They expected to be able to protract the discussion of terms throughout the day, and their plan was to slip away during the night and disperse to their various homes. Alexander, however, was informed of their intention; giving them plenty of time to get away and to remove the pickets which were stationed all round the Rock, he waited till the actual withdrawal began, and then, with a party of 700 of the Longshields and his personal guard, moved forward to that part of the Rock which was now undefended. He was himself the first to set foot upon it, and his men followed, hauling each other up.

At a given signal they turned upon the retreating Indians and killed many of them as they tried to escape; others in sudden desperation flung themselves over the cliffs.

Thus Alexander was left in possession of the Rock which had baffled Heracles himself. Upon it he offered sacrifice, and then garrisoned it with troops under the command of Sisicottus, an Indian who some time previously had deserted to Bessus in Bactria and had subsequently taken service under Alexander, after his conquest of Bactria, and proved himself highly trustworthy.

Leaving Aornos, Alexander entered the territory of the Assacenians on the strength of a report that Assacenus' brother with his elephants and a large number of natives proposed to defend themselves in the mountains there. The town of Dyrta he found empty and abandoned, as was the country in the immediate neighbourhood, and the day after his arrival there he detached Nearchus with the light-armed units and the Agrianes, and Antiochus with his own regiment and two others and sent them out to reconnoitre. Their orders were also to capture and question any natives they could lay hands on, and, in particular,

F

to get what information they could about elephants, as this interested him more than anything.

He now marched for the Indus. It was difficult country, and troops went on ahead to make a practicable route. A few natives were captured, and from them he learned that the Indians of the district had fled to Abisarus, leaving their elephants where they were to feed by the river. He ordered the men to take him to the elephants.

Many Indians hunt elephants, and Alexander greatly liked to have elephant-hunters in his retinue. On this occasion, too, he went hunting with his guides; two of the beasts, in the course of the hunt, jumped over a cliff and were killed, but the rest were caught. They permitted riders to mount them and were attached to the army.

There was a wood by the river, and as the timber was of good quality Alexander had it felled and boats built. The boats were taken down-river to the bridge, the construction of which Hephaestion and Perdiccas had some time ago completed.

BOOK FIVE

I̶N̶ the country on Alexander's route between the river Cophen and
the Indus lay the city of Nysa, supposed to have been founded by
Dionysus, at the time of his conquest of the Indians. Nobody knows,
however, who this Dionysus was, nor the date of his invasion of India,
nor where he started from, and I myself should hardly care to say if
this Theban deity marched with his army against the Indians from
Thebes or from Tmolus in Lydia, or how it was that after passing
through the territories of so many warlike peoples unknown to the
Greeks of that date, he fought and conquered only the Indians. However, one should not inquire too closely where ancient legends about
the gods are concerned; many things which reason rejects acquire
some colour of probability once you bring a god into the story.

The people of Nysa, upon Alexander's approach, sent their chief,
Acuphis, to him accompanied by thirty of their most distinguished
men with instructions to ask him to leave their city to its god. The
story is that when they entered Alexander's tent, they found him sitting there dusty and travel-stained, still wearing his equipment, his
helmet on his head and a spear in his hand. The sight of him sitting
thus surprised them so much that they prostrated themselves upon the
ground and for a long time spoke never a word. At last, however,
Alexander bade them get up and not be alarmed; whereupon Acuphis
addressed him in the following words: 'Sire, it is the request of the
people of Nysa that you show your reverence for Dionysus by leaving
them free and independent. For when Dionysus, after his conquest of
the Indians, was on his way homeward towards the Grecian sea, he
founded this city as a memorial of his long journey and his victory,
leaving to inhabit it those of his men who were no longer fit for service – who were also his Priests. He did but as you have done; for
you too founded Alexandria in the Caucasus and Alexandria in
Egypt and many other cities as well, and will found yet more here-
after, in that you will have surpassed the achievements of Dionysus.

'Dionysus named this city Nysa and this land Nysaea in memory of
his nurse, who bore that name; and to the mountain near the city he

gave the name Merus – or the Thigh – because legend has it that he
grew in the thigh of Zeus. Ever since that time Nysa has been free;
we who live in it have made our own laws – and obeyed them, as
good men should. If you wish for a proof that Dionysus was our
founder, here it is: this is the only place in India where ivy grows.'

Alexander found what Acuphis said highly agreeable; he would
have liked very much to believe the old tale about Dionysus' journey
and his founding of Nysa, for then he would have had the satisfaction
of knowing that he had already penetrated as far as Dionysus did,
and would presently advance yet further; he felt moreover that his
Macedonian troops would consent to share his hardships a little
longer, if they knew they were in competition with Dionysus. Accordingly he granted to the people of Nysa the continuance of their
freedom and autonomy.

He inquired about the nature of their institutions, and on being told
that the government was aristocratic in form, he expressed approval
and asked that 300 of their mounted troops should be sent to join him
together with 100 men chosen from the most distinguished in the
governing class (which also happened to consist of 300 men). Acuphis, whom Alexander appointed governor of Nysaea, was to select
them. Acuphis is said to have smiled at this request, and on being
asked by Alexander what it was that amused him, the story goes that
he replied: 'But how, my lord, do you suppose that a city can lose a
hundred good men and still be well governed? If you have our interest at heart, we will, indeed, send for the three hundred cavalrymen,
and more, if you want them; but instead of the hundred able and distinguished citizens whom you ask me to select, take, I beg you,
double the number of the inferior sort, so that when you come again
to visit us you may find us as well governed as we are now.'

Alexander acceded to the request, which he thought a sensible one.
He repeated his order that Acuphis should send the cavalrymen to accompany him, but neither the select hundred nor any substitutes for
them. Acuphis, however, sent him his son and grandson.

There was a certain spot which the people of Nysa were very proud
of because of its connexions with Dionysus. Alexander was extremely
anxious to visit it; he longed to go with the mounted troops of the
Hetaeri and his Guard of infantry to Mount Merus and see with his
own eyes the ivy and laurel which grew there in such abundance, the

groves of various trees which covered it, and the dense woodland full
of game of all kinds for hunting. Accordingly they went, and the
Macedonians were delighted with the ivy, which they had not seen
for so long – there is none in India elsewhere, not even in districts
where the vine grows – and at once eagerly set themselves to make
wreaths of it which they put on their heads while they sang songs of
praise to Dionysus and called upon him by his many names. Alexander offered sacrifice on the sacred spot and made merry with his
friends – and there is a story (which you may believe if you like) that
a number of distinguished Macedonian officers, once the ivy crown
was on their heads and the god invoked, were possessed by his spirit
and with cries of *Euoi, Euoi*, lost their wits in the true Bacchic frenzy.

These tales, however, you may believe or not, as you think fit. Personally I do not completely accept the view of Eratosthenes of Cyrene,
who tells us that everything attributed by the Macedonians to the
divine influence was grossly exaggerated in order to please Alexander.
For instance, there is the case of the cave in the territory of the Parapamisidae: according to Eratosthenes, the Macedonians saw this
cave and on the strength of some local legend – which they may well
have invented – put it about that it was the cave where Prometheus
was hung in chains when the eagle used to come to feed on his guts,
and that Heracles came thither to kill the eagle and set Prometheus
free; so that by means of this tale the Macedonians transferred Mount
Caucasus from Pontus to the far east, fixing it in India in the country
of the Parapamisidae, and gave the name Caucasus to what was in
reality the Parapamisus range simply to flatter Alexander by the inference that he had crossed Caucasus. Again, having seen Indian cattle
branded with the image of a club, they used this as an argument to
prove that Heracles had visited India. Eratosthenes is equally sceptical
about similar tales of Dionysus' wanderings – but, for my own part,
I am content to maintain neutrality in these matters.

On reaching the Indus, Alexander found that Hephaestion had already bridged it and collected a large number of small boats and two
thirty-oared galleys. Gifts from Taxiles the Indian were awaiting
him: 200 talents of silver, 3,000 oxen and over 10,000 sheep for sacrificial purposes, and some thirty elephants. A cavalry contingent 700
strong also came from Taxiles to join Alexander's forces, and the
town of Taxila, which is the most considerable between the Indus and

the Hydaspes, was given into his hands. Here Alexander offered sacrifice to the gods whom it was his custom to honour, and held a contest of athletics and horsemanship by the river. The omens from the sacrifice were favourable for the crossing.

The Indus is bigger than any river in Europe, and than any other in India except the Ganges; it rises somewhere west of the Parapamisus (or Caucasus) range and flows into the Indian Ocean to the southward; it has two mouths and in both of them the lower reaches are swampy, like the five mouths of the Danube; it forms a delta (called Pattala in the Indian language) similar to the delta of the Nile in Egypt: all these are accepted facts, and I take the opportunity of recording them here. The four Indian rivers, Hydaspes, Acesines, Hydraotes, and Hyphasis, though much greater than the other Asian rivers, are nevertheless smaller – indeed much smaller – than the Indus, as the Indus itself is smaller than the Ganges. Ctesias indeed (if his report is worth anything as evidence) says that at its narrowest part the breadth of the Indus is about five miles, at its widest about twelve miles, while for most of its course it is somewhere between the two. This, then, was the river which early one morning Alexander crossed with his army, and so entered India.

I have not included in this book an account of the Indian way of life, or any description of the strange animals to be found, or of the variety and size of the fish and other aquatic creatures in the Indus, the Hydaspes, the Ganges, and elsewhere; nor have I mentioned gold-mining ants and gold-guarding griffons and other queer things which people have invented rather for diversion than as serious history, in the belief that none of the absurd stories they tell about India are likely to be brought to the test of truth. Actually, however, most of these fables were indeed proved or disproved by Alexander and his men – except in a few cases where they themselves were guilty of invention. They proved, for instance, that the Indians have no gold – at any rate the very considerable section of them which Alexander visited in the course of his campaign – and that their domestic arrangements are far from luxurious. The men are taller than any other Asiatics, most of them being over seven feet, or not much less; they are darker-skinned than any other race except the Ethiopians, and the finest fighters to be found anywhere in Asia at that time. I cannot satisfactorily compare them with the ancient Persians who marched with Cyrus, son of

Cambyses, when he wrested the sovereignty of Asia from the Medes and established his control either by force or by consent over so many other peoples as well; for the Persians at that period of their history were a poor nation and lived in a harsh land, and their way of life was as near as may be to the stern discipline of Sparta; nor can I make any certain inference from the Persian disaster in Scythia, not knowing if the cause of it was the unfavourable nature of the ground where the battle was fought, or some mistake made by Cyrus, or the actual military inferiority of the Persian soldiers to the Scythians of those parts.

However, about India it is my intention to write a special account based on the most reliable reports from Alexander's expedition and the discoveries of Nearchus, who sailed along the northern coasts of the Indian Ocean, and including facts recorded by the two distinguished writers Megasthenes and Eratosthenes. My account will cover the Indian way of life, any strange creatures to be found in the country, and the actual coastal voyage in the Southern Ocean. For the present I must be content with what I have felt to be adequate simply for the illustration of Alexander's achievements: namely, that the boundary of Asia is the Taurus range, beginning at Mycale opposite the island of Samos, running north of Pamphylia and Cilicia, and thence to Armenia, whence it continues by way of Parthia and Chorasmia to Media, and in Bactria joins the Parapamisus range. It was this latter range which Alexander's men called the Caucasus, apparently for the purpose of magnifying his achievement by the suggestion that he reached the further side of the Caucasus in his triumphant advance. It is possible, however, that there is no real break between this Indian Caucasus and the Scythian Caucasus, any more than there is between it and Taurus, and it is for that reason that I have already used the name Caucasus for it, and shall continue to do so. It runs down to the Indian Ocean.

Thus all the important rivers of Asia rise either in the Taurus or in the Caucasus Mountains, some of them flowing north and entering either Lake Maeotis or the so-called Hyrcanian Sea – itself a gulf of the Indian Ocean – others flowing south, such as the Euphrates, Tigris, Indus, Hydaspes, Acesines, Hydraotes, Hyphasis, and all the rest between these and the Ganges, which either empty themselves into the sea or disperse into swamp and disappear, as the Euphrates does.

Imagine Asia as divided by the Taurus and Caucasus ranges, running in an east–west direction, and you will see that the two main
divisions are formed by the Taurus, one lying north of it, the other
south; the southern part may then again be divided into four, the
largest of which is, according to Eratosthenes and Megasthenes, India;
(Megasthenes, by the way, spent much time in Arachosia with its
governor Sibystius, and tells us that he frequently visited the Indian
King Sandracottus); the smallest division, bounded on the east by the
Euphrates, lies towards the Aegean, and the two remaining divisions,
lying between the Euphrates and the Indus, can hardly, when put together, be compared in extent with India. India itself, east and west
and right down to the south, is bounded by the Indian Ocean, and on
the north by the Indian Caucasus as far as its junction with the Taurus
range; from these mountains to the Indian Ocean its western boundary is the Indus. Most of the country is plain, generally supposed to
be alluvial; and it is a fact that elsewhere, too, the majority of coastal
plains have been formed by the silt of rivers – which was also, presumably, the reason why in ancient times the name of the country was
the same as that of its river: for example, there is a plain of Hermus, a
river which rises in the mountain of Dindymene the Great Mother,
in Asia, and flows into the sea near Smyrna in Aeolia; then there is the
Cayster, which gives its name to a plain in Lydia, the Caïcus in Mysia,
and the Maeander in Caria, after which is named the whole coastal
strip as far as Miletus in Ionia. The historians Herodotus and Hecataeus
(if the latter is indeed the author of the book in question) both call
Egypt 'the gift of the river', and Herodotus has proved the point by
very clear evidence. In this case, too, the river gave its name to the
country, for that Aegyptus was originally the name of the river now
known both in Egypt and elsewhere in the world as the Nile there is
sufficient evidence in Homer, where we find the statement that Menelaus brought up 'at the mouth of the Aegyptus'.

If, therefore, in various parts of the world one river, and a comparatively small one at that, can on its course to the sea build up a
large area of land by means of the mud and silt which it brings down
from the uplands where it rises, there is surely no reason why one
should not admit that India, too, is for the most part an alluvial plain;
for if one added together the Hermus, Cayster, Caïcus, Maeander,
and all the other Asian rivers which flow into the Aegean, they would

not, for sheer volume of water, compare with any single one of the rivers of India – to say nothing of the greatest, the Ganges, with which not even the Egyptian Nile or the great European river the Danube is to be mentioned in the same breath: indeed, combine all those rivers into one and they would not equal in volume even the Indus, which is a mighty stream right from its source and receives the waters of fifteen tributaries, all of them bigger than the rivers of Asia, and imposes its name upon the country as it flows down to meet the sea. That is all I will say here about this great country. I must keep the rest for my other book, *The History of India*.

There is no mention in the accounts either of Aristobulus or Ptolemy (my two principal authorities) of the method employed by Alexander in bridging the Indus, and I should myself hesitate to express an opinion as to whether a permanent bridge was constructed or a bridge of boats such as Xerxes made for crossing the Hellespont or Darius for crossing the Bosphorus and the Danube. Nevertheless I am inclined to think that the latter method was used, if only because the depth of water is too great to allow the construction of a permanent bridge, and because, even had so astonishing a feat been accomplished, it could not possibly have been completed so quickly. Again, granting that boats were used, I still cannot say for certain whether they were lashed together and moored in line as in the bridge over the Hellespont which Herodotus describes, or whether the method was that employed by the Romans in their bridges over the Danube and the Celtic Rhine, or on the various occasions when they had to bridge the Tigris and the Euphrates; in any case, the Roman method of bridging by boats is the quickest I know of, and I shall describe it here, if only for its interest.

At the word of command, the boats are allowed to float downstream, stern first, while their way is checked by a rowing-boat which manœuvres them into position. Once they are in position, pyramid-shaped wicker baskets filled with rough stones are lowered from the bows to hold them against the current. As soon as one vessel is securely moored, another is brought up alongside of it, bows-on to the current, at the proper distance to ensure a sufficiently strong base for the superstructure; then timbers are rapidly laid athwartships from one vessel to the other with planks across them to make the structure rigid. The same process is repeated from vessel to vessel, as many as are needed to complete the bridge. On both sides of it ladders are fixed to serve as a bulwark and render the passage safer for horses and pack-animals, and also to strengthen the structure still further. The whole operation takes little time, and is carried out in an orderly manner, in spite of much noise and bustle; shouts of encouragement there may be, on one vessel or another, or loud comments on bad work – but through it all the words of command can be heard well enough, and the rapid progress of the work is not impaired.

Such, then, is the traditional method employed by the Romans. Precisely how Alexander bridged the Indus I do not know, for there is no contemporary account; none the less, I expect it was by some very similar method. Perhaps it was not – but no matter.

Once across the river, Alexander offered his customary sacrifice and continued his march to Taxila, a large and prosperous town – indeed, the largest between the Indus and the Hydaspes. Here he was courteously received by Taxiles, the governor, and the Indians of the district, and he granted them, in return, as much of the territory bordering on their own as they asked for. He was also visited by representatives from Abisarus, King of the Indian hill-tribes, with his brother and other distinguished personages among them, and by representatives from the local governor Doxareus. All of them brought presents. Here as elsewhere Alexander offered his usual sacrifices, and held public games with contests in athletics and riding; then, after appointing Philip, son of Machatas, as governor of this district, he proceeded to the Hydaspes, leaving in Taxila any men who were sick and unfit for service.

News had already reached him that Porus with all the troops he could muster was on the other side of the Hydaspes, determined either to prevent his crossing or to attack him should he attempt it. Alexander, accordingly, sent Coenus, son of Polemocrates, back to the Indus with orders to cut into sections the boats which had been used at the crossing of that river and transport them to the Hydaspes; the order was carried out, the smaller vessels being cut in half, the thirty-oared galleys into three, and the sections carried in carts to the bank of the Hydaspes, where they were re-assembled, so that the whole flotilla was once again to be seen, as it had been seen upon the Indus. Then, with the force he had brought to Taxila and 5,000 Indian troops under Taxiles and the local chieftains, he marched for the Hydaspes.

From the position he took up on the bank of this river he was able to see Porus, with all his forces, including his squadron of elephants, on the further side. At the point immediately opposite Alexander, Porus remained on guard in person, and sent pickets, each under command of an officer, to the various other points along the river where a crossing was practicable; for he was determined to stop the Macedonians from getting over. Alexander's answer was by continual movement of his own troops to keep Porus guessing: he split his force into a number of detachments, moving some of them under his own command hither and thither all over the place, destroying enemy possessions and looking for places where the river might be crossed, and putting others under the command of various officers with instructions to keep constantly on the move, now in this direction, now in that. As supplies continued to come in for his army from all parts of the country west of the Hydaspes, it was clear to Porus that he meant to remain in the neighbourhood of the river, until in the course of the winter the water fell sufficiently to enable him to effect a crossing at any one of a number of places. Moreover, the continual movement of Alexander's boats up or down stream, the manufacture of skin floats filled with chaff, and the sight of troops, cavalry, and infantry, constantly massed on the river-bank, gave Porus no chance to relax his vigilance or to concentrate his defensive preparations upon any one point rather than another.

The water was high at that time of year – the summer solstice – in all the Indian rivers, and the current in them swift and turbulent; for there are heavy rains at this season, and these, added to the melting snow from the Caucasus, where most of the rivers rise, greatly increase the volume of water, while during the winter the flow is checked again, the water becomes less turbid, and the level of it drops, so that here and there it is possible to get across. The Indus and the Ganges (and perhaps one other) are never fordable – but what I have said is certainly true of the Hydaspes.

Alexander openly declared his intention of waiting for the season in which the water in the river should fall, if he were prevented from crossing immediately; nevertheless he remained in the neighbourhood and kept a sharp look-out for any possible opportunity of getting his men over by a swift and unexpected movement. It was clear to him that he could not effect the crossing at the point where Porus held the

opposite bank, for his troops would certainly be attacked, as they tried
to gain the shore, by a powerful and efficient army, well-equipped and
supported by a large number of elephants; moreover, he thought it
likely that his horses, in face of an immediate attack by elephants,
would be too much scared by the appearance of these beasts and their
unfamiliar trumpetings to be induced to land – indeed, they would
probably refuse to stay on the floats, and at the mere sight of the elephants in the distance would go mad with terror and plunge into the
water long before they reached the further side.

The river had to be crossed, so, as it could not be done openly,
Alexander determined to attain his object by cunning. Every night he
kept moving the greater part of his mounted troops up and down the
bank of the river, making as much noise as possible – shots, war-cries,
and every sort of clatter and shindy which might be supposed to pre-
cede an attempted crossing. Porus, bringing up his elephants, followed
these movements, guided by the noise, and Alexander gradually led
him to make these marches, parallel to his own, a regular thing. This
went on for some time, until Porus, finding that the Greeks never
went beyond shouts and yells, gave it up. Clearly, it was a false alarm;
so he ceased to follow the movements of the Greek cavalry and stayed
where he was, in his original position, with look-outs posted at
various points along the river. Thus Porus, no longer expecting a sudden attempt under cover of darkness, was lulled into a sense of
security – and this was Alexander's opportunity.

At a sharp bend in the river there was a projecting spit of land,
thickly wooded with different sorts of timber; and just off this promontory lay an uninhabited island, also well wooded. Alexander did
not fail to observe the opportunity which this offered: the dense woodland both on the island and on the river-bank beyond it was just the
thing to conceal his attempt, so this was the spot where he determined
to make the crossing. It was some eighteen miles from his main position, and all along the river he had stationed pickets, close enough to
enable them to keep contact with each other both by sight and sound
and to hear without difficulty any orders passed from any point along
the line. For several nights in succession over a wide area noise and
bustle were kept going and fires burning.

The decision once made, Alexander began his preparations openly.
Craterus was left in charge of the original position with his own

cavalry regiment, the mounted contingents from Arachotia and the Parapamisidae, part of the Macedonian infantry consisting of the brigade of Alcetas and Polysperchon, the local Indian chieftains, and the 5,000 troops under their command. His orders were not to attempt a crossing until Porus had moved from his position to attack Alexander, or until he was sure that Porus was in retreat and the Greeks victorious. 'But if,' Alexander added, 'Porus opposes me with a part only of his force and leaves the rest, together with elephants, where it now is, you must stay where you are; if, on the other hand, he moves his whole contingent of elephants against me, leaving in his present position only some portion of his other forces, then you must lose no time in getting across. The only real danger to our horses, as we put them ashore, is elephants. Nothing else will worry them.'

Between the island and the main camp of which Craterus was left in charge, Meleager, Attalus, and Gorgias were posted with the mercenary cavalry and infantry; their instructions, too, were to effect a crossing in sections as soon as they saw that the Indians were fairly engaged. The mounted troops which Alexander selected to operate under his own command consisted of the special squadron of the Hetaeri, the cavalry regiments of Hephaestion, Perdiccas, and Demetrius, the contingents from Bactria and Sogdiana, the Scythian cavalry, and the mounted archers of the Daae; from the infantry units he chose the Longshields, the brigade of Cleitus and Coenus, the archers, and the Agrianes. He took the precaution of moving at some distance from the river, in order to conceal his march to the point where he proposed to cross – the island, namely, and the spit of land opposite to it. To this point the floats had already been conveyed some time previously, and now, under cover of darkness, they were filled with chaff and carefully sewn up. During the night a deluge of rain helped to conceal the preparations for the coming attempt; the clatter of arms, shouted orders, and the commotion they caused could not be heard across the river through the noise of the storm and the claps of thunder. Besides the skin-floats, most of the boats, including the thirty-oared galleys, had already arrived. These had been cut into sections, and were now re-assembled and concealed among the trees.

Just before dawn the rain stopped and the wind fell light. The mounted troops were embarked on the floats, the boats taking as many of the infantry as they would hold, and the crossing began –

screened by the island, to prevent discovery by Porus' scouts before
he island was passed and the whole flotilla already near the opposite
bank. Alexander himself crossed in one of the galleys with half the
regiment of Longshields, the remainder following in other galleys.
He was accompanied by three officers of his personal guard – Ptolemy,
Perdiccas, and Lysimachus – and by Seleucus (the Seleucus who afterwards became King).

Once past the island, the approach to the river-bank was in full
view of the enemy patrols, who galloped off with all the speed their
horses could muster, to report to Porus. Alexander was the first
ashore, and promptly took charge of the troops from the other
galleys; the cavalry had had orders to disembark first, and these he
proceeded to marshal as each squadron came off the floats. He then
moved forward in battle order.

To Alexander this was all strange country, and it so happened that
he had, without knowing it, landed on another island, and not on the
mainland at all. It was an island of considerable extent – and therefore
all the more difficult to recognize as such – and was separated from the
mainland beyond by a branch of the river of no very great size. Nevertheless the torrential rain throughout the previous night had increased
the volume of water, and the mounted troops were unable to find a
practicable place for crossing. For a time they were faced with the dis-
agreeable prospect that all the labour they had gone through would
have to be repeated; at last, however, a ford was found, and Alexander led the way over. It was no easy task, as the water in the deepest
part was up to the men's armpits and the horses' necks.

Once this second crossing was successfully accomplished, Alexander again marshalled his troops. His picked cavalry and the best of the
other mounted regiments he brought round to the right wing,
stationing the mounted archers in the van; in the rear of the cavalry
he posted the Royal Regiment of Longshields under Seleucus, then
the Royal regiment of the heavy infantry, in close touch with the
other Longshields divisions, according to their precedence for that
day. The archers, Agrianes, and Javelins took their position on either
wing of the main body of infantry. Having thus made his dispositions,
he gave orders for the infantry, nearly 6,000 strong, to follow in order
of march, while he himself, with only the cavalry (numbering some
5,000) in which he thought he had the advantage over the enemy,

moved forward rapidly. Tauron, captain of the archers, was instructed to advance in the rear of the cavalry with all the speed he could make.

The idea in Alexander's mind was that if Porus' army should attack in force he would either settle them straight away by a cavalry charge, or, failing that, fight a delaying action until his infantry could come to his support; if, on the other hand, the Indians proved to be so badly shaken by the bold and unexpected crossing of the river that they took to their heels, he would be able to press hard on the retreating army, and the more men they lost during their withdrawal, the lighter his own task would subsequently be.

There are, however, somewhat conflicting accounts of these operations. According to Aristobulus, Porus' son arrived on the scene with sixty chariots before Alexander effected his second crossing – from the large island, that is; and in view of the fact that the crossing was no easy matter even without opposition, he might have prevented it altogether if his Indians had left their chariots and attacked on foot Alexander's leading troops as they were trying to get on shore. But in point of fact he merely drove past, and permitted Alexander to cross without molestation. Against this force Alexander sent his mounted archers, and it was broken up without difficulty, many of the men being wounded. Other writers state that there was a fight at the actual landing between Alexander's cavalry and a force of Indians commanded by Porus' son, who was there ready to oppose them with superior numbers, and that in the course of the fighting he wounded Alexander with his own hand and struck the blow which killed his beloved horse Bucephalus.

Ptolemy, son of Lagus, gives a different account, which I myself accept. According to him, Porus did, as other writers relate, send his son, but not with only sixty chariots. For it is hardly likely that, on a report from his scouts that either Alexander himself or, at any rate, some portion of his army, had crossed the Hydaspes, he would have sent his own son to oppose the landing with so trivial a force – a force, on the one hand, unnecessarily large for mere reconnaissance and unsuitably equipped for a rapid withdrawal, and, on the other, totally inadequate either to prevent a proposed crossing or to attack an enemy which had already succeeded in getting over. Ptolemy's actual statement is that Porus' son had with him 2,000 mounted troops and 120 chariots when he reached the spot; but Alexander had been too

quick for him and had already effected his final crossing from the
island. Against this force Alexander first sent his mounted archers,
while he himself moved on with the cavalry, thinking that Porus was
on the way to engage him with the main strength of his army. This
cavalry contingent, posted in the van, preceded the rest of the Greek
troops; but as soon as Alexander received an accurate report of the
enemies' numbers, he attacked at once, and the Indians, seeing Alexander there in person and his massed cavalry coming at them in successive charges, squadron by squadron, broke and fled. The Indians'
losses in the action were some 400 mounted men, Porus' son being
himself among the killed; their chariots and horses were captured as
they attempted to get away – speed was impossible, and the muddy
ground had rendered them useless even during the fight.

The Indians who did succeed in getting away reported to Porus
that Alexander had crossed the river in force and that his son had been
killed in the action. Porus was faced with a difficult choice, for the
troops under Craterus, who had been left behind in Alexander's
original position opposite the main Indian army, could now be seen
making their way over the river. Swiftly he made up his mind; he
determined to move in force against Alexander, and to fight it out
with the King of Macedon himself and the flower of his men. Then,
leaving behind a small force with a few elephants to spread alarm
among Craterus' cavalry as they attempted to land on the river-bank,
he marched to meet Alexander with all his cavalry, 4,000 strong, all
of his 300 chariots, 200 elephants, and the picked contingents of his
infantry, numbering some 30,000 men.

Much of the ground was deep in soft mud, so he continued his
advance till he found a spot where the sandy soil offered a surface
sufficiently firm and level for cavalry manœuvre, and there made his
dispositions. In the van he stationed his elephants at intervals of
about 100 feet, on a broad front, to form a screen for the whole body
of the infantry and to spread terror among the cavalry of Alexander.
He did not expect that any enemy unit would venture to force a way
through the gaps in the line of elephants, either on foot or on horse-
back; terror would make the horses uncontrollable, and infantry units
would be even less likely to make the attempt, as they would be met
and checked by his own heavy infantry and then destroyed by the
elephants turning upon them and trampling them down. Behind the

elephants were the foot-soldiers, though not on a front of equal extent: the various units, forming a second line, were so disposed as to fill the intervals in the line of elephants. There was infantry on both wings as well, outflanking the elephants, and, finally, on both flanks of the infantry were the mounted units, each with a screen of war-chariots.

Noting that the enemy was making his dispositions for battle, Alexander checked the advance of his cavalry to allow the infantry to come up with him. Regiment by regiment they made contact, moving swiftly, until the whole force was again united. Alexander had no intention of making the fresh enemy troops a present of his own breathless and exhausted men, so he paused before advancing to the attack. Meanwhile he kept his cavalry manœuvring up and down the line, while the infantry units were allowed to rest until they were once more in good heart for battle.

Observation of the Indian dispositions decided him against attempting an assault upon their centre, where the heavy infantry was massed in the intervals of the protecting screen of elephants, and his reluctance to take this course was based precisely upon Porus' own calculations; relying, instead, on his superiority in cavalry, he moved the major portion of his mounted troops towards the enemy's left wing, to make his assault in that sector. Coenus was sent over to the Indians' right with Demetrius' squadron and his own, his orders being that when the enemy moved their cavalry across to their left to counter the massed formations of the Macedonian mounted squadrons, he should hang on to their rear. The heavy infantry was put in charge of Seleucus, Antigenes, and Tauron, with orders not to engage until it was evident that the Indians, both horse and foot, had been thrown into confusion by the Macedonian cavalry.

Once the opposing armies were within range, Alexander launched his mounted archers, 1,000 strong, against the enemy's left wing, hoping to shake it by the hail of their arrows and the weight of their charge, and immediately afterwards himself advanced with the mounted Hetaeri against the Indian left, intent upon making his assault while they were still reeling under the attack of the mounted archers and before their cavalry could change formation from column into mass.

The Indians meanwhile withdrew all the cavalry from other sections of their line, and moved it across to meet and counter Alexander's

movement towards their flank, and it was not long before Coenus'
men could be seen following, according to orders, close in their
rear. The Indians were thereupon compelled to split their force
into two; the larger section, containing the best troops, continued to
proceed against Alexander, while the remainder wheeled about in
order to deal with Coenus. This, of course, was disastrous not only to
the effectiveness of the Indians' dispositions, but to their whole plan of
battle. Alexander saw his chance; precisely at the moment when the
enemy cavalry were changing direction, he attacked. The Indians did
not even wait to receive his charge, but fell back in confusion upon
the elephants, their impregnable fortress – or so they hoped. The elephant-drivers forced their beasts to meet the opposing cavalry, while
the Macedonian infantry, in its turn, advanced against them, shooting
down the drivers, and pouring in a hail of missiles from every side
upon the elephants themselves. It was an odd bit of work – quite unlike any previous battle; the monster elephants plunged this way and
that among the lines of infantry, dealing destruction in the solid mass
of the Macedonian phalanx, while the Indian horsemen, seeing the infantry at one another's throats, wheeled to the assault of the Macedonian cavalry. Once again, however, the verve and experience of Alexander's mounted troops were too much for them, and they were
forced back a second time on the elephants.

During the action all the Macedonian cavalry units had, by the exi-
gencies of the fighting rather than deliberate orders, concentrated into
a single body; and now its successive charges upon this sector or that
inflicted heavy losses on the enemy. By this time the elephants were
boxed up, with no room to manœuvre, by troops all round them, and
as they blundered about, wheeling and shoving this way and that,
they trampled to death as many of their friends as of their enemies.
The result was that the Indian cavalry, jammed in around the elephants and with no more space to manœuvre than they had, suffered
severely; most of the elephant-drivers had been shot; many of the
animals had themselves been wounded, while others, riderless and
bewildered, ceased altogether to play their expected part, and, maddened by pain and fear, set indiscriminately upon friend and foe,
thrusting, trampling, and spreading death before them. The Macedonians could deal with these maddened creatures comfortably
enough; having room to manœuvre, they were able to use their

judgement, giving ground when they charged, and going for them with their javelins when they turned and lumbered back, whereas the unfortunate Indians, jammed up close among them as they attempted to get away, found them a more dangerous enemy even than the Greeks.

In time the elephants tired and their charges grew feebler; they began to back away, slowly, like ships going astern, and with nothing worse than trumpetings. Taking his chance, Alexander surrounded the lot of them – elephants, horsemen, and all – and then signalled his infantry to lock shields and move up in a solid mass. Most of the Indian cavalry was cut down in the ensuing action; their infantry, too, hard pressed by the Macedonians, suffered terrible losses. The survivors, finding a gap in Alexander's ring of cavalry, all turned and fled. Craterus and the other officers who had been left on the bank of the river began to cross as soon as they saw Alexander's triumphant success, and their fresh troops, taking over the pursuit from Alexander's weary men, inflicted upon the vanquished Indians further losses no less severe.

Nearly 20,000 of the Indian infantry were killed in this battle, and about 3,000 of their cavalry. All their war-chariots were destroyed. Among the dead were two sons of Porus, Spitaces the local Indian governor, all the officers in command of the elephants and chariots, and all the cavalry officers and other commanders of high rank. The surviving elephants were captured. Out of Alexander's original 6,000 infantry, some eighty were killed; in addition to these he lost ten of the mounted archers, who were the first unit to engage, about twenty of the mounted Hetaeri, and 200 of the other cavalry.

Throughout the action Porus had proved himself a man indeed, not only as a commander but as a soldier of the truest courage. When he saw his cavalry cut to pieces, most of his infantry dead, and his elephants killed or roaming riderless and bewildered about the field, his behaviour was very different from that of the Persian King Darius: unlike Darius, he did not lead the scramble to save his own skin, but so long as a single unit of his men held together, fought bravely on. It was only when he was himself wounded that he turned the elephant on which he rode and began to withdraw. The wound was in his right shoulder, the only unprotected part of his body; no missile, as he moved here and there in the thick of the fighting, could touch him anywhere else because of the corselet which he wore – a corselet exceedingly tough and closely fitting, as all who subsequently saw him could observe.

Alexander, anxious to save the life of this great and gallant soldier, sent Taxiles the Indian to him. Taxiles rode up as near as he dared and requested him to stop his elephant and hear what message Alexander sent him, as escape was no longer possible. But Taxiles was an old enemy of the Indian King, and Porus turned his elephant and drove at him, to kill him with his lance; and he might indeed have killed him, if he had not spurred his horse out of the way in the nick of time. Alexander, however, far from resenting this treatment of his messenger, sent a number of others, the last of whom was an Indian named Meroes, a man he had been told had long been Porus' friend. Porus listened to Meroes' message, stopped his elephant, and dismounted; he was much distressed by thirst, so when he had revived himself by drinking, he told Meroes to conduct him with all speed to Alexander.

Alexander, informed of his approach, rode out to meet him, accompanied by a party of the mounted Hetaeri. When they met, he reined in his horse, and looked at his adversary with admiration: he was a magnificent figure of a man, over seven feet high and of great personal beauty; his bearing had lost none of its pride; his air was of one brave man meeting another, of a king in the presence of a king, with whom he had fought honourably for his kingdom.

Alexander was the first to speak. 'What,' he said, 'do you wish that I should do with you?'

'Treat me as a king ought,' Porus is said to have replied.

'For my part,' said Alexander, pleased by his answer, 'your request shall be granted. But is there not something you would wish for yourself? Ask it.'

'Everything,' said Porus, 'is contained in this one request.'

The dignity of these words gave Alexander even more pleasure, and he restored to Porus his sovereignty over his subjects, adding to his realm other territory of even greater extent. Thus he did indeed use a brave man as a king ought, and from that time forward found him in every way a loyal friend. Such was the result of the battle with Porus and the Indians beyond the Hydaspes. It was fought in the month of May, during the archonship of Hegemon at Athens.

Near the scene of the battle and the spot where he crossed the Hydaspes, Alexander founded two cities; one he called Nicaea, to commemorate his victory, the other Bucephale, in memory of his horse Bucephalus, who died in that country – not of hurts received in battle, but of old age and exhaustion. He was about thirty and worn out. In former days he had shared with Alexander many a danger and many a weary march. No one ever rode him but his master, for he would never permit anyone else to mount him. He was a big horse, high-spirited – a noble creature; he was branded with the figure of an ox-head, whence his name – though some have said that the name came from a white mark on his head, shaped like the head of an ox. This was the only bit of white on his body, all the rest of him being black. In Uxia, once, Alexander lost him, and issued an edict that he would kill every man in the country unless he was brought back – as he promptly was. The story is evidence both of the fear which Alexander inspired and of his devotion to Bucephalus. But I must say no more: what I have written in Bucephalus' praise, I have written for Alexander's sake.

When the funeral rites for the men who fell in the battle had been duly performed, Alexander offered the customary sacrifices in thanksgiving for victory and celebrated games, with athletic and equestrian contests, at the place of his first crossing of the Hydaspes. Then, leaving Craterus with part of the army to superintend the building and fortification of the newly founded settlements, he proceeded against the Indians across the border of Porus' kingdom. Aristobulus calls this tribe Glauganicae, Ptolemy Glausae – but never mind that; the name hardly matters. Alexander entered their territory with half of the mounted Hetaeri, picked troops from each division of heavy infantry, the archers, the Agrianes, and the whole contingent of the mounted archers. The natives surrendered to a man. Some thirty-seven towns were taken, the smallest having not less than 5,000 inhabitants and many of them more than double that; a large number of villages hardly less populous also fell into Alexander's hands. All this territory he handed over to Porus. He also brought about a reconciliation between Porus and Taxiles, and sent Taxiles back to his own people.

About this time Alexander was visited by a delegation from Abisares offering the surrender of himself and his territory, and this in spite of the fact that before the battle on the Hydaspes his intention had been to join Porus. His own brother was now among the envoys, entrusted with a gift of money and forty elephants for Alexander. The free Indians also sent a delegation, and yet another came from a chieftain who also bore the name Porus. Alexander promptly sent for Abisares, adding a threat that, should he fail to appear, he would soon see the Greek army and its commander-in-chief in an unwelcome spot.

Meanwhile Phrataphernes, the satrap of Parthia and Hyrcania, arrived with Thracians left there under his command, and at about the same time a message came through from Sisicottus, the satrap of Assacenia, that the Greek governor had been assassinated, and the people had thrown off their allegiance to Alexander. Alexander, accordingly, dispatched a force under the command of Philip and Tyriaspes to restore order in the province. He then marched for the river Acesines.

The Acesines is the only Indian river of which Ptolemy, son of Lagus, has mentioned the size. By his account, at the point where Alexander's men crossed it on boats and floats it is a little under two miles wide and very swift; it is fouled by large jagged rocks over which the water pours violently with much noise and commotion. The floats got over easily enough, but of the boats a number came to grief, being swept on to the rocks, where they were broken up and their occupants drowned. From this description it is reasonable to infer that other writers are pretty accurate when they give the average breadth of the Indus as five miles, contracting to two at the points where it is narrowest and deepest. Indeed, two miles is its breadth over a good part of its course. I am inclined to think, moreover, that Alexander deliberately crossed the Acesines at its widest point, to take advantage of the slower current.

After crossing he left Coenus with his own brigade to superintend the passage of the remainder of the troops who were to bring up the grain and other supplies from those parts of the country which were already in his hands. Porus was then sent back to his people with instructions to rejoin later with the pick of his troops and any elephants he happened to have. The other Porus – the one who had disgraced himself, and was reported to have fled his country – Alexander proposed to pursue with the lightest units of his army. This second

Porus, so long as there was hostility between Alexander and his nobler namesake, had sent Alexander repeated offers to surrender himself and his territory – not, indeed because he liked Alexander, but because he hated his namesake; then, learning that the latter had not only been released but had also been granted a large accession of new territory, he became alarmed, and fled his country with as many fighting men as he could persuade to share his fortunes. What frightened him was not Alexander so much as the threat to himself of his rival's increase in power.

Alexander's route in pursuit of him brought him first to the Hydraotes, a river as broad as the Acesines but not so swift. At all strategic points throughout the territory on the hither side of the Hydraotes he left troops, so that Craterus and Coenus in their foraging expeditions might be able to go pretty well anywhere without risk. He then instructed Hephaestion to proceed with two regiments of infantry, his own and Demetrius' cavalry regiment, and half the contingent of archers to the territory of the renegade Porus, which he was to hand over to the other Porus, together with any independent Indian tribes he might find on the Hydaspes; these, too, were to be taken over and submitted to Porus' authority. These arrangements made, he crossed the Hydraotes, which, unlike the Acesines, caused him no trouble, and advanced along the further bank. Most of the tribes in this region surrendered to him without resistance, including a few who had begun by offering a certain show of hostility; a few others tried to elude him, but were caught and subdued by force of arms.

It was reported to Alexander that a tribe of independent Indians known as Cathaei was, among certain others, preparing resistance in the event of an invasion, and calling for the support of its neighbours. Sangala, the town where they were proposing to make their stand, was said to be a strong one, and they themselves were reputed to be excellent soldiers and brave men. The defiant attitude of these people was shared by two other tribes, the Oxydracae and Malli. Not long before, Porus and Abisares had undertaken an expedition against these people; they had induced a number of other independent tribes to support the attempt, but even so they had achieved nothing – nothing, at any rate, commensurate with the magnitude of their preparations.

The effect of this report was to put Alexander on the move against
the Cathaei without an instant's delay. Two days' march from the
Hydraotes he reached a town named Pimprama, belonging to a tribe
known as the Adraistae. They offered no resistance. On the following
day he rested his men, and then proceeded against Sangala. The
Cathaei with the neighbouring tribes who had joined them had taken
up a position on a hill in front of the town; the hill was less steep in
some places than in others, and all round it they had put carts to form
a triple defensive ring, within which they lay encamped.

Alexander modified his tactics to suit the circumstances. In view of
the enemy's strength and the nature of his position, he immediately
ordered forward the mounted archers with instructions to ride along
the enemy's front, shooting at long range, to prevent a sortie before
the rest of his troops were in position, and to cause as much damage as
possible before they left their defensive position to engage in force.
Meanwhile he brought Cleitus' mounted regiment and the special
cavalry squadron round to the right wing of his army, with the Longshields and Agrianes in close touch; and on the left posted Perdiccas'
cavalry regiment and the infantry brigades of the Hetaeri. The archers
were in two divisions, one on each wing. Before his dispositions were
completed, the rear-guard, both horse and foot, arrived on the scene;
the cavalry was used to strengthen the wings, and the additional infantry units to increase the solidity of the phalanx. This done, Alexander took control of the mounted troops on his right and advanced
against the line of baggage-carts on the Indian left, where they were
spaced out somewhat more widely and the conformation of the
ground seemed to offer not too awkward an approach.

The cavalry threat did not draw the Indians out from their defences;
they climbed on to the carts and met the advance with bows and
arrows at long range. Alexander saw that cavalry in these circumstances would be ineffective, so he promptly dismounted and in person led his infantry to the assault. The enemy was driven without difficulty from the first line of carts, but, falling back on the second, they
rallied and were better able to defend themselves. Holding a smaller
ring, they were consequently in closer order, and the Macedonians
had no longer the advantage of advancing over open ground: on the
contrary, they had to clear the outer ring of carts out of their way and
push through individually as best they could, wherever there was

room. They managed it, however, and once again the Indians were forced to withdraw. This time they made no further stand; without attempting to hold the third line of carts, they hurriedly retreated and shut themselves up in the town.

Alexander did not press his offensive any more that day. So far as he could with the number of infantry troops at his disposal he surrounded the town, but the extent of its defences was too great to allow a complete encirclement. At one point there was a break in the defences, and in front of this at no great distance was a lake; round this lake Alexander took the precaution of posting his mounted men, as the water was evidently shallow, and he guessed that the Indians, severely shaken as they were by their previous defeat, would attempt to get out of the town under cover of darkness. His guess proved right: about the second watch most of them slipped out, and fell into the arms of the cavalry patrols. Many were killed, and the rest, realizing that there were enemy patrols all round the lake, retired into the town again.

All round the town, except where the lake formed a natural barrier, Alexander now erected a double stockade, and saw to it that the lake itself was more efficiently guarded. His intention had been to bring up siege-engines to breach the town's defences, but he was informed by deserters that the Indians had decided to make their escape that very night: their purpose was to slip out by the lake, where there was a break in the stockade. Accordingly he ordered Ptolemy, son of Lagus, to take up his position at that point with three regiments of Long-shields, all the Agrianes, and a brigade of archers. Pointing to the place where he guessed the enemy would make their attempt to get through. 'The instant,' he said to Ptolemy, 'you see them at it, stop them, and order the trumpeter to sound the alarm. On this signal, the rest of you officers will take your men promptly to the scene of action, wherever the trumpet calls you. And, mark you, I shall be there myself.'

Ptolemy collected all the carts he could out of those the Indians had left behind after their initial repulse and sent them across the line of the Indians' escape, to act as booby-traps in the darkness and confusion; he also gave orders that the posts which had been cut for the stockade but not yet erected should now be used to construct a barrier on either side between the lake and the wall of the town. His men completed the work, despite the fact that most of it was done in darkness.

At approximately the fourth watch the Indians, just as Alexander's informants had said they would do, opened the town gates which led to the lake and made their way with all speed towards it. Ptolemy and his guards were ready for them. At once the trumpeters sounded the alarm, and Ptolemy led his men fully armed and in good order against the enemy; their way of escape was already blocked by the carts and the new section of palisade, and when the trumpets sounded and they found Ptolemy's troops on top of them, cutting down every man who managed to struggle through between the carts, they gave it up and withdrew once more into the town, with a loss during their retreat of some 500.

By this time Porus had arrived with the rest of his elephants and 5,000 Indian troops. Alexander had had his siege-engines assembled and they were already being brought into position; but they proved unnecessary, for before a breach was made in the wall – which was of brick – the Macedonians undermined it, erected scaling-ladders at numerous points all round, and took the town by assault. Up to 17,000 Indians were killed in this operation and over 70,000 taken prisoner. Five hundred mounted men and 300 war chariots were also captured. Throughout the siege Alexander lost a little under 100 men; the number of wounded, however, was disproportionately large – over 1,200 – among them being Lysimachus, of Alexander's personal guard, and other officers.

After the burial of the dead with all customary ritual, Alexander sent his secretary, Eumenes, with 300 mounted men to the two towns which had joined Sangala in refusing submission. His instructions were to report the capture of Sangala and to give the people an assurance that if they stayed where they were, and admitted Alexander as a friend within their gates, they would have nothing to complain of in their treatment – no more, indeed, than any of the other independent tribes which had voluntarily submitted to him. Both towns, however, had already had the news that Sangala had been taken by assault, and such was the consternation it caused that the people had fled. Alexander pursued them hotly as soon as he knew that they were on the move, but, as the report took some time to reach him, most of them had had time to get clear away. A certain number of sick, perhaps 500, had been abandoned by their comrades in their dash for safety, and these were caught and killed. Alexander soon broke off the pursuit, returned to Sangala, and razed it to the ground. The land belonging to it he handed over to the Indian tribes who had given up their former independence and voluntarily attached themselves to his cause. Porus was then sent with his troops to the towns which had surrendered, with orders to garrison them, and Alexander himself marched for the river Hyphasis, bent upon still further conquest. So long as a single hostile element remained, there could, he felt, be no end to the war.

Reports had come in that the country beyond the Hyphasis was rich and productive; the people were good farmers and fine soldiers and lived under an orderly and efficient social system. The governments in that region were mostly aristocratic, but by no means oppressive. The elephants there were more numerous than elsewhere in India, and conspicuous both for size and courage. Such stories could not but whet Alexander's appetite for yet another adventure; but his men felt differently. The sight of their King undertaking an endless succession of dangerous and exhausting enterprises was beginning to depress them. Their enthusiasm was ebbing; they held meetings in camp, at which even the best of them grumbled at their fate, while others swore that they would go no further, not even if Alexander himself led them. This state of affairs was brought to Alexander's notice, and before the alarm and despondency among the men could go still further, he called a meeting of his officers and addressed them in the following words:

'I observe, gentlemen, that when I would lead you on a new venture you no longer follow me with your old spirit. I have asked you to meet me that we may come to a decision together: are we, upon my advice, to go forward, or, upon yours, to turn back?

'If you have any complaint to make about the results of your efforts hitherto, or about myself as your commander, there is no more to say. But let me remind you: through your courage and endurance you have gained possession of Ionia, the Hellespont, both Phrygias, Cappadocia, Paphlagonia, Lydia, Caria, Lycia, Pamphylia, Phoenicia, and Egypt; the Greek part of Libya is now yours, together with much of Arabia, lowland Syria, Mesopotamia, Babylon, and Susia; Persia and Media with all the territories either formerly controlled by them or not are in your hands; you have made yourselves masters of the lands beyond the Caspian Gates, beyond the Caucasus, beyond the Tanais, of Bactria, Hyrcania, and the Hyrcanian sea; we have driven the Scythians back into the desert; and Indus and Hydaspes, Acesines and Hydraotes flow now through country which is ours. With all that accomplished, why do you hesitate to extend the power of Macedon – *your* power – to the Hyphasis and the tribes on the other side? Are you afraid that a few natives who may still be left will offer opposition? Come, come! These natives either surrender without a blow or are caught on the run – or leave their country undefended for your taking; and when we take it, we make a present of it to those who have joined us of their own free will and fight at our side.

'For a man who *is* a man, work, in my belief, if it is directed to noble ends, has no object beyond itself; none the less, if any of you wish to know what limit may be set to this particular campaign, let me tell you that the area of country still ahead of us, from here to the Ganges and the Eastern ocean, is comparatively small. You will undoubtedly find that this ocean is connected with the Hyrcanian Sea, for the great Stream of Ocean encircles the earth. Moreover I shall prove to you, my friends, that the Indian and Persian Gulfs and the Hyrcanian Sea are all three connected and continuous. Our ships will sail round from the Persian Gulf to Libya as far as the Pillars of Hercules, whence all Libya to the eastward will soon be ours, and all Asia too, and to this empire there will be no boundaries but what God Himself has made for the whole world.

'But if you turn back now, there will remain unconquered many warlike peoples between the Hyphasis and the Eastern Ocean, and many more to the northward and the Hyrcanian Sea, with the Scythians, too, not far away; so that if we withdraw now there is a danger that the territory which we do not yet securely hold may be stirred to revolt by some nation or other we have not yet forced into submission. Should that happen, all that we have done and suffered will have proved fruitless – or we shall be faced with the task of doing it over again from the beginning. Gentlemen of Macedon, and you, my friends and allies, this must not be. Stand firm; for well you know that hardship and danger are the price of glory, and that sweet is the savour of a life of courage and of deathless renown beyond the grave.

'Are you not aware that if Heracles, my ancestor, had gone no further than Tiryns or Argos – or even than the Peloponnese or Thebes – he could never have won the glory which changed him from a man into a god, actual or apparent? Even Dionysus, who is a god indeed, in a sense beyond what is applicable to Heracles, faced not a few laborious tasks; yet we have done more: we have passed beyond Nysa and we have taken the rock of Aornos which Heracles himself could not take. Come, then; add the rest of Asia to what you already possess – a small addition to the great sum of your conquests. What great or noble work could we ourselves have achieved had we thought it enough, living at ease in Macedon, merely to guard our homes, accepting no burden beyond checking the encroachment of the Thracians on our borders, or the Illyrians and Triballians, or perhaps such Greeks as might prove a menace to our comfort?

'I could not have blamed you for being the first to lose heart if I, your commander, had not shared in your exhausting marches and your perilous campaigns; it would have been natural enough if you had done all the work merely for others to reap the reward. But it is not so. You and I, gentlemen, have shared the labour and shared the danger, and the rewards are for us all. The conquered territory belongs to you; from your ranks the governors of it are chosen; already the greater part of its treasure passes into your hands, and when all Asia is overrun, then indeed I will go further than the mere satisfaction of your ambitions: the utmost hopes of riches or power which each one of you cherishes will be far surpassed, and whoever wishes to return home will be allowed to go, either with me or without me. I will make those who stay the envy of those who return.'

When Alexander ended, there was a long silence. The officers present were not willing to accept what he had said, yet no one liked to risk an unprepared reply. Several times Alexander invited comment, should any wish to give it and genuinely hold different views from those he had expressed; but in spite of his invitation nothing was said, until at last Coenus, son of Polemocrates, plucked up his courage to speak.

'Sir,' he said, 'we appreciate the fact that you do not demand from us unreasoning obedience. You have made it clear to us that you will lead us on only after winning our consent, and, failing that, that you will not use compulsion. This being so, I do not propose to speak on behalf of the officers here assembled, as we, by virtue of our rank and

authority, have already received the rewards of our services and are
naturally concerned more than the men are to further your interests.
I shall speak, therefore, for the common soldiers, not, by any means,
with the purpose of echoing their sentiments, but saying what I believe will tend to your present advantage and our future security. My
age, the repute which, by your favour, I enjoy among my comrades,
and the unhesitating courage I have hitherto displayed in all dangers
and difficulties give me the right to declare what I believe to be the
soundest policy. Very well, then: precisely in proportion to the number and magnitude of the achievements wrought by you, our leader,
and by the men who marched from home under your command, I
judge it best to set some limit to further enterprise. You know the
number of Greeks and Macedonians who started upon this campaign,
and you can see how many of us are left today: the Thessalians you
sent home from Bactria because you knew their hearts were no longer
in their work – and it was wisely done; other Greeks have been settled
in the new towns you have founded, where they remain not always
willingly; others, again, together with our own Macedonians, continue to share with you the dangers and hardships of war, and of these
some have been killed, some, disabled by wounds, have been left behind in various parts of Asia, and more still have died of sickness, so
that only a few from that great army are left, a small remnant broken
in health, their old vigour and determination gone. Every man of
them longs to see his parents again, if they yet survive, or his wife, or
his children; all are yearning for the familiar earth of home, hoping,
pardonably enough, to live to revisit it, no longer in poverty and ob-
scurity, but famous and enriched by the treasure you have enabled
them to win. Do not try to lead men who are unwilling to follow
you; if their heart is not in it, you will never find the old spirit or the
old courage. Consent rather yourself to return to your mother and
your home. Once there, you may bring good government to Greece
and enter your ancestral house with all the glory of the many great
victories won in this campaign, and then, should you so desire it, you
may begin again and undertake a new expedition against these Indians of the East – or, if you prefer, to the Black Sea or to Carthage
and the Libyan territories beyond. It is for you to decide. Other
troops, Greek and Macedonian, will follow you – young, fresh troops
to take the place of your war-weary veterans. Still ignorant of the

horrors of war and full of hope for what the future may bring, these men will follow you with all the more eagerness in that they have seen your old campaigners come safely home again no longer poor and nameless but loaded with money and fame. Sir, if there is one thing above all others a successful man should know, it is *when to stop*. Assuredly for a commander like yourself, with an army like ours, there is nothing to fear from any enemy; but luck, remember, is an unpredictable thing, and against what it may bring no man has any defence.'

Coenus' words were greeted with applause. Some even wept, which was proof enough of their reluctance to prolong the campaign and of how happy they would be should the order be given to turn back. Alexander resented the freedom with which Coenus had spoken and the poor spirit shown by the other officers, and dismissed the conference. Next day he summoned the same officers to his presence and angrily declared that, though he would put pressure on no Macedonian to accompany him, he himself was resolved to go on.

'I shall have others,' he cried, 'who will need no compulsion to follow their King. If you wish to go home, you are at liberty to do so – and you may tell your people there that you deserted your King in the midst of his enemies.'

Thereupon he withdrew to his tent, and for the rest of that day, and for two days following, refused to allow anyone to see him, even members of the Hetaeri; his hope was that the various commanders, both of his Macedonian and allied contingents, might change their minds and become readier to listen to him – for, after all, in a crowd of soldiers such sudden reversals of feeling are common enough. The silence, however, remained absolute and unbroken; the men were angry at Alexander's burst of temper and determined not to let it influence them. But in spite of their obvious hostility Alexander (according to Ptolemy's account of the incident) none the less offered sacrifice in the hope of favourable omens for the crossing. When, however, the omens proved to be against him, he at last submitted, and, having sent for the most senior officers of the Hetaeri and those who were his own closest friends, made a public announcement that, as all circumstances combined to dissuade him from a further advance, he had decided upon withdrawal.

One can imagine the shouts of joy which rose from the throats of that heterogeneous host. Most of them wept. They came to Alexander's tent and called down every blessing upon him for allowing them to prevail – the only defeat he had ever suffered.

The decision made, Alexander divided his men into companies and ordered the construction of twelve altars, as high as the loftiest siege-towers and even broader in proportion, as a thank-offering to the gods who had brought him so far in his victorious progress, and as a memorial of all he had so laboriously achieved. The altars were duly raised, and he offered sacrifice upon them as his custom was, and held games with contests for both horse and man. The territory as far as the river Hyphasis he added to Porus' dominions, and then began his own withdrawal towards the Hydraotes. Crossing this river, he re-traced his steps to the Acesines, where he found already complete the settlement which Hephaestion had been instructed to build and fortify. Here he settled volunteers from the neighbouring Indian tribes and those of his mercenary troops who were disabled by wounds or sickness, and then began his preparations for the voyage down-river to the Indian Ocean.

Meanwhile Arsaces, governor of the territory which bordered on that of Abisares, presented himself. He was accompanied by Abisares' brother and other relatives, and brought presents for Alexander of the kind most esteemed by the Indians, together with thirty of Abisares' elephants. Abisares himself, he reported, was too ill to come in person. At the same time Alexander's envoys to Abisares also presented themselves. Alexander readily believed that the facts were as stated, and allowed Abisares to continue to govern his own province, with Arsaces attached to the administration. He assessed the amount of tribute they should pay, and again offered sacrifice; then, having crossed the Acesines, he marched to the Hydaspes, where he made good the damage done by heavy rains to the two settlements of Nicaea and Bucephala, and saw to any other matters which required attention in that part of the country.

BOOK SIX

On the Hydaspes, Alexander's preparations were now complete. The various craft for the passage included a number of galleys, some of thirty oars, some smaller, barges for horse transport, and other craft likely to be of service in moving an army by river. The decision was accordingly made to begin the voyage down the Hydaspes to the Indian Ocean.

Alexander fancied at this time that he had discovered the source of the Nile, his reasons being that he had, on a previous occasion, seen crocodiles in the Indus, and in no other river except the Nile, and had also observed a kind of bean like the Egyptian bean growing on the banks of the Acesines, which, he was told, flowed into the Indus. His notion was that the Nile (under the name of Indus) rose somewhere in that part of India and then flowed through a vast desert tract, where it lost its original name and received that of Nile from the Ethiopians and Egyptians at the point where it began to flow through inhabited country again, ultimately debouching into the Mediterranean. Homer, he remembered, called it Egyptus, after the country through which it ran.

Indeed, in a letter to Olympias on the subject of India, Alexander made a special point of mentioning his belief that he had found the source of the Nile, though in actual fact he based this important conclusion upon the slenderest evidence. Later he went more thoroughly into the question of the geography of the Indus, and learned from the natives that the Hydaspes ceases to be so named at its junction with the Acesines, just as the latter does at its junction with the Indus, which, in its turn, flows out by two channels into the Indian Ocean, and has no connexion with Egypt whatever. This information led him to cut out the passage about the Nile from his letter to his mother. He then gave orders for the preparation of the fleet for the proposed voyage down the rivers to the Ocean. The crews of the various craft were drawn from the Phoenicians, Cyprians, Carians, and Egyptians serving in the forces.

It was at this time that Coenus fell sick and died. He was one of the

G

most loyal and trusted officers of the Hetaeri, and so far as circumstances permitted Alexander gave him a splendid funeral. He then
summoned to his presence the Hetaeri and such Indian envoys as happened to be present to pay their respects, and proclaimed Porus
monarch of all the Indian territory he had by that time conquered.
This included seven nations and a grand total of over 2,000 towns.

The army for the coming expedition was organized in three divisions: all the Longshields, the archers, the Agrianes, and the picked
cavalry squadrons were embarked in the transports under Alexander's
personal command; Craterus was instructed to march a part of the infantry and cavalry along the right bank of the Hydaspes, while the
bulk of the best fighting troops, together with the elephants, now
about 200 in number, were to proceed along the left bank under the
command of Hephaestion. This latter division had orders to march
with all speed for the palace of Sopeithes. Philip, governor of the territory on the west, or Bactrian, side of the Indus, was to wait three days
and then follow with his troops. The mounted troops from Nysa were
sent home. Nearchus was appointed Admiral of the fleet, and the
helmsman of Alexander's own vessel was Onesicritus, the man who
wrote a memoir about Alexander full of lies – among them the statement that he was an admiral. However, he wasn't: he was just a
helmsman. According to Ptolemy, son of Lagus, my principal authority, the river fleet consisted of eighty thirty-oared galleys, while the
total number of boats of all sorts, including horse-transports, light
galleys, and other river craft, some already in service, others specially
built for the occasion, was not far short of 2,000.

The final preparations made, the embarkation began at dawn, and
Alexander offered his customary sacrifice, not omitting a special offering to the river Hydaspes according to the soothsayers' instructions.
Stepping aboard, he stood in the bows of his vessel and from a golden
bowl poured a libation into the water, solemnly invoking the river
and joining with its name the name of Acesines, which he now knew
to be the greatest of its tributaries, with the meeting of the waters not
far away, and, finally, calling upon the Indus too, into which both
Acesines and Hydaspes run. Then, after a libation to Heracles his ancestor and to Ammon and the other gods it was his custom to honour,
he ordered the trumpets to sound the signal for departure, and the
whole fleet, each vessel in her proper station, began to move down-

river. To avoid the danger of running foul of each other, all craft –
carriers, horse-transports, and warships – had instructions to keep their
exact distances, the faster vessels being ordered to check their speed so
as not to break formation. One may imagine the noise of this great
fleet getting away under oars all together: it was like nothing ever
heard before, what with the coxswains calling the *in ... out: in ... out*
for every stroke and the rowers' triumphant cries as, like one man,
they flung themselves upon the swirling water. The lofty banks, often
towering above the ships, caught the clamour, and held it and intensi-
fied it, tossing it to and fro across the stream, echoing and re-echoing,
while silent and deserted glens on one side or other of the river rever-
berated with the din and helped to swell it. The natives (who had no
tradition that Dionysus' expedition to India had been by water) had
never before seen horses on shipboard, and the sight of them crowd-
ing the barges filled them with such amazement that all who wit-
nessed the departure of the fleet followed it along the banks for miles,
and other friendly tribesmen who were near enough to hear the cries
of the rowers and the dash and clatter of the oars came running to the
river-bank and joined in the procession, singing their barbaric songs.
For the Indians, be it said, are an extremely musical race and have
loved dancing ever since the days when Dionysus came with his wild
revellers to their country.

On the third day the fleet brought up at the spot where Hephaestion and Craterus had been ordered to halt their forces, one on each
side of the river. Alexander waited there two days, and when Philip
joined him with the rest of the troops, he sent him to the Acesines
with orders to proceed with his men along its banks. Craterus and
Hephaestion were also ordered on again, with careful instructions on
the route they were to follow. Then the descent of the Hydaspes was
resumed, and was found to be nowhere less than two and a half miles
wide. In the course of the voyage Alexander put in, when opportunity offered, to the river-bank, to deal with the natives of the
vicinity. Some surrendered voluntarily; others, who had offered resistance, he had already subdued.

He was, however, anxious to hurry on to the territory of the Mallians and Oxydracae. Information had reached him that these people
were the most numerous and warlike of the Indians in that part of the
country, and it was further reported that they had shut up their

women and children in their most strongly fortified towns with the
intention of making a stand against him. Accordingly he made all
possible speed, in order to get at them before they were ready to receive him, and while their preparations were still inadequate and incomplete.

Getting under way again, on the fifth day he reached the junction
of the Hydaspes and the Acesines. At the place where the two streams
unite, the river is very narrow, and the current, in consequence, extremely rapid; the surface is roughened and broken, there are dangerous eddies and whirlpools, and the roaring of the water can be heard
for many miles. Alexander had been forewarned of these conditions
by the natives, and he had told his men what to expect; none the less,
when the flotilla approached the junction, the water made such an
appalling shindy that the men at the oars stopped rowing in sheer
panic, and the coxswains, dumb with astonishment, ceased to call the
time. Presently, however, just above the actual point of meeting, the
men at the helm of the various craft shouted orders to the rowers to
put their backs into it and drive through the narrows with all speed,
in the hope that if they kept good way on they might prevent their
vessels from being spun round by the swirling eddies. The barges and
short, beamier craft were, indeed, spun about like tops, but, apart
from the anxiety of their crews, came to no harm, as the current
swept them, stern-first or broadside-on, in a direct line through the
narrows; the warships, on the contrary, got off by no means so
lightly: their inferior bouyancy made it harder for them to cope
with the hubbub, and those with two banks of oars had great difficulty in keeping the lower tier clear of the water. Some, unable to
keep sufficient way on to shoot the rapids successfully, were badly
caught and got their oars broken off as they came broadside on to the
eddies, and many other craft were in distress, two of them running
foul of one another and sinking with the loss of many lives. At last,
when the narrows were passed, the stream slackened and the swirls
and eddies were much less violent, so that Alexander was able to land
his men on the right bank of the river just below a headland where the
force of the current was not felt and the ships could be beached and
floating wreckage collected, together with any survivors who might
still be clinging to it. These were accordingly brought to safety and
the damaged vessels repaired, after which Nearchus was ordered to

continue down-stream as far as the territory of the Mallians, while
Alexander himself carried out a rapid raid against the natives who
had not submitted to him, and thus prevented them from bringing
help to the Mallians. That done, he returned to the flotilla.

At this point he was rejoined by Hephaestion, Craterus, and Philip.
Sending the elephants, Polysperchon's brigade, the mounted archers,
and Philip's contingent over to the other side of the river, he put them
under Craterus' command and at the same time instructed Nearchus
to proceed down the river, keeping three days' march ahead of the
army, which he then split into three divisions: Hesphaestion was ordered to march five days in advance, with the object of intercepting
and capturing any native troops which, in their attempt to escape
Alexander's own contingent, might be moving rapidly forward;
Ptolemy, son of Lagus, with another division, had orders to wait three
days and then follow, in order to be in a position to catch any of
the enemy who, to avoid Alexander, turned back upon their
tracks. Further instructions were that, on reaching the junction of
the Acesines and Hydraotes, the leading division was to wait till
Alexander should himself arrive and Craterus and Ptolemy join up
with him.

Under his personal command Alexander took the Longshields,
archers, Agrianes, Peitho's brigade of what were known as Foot-
Guards, all the mounted archers, and half of the mounted Hetaeri.
With these troops he marched for the territory of the Mallians, a
branch of the independent Indians. His route lay over almost waterless country, but in the course of the first day's march he halted by a
pond about a dozen miles from the Acesines; there, after a meal and a
brief rest for the men, he ordered every available receptacle to be
filled with water before proceeding, when, having covered fifty miles
during the remainder of the day and the whole of the following night,
he reached a town where many of the Mallians had taken refuge. The
last thing they expected was that Alexander would come by way of
this waterless region, and most of them were, in consequence, unarmed and outside the defences of their walls. Obviously this was the
very reason why Alexander had chosen this route: it was a difficult
one, and the enemy never thought it possible that he would choose it.
He took them completely by surprise, and most of them, unarmed as
they were, offered no resistance and were killed. Some shut themselves

up in the town, whereupon Alexander, whose infantry had not yet
arrived upon the scene, blocked them up there by throwing a cordon
of mounted troops round the walls. As soon as the infantry joined
him, he dispatched Perdiccas with his own and Cleitus' cavalry regiments and the Agrianes to another Mallian town at which large numbers of the Indians had concentrated, and ordered him not to attack
till he himself should arrive, but to keep his eyes open to prevent anyone from slipping out of the town and informing the other natives
that he was already on the way.

He then launched his own attack. The Indians, who had already lost
a great many men either killed or wounded in the first surprise attack,
abandoned their outer defences, which they had no hope of holding,
and took refuge within their inner fortifications, where, as the position was a commanding one and difficult to assault, they managed for
a time to hold out; but the strong pressure exerted on every side by
the Macedonians and the ubiquitous pressure of Alexander in the
thick of the fighting soon proved too much for them. The inner fortress was stormed and all its defenders, about 2,000 in number, were
killed.

Perdiccas, meanwhile, had reached his objective. He found the
town deserted, and learning that it was not long since the inhabitants
had fled, he rode with all speed in pursuit of them, his light infantry
following at the best pace they could make. Some of the fugitives
managed to escape into the marshes; the rest were overtaken and
killed.

After his meal and a rest for his men, Alexander set forward again
at about the first watch. He covered many miles in the course of the
night, and at daybreak reached the Hydraotes, where he learned that
most of the Mallians had already crossed to the other side; some were
still on their way over, and many of these he caught and destroyed –
indeed, without a moment's hesitation he went over the river among
them and then continued to press his pursuit of those who had got
away ahead of him. Many of these too he caught and killed, and took
a number of prisoners; but the majority of them succeeded in making
their escape to a strongly fortified position. Against these, as soon as
the infantry rejoined him, he sent Peitho with his own brigade and
two regiments of cavalry. The attack was successful; they captured
the position and reduced to the status of slaves every man who sur-

vived the assault. After this exploit Peitho and his troops rejoined the
main body of the army.

A report had reached Alexander that a Mallian force was preparing
to defend itself in one of the Brahmin towns and he was now on his
way thither. On reaching it, he stationed his infantry in a ring round
the outer defences and moved up in close formation. The defenders
soon saw that their walls were being sapped, and this, together with
the weight of the enemy missiles, induced them (as in Alexander's
previous operation) to abandon their position and take refuge in their
inner stronghold; here they continued to resist, and not without some
success, for they turned and fell upon a small party of Macedonians
who had forced their way in with them, driving some of them
out again and killing about twenty-five before they could get
away.

Alexander meanwhile brought the scaling-ladders into position all
round the inner stronghold and ordered sapping operations to begin.
A tower soon fell and the collapse of a section of the wall laid the fortress open to assault, whereupon Alexander, ahead of his men, was up
in the moment, and stood there alone, a conspicuous figure, holding
the breach. The sight of him struck shame into his troops, so up they
went after him in scattered groups, some here, some there. Soon the
fortress was in their hands. Some of the Indians set fire to their houses
or were caught in them and killed; most died fighting. In all they lost
about 5,000 men; they had fought too well for more than a handful to
be taken alive.

After waiting there a day to rest his troops Alexander began his
advance against the remaining Mallian forces. He found their settlements deserted and gathered by report that they had all fled into uninhabited country; accordingly, after another day's rest for his men,
he sent Peitho and Demetrius, the cavalry officer, back to the river
with the troops already under their command together with some
companies of light infantry sufficient for the task in hand: this was, to
march along the river and keep a look out for any of the enemy who
might have fled to the woods there (they were very extensive along
the river-bank) and to kill all of them who refused to give themselves
up. They did, in fact, catch and kill a great many of them.

Alexander's own next objective was the principal town of the Mallian people. It had been reported to him that many of the Mallians had

left their own settlements and joined their kinsmen there; nevertheless, on the news of Alexander's approach, this town, too, was abandoned, and the Indians, having crossed the Hydraotes, took up a
strong position on the high ground of the opposite bank, evidently intending to prevent Alexander from coming over. Learning of this
movement, Alexander at once advanced with all his available cavalry
to the point on the Hydraotes where the Mallians had massed, and
gave orders for the infantry to follow. Reaching the river and observing the enemy in position on the further bank, though he still had
only the cavalry with him, he plunged, without even waiting to re-
form after his march, into the ford. When he was half-way over, the
enemy withdrew from the river-bank rapidly but in good order.
Alexander followed them up, and as soon as they realized that he had
only mounted troops with no infantry in support, they checked their
withdrawal, turned, and offered a vigorous resistance. Their force was
some 50,000 strong. Alexander's infantry had not yet joined him; accordingly, as the Indians were massed in close formation, he held off
for the time being, keeping his cavalry continually manœuvring and
making an occasional probe; presently, however, the Agrianes
arrived on the scene together with the archers and some picked units
of light infantry which were serving under his personal command,
while at the same time the heavy infantry was already visible at no
great distance. Faced by these simultaneous threats the Indians broke
and hurriedly withdrew to the shelter of one of the neighbouring
settlements which was strongly fortified. Alexander followed close on
their heels, inflicting a number of casualties, and when the fugitives
had shut themselves up inside the defences of the town, he promptly
ordered his cavalry to draw a cordon round it; then, when his infantry joined him, he took up a position completely encircling the
outer defences, and suspended operations for the day. There were two
reasons for the pause: insufficient daylight left for an immediate attack, and the fact that all his men were pretty well exhausted – the
infantry by their long march, the mounted troops by their protracted
pursuit, and both not least by their crossing of the river.

Next day when the attack began, with Alexander himself in command of one division of the army and Perdiccas of the other, the Indians did not hold their positions on the outer defences to receive the
Macedonian onset, but withdrew their entire force to the inner fort-

ress of the town. Alexander and his men by wrenching a gate from its hinges penetrated into the town far in advance of the troops under Perdiccas, who had met trouble in trying to get over the wall and were, in consequence, slow off the mark; most of them, moreover, carried no ladders, as the sight of the wall bare of defenders led them to believe that the town was already taken. But they soon realized their mistake, and seeing that the enemy held the inner fortress, with large numbers of men posted in front of it bent upon its defence, they at once began sapping operations and got scaling-ladders into position wherever they could, in an attempt to force their way in. The men with the ladders were not quick enough to satisfy Alexander; in his impatience he snatched one from the fellow who carried it and with his own hands reared it against the fortress wall; then, crouched under his shield, up he went. Peucestas followed him with the 'sacred shield' – the shield from the temple of Athene at Troy, which Alexander kept by him and had carried before him in battle. Peucestas was followed by Leonnatus, an officer of the Guard; then Abreas, one of the picked soldiers on double pay, mounted by a second ladder.

The King had now reached the top. Laying his shield on the coping of the wall, he forced some of the defenders back into the fortress, cut down others with his sword, till he stood there on the battlements alone, not one of the enemy within his reach. The sight of him filled the men of the Longshields with terror for his safety; scrambling for precedence, they made a dash for the ladders, but under the excessive load they broke and hurled the climbers to the ground. The rest were helpless.

No Indian ventured to approach Alexander as he stood on the fortress wall; but he was the target of every marksman in the neighbouring towers; men in the town shot at him too – and from no great distance either, as raised ground near the fortress wall brought them within closer range. That it was indeed Alexander who stood there was plain to all: his almost legendary courage no less than his shining armour proclaimed him.

Suddenly a thought crossed his mind: by staying where he was he might well be killed with nothing accomplished; but if he leapt down into the fortress, he might by that very act spread consternation among the enemy, or at least, if it was his fate to die, death would come not without a struggle and as the crown of an exploit which would live upon the lips of men. To think was to act: without further hesitation he made his leap.

Once inside the fortress, he put his back to the wall and made ready to fight. A party of Indians came at him, and he cut them down; their commander rushed forward, all too rashly, and he, too, fell. First one, then a second, who tried to approach him he stopped with a well-aimed stone. Others pressed within striking distance, and fell victims to his sword. After that none ventured again to attack him hand to hand; keeping their distance, they formed a half-circle round where he stood and hurled at him whatever missiles they had or could find.

By this time Peucestas, Abreas, and Leonnatus, the only men who succeeded in scaling the wall before the ladders collapsed, had got inside the fortress and were fighting in defence of their King. Abreas was shot in the face and killed and Alexander himself was hit, the arrow penetrating his corselet and entering his body above the breast. Ptolemy tells us that the blood from the wound was mixed with air breathed out from the pierced lung. Despite the pain he continued to defend himself so long as the blood was warm; but there was soon a violent haemorrhage, as was to be expected with a pierced lung, and overcome by giddiness and faintess he fell forward over his shield. Peucestas stood astride of his body holding up before him the sacred shield from Troy, and Leonnatus took his stand on the other side, both men being now the target for the enemy missiles, while Alexander himself was almost unconscious from loss of blood.

The Macedonian assault upon the fortress was by now thoroughly out of hand; the men had seen Alexander as he stood on the battlements, the mark of the enemy's missiles; they had seen him leap down on the other side; and now, afraid lest his rash act should be the end of him and eager to bring help in time, they made a rush for the fortress wall. The ladders were smashed and useless, but, on the spur of the moment, they used whatever means they could to get up and over: some drove stakes into the clay of the wall and dragged themselves slowly and laboriously up; others struggled up by standing on their comrades' shoulders. Each man as he got to the top flung himself down on the further side into the fortress. There they saw the King on the ground, and a cry of grief and a shout of rage rose from every throat. Soon a fierce battle was raging, one man after another holding his shield over Alexander's prostrate body, until at last the troops outside had smashed the bolt of the gate in the curtain-wall and were beginning to come in, a few at a time. Others then got their shoulders to the half-opened gate, forced it inwards, and so laid the fortress open.

Now the slaughter began; neither women nor children were spared. A party of men carried away the King on his shield; his condition was critical and no one, at this time, thought he could live. Some writers have stated that the arrow which hit him was cut out by Critodemus, a doctor from the island of Cos, of the family of Asclepius; others that Perdiccas, of the King's Guard, cut it out with his sword at Alexander's request, no doctor being at hand in this emergency. There was a rush of blood as the arrow was drawn out, and Alexander fainted again, thus checking the haemorrhage. All sorts of other stories about this grave incident have been put on record, most of them false, and tradition has taken them over in their original form and still preserves them; and doubtless it will continue to pass them on to future generations, unless a stop is put to it by the account I give in this book.

In the first place, it is universally supposed that it was among the Oxydracae that Alexander received his almost fatal wound: but it was not – it was in the territory of the Mallians, an independent Indian tribe. The town was a Mallian town, and it was the Mallians who shot Alexander. They had, to be sure, intended to join the Oxydracae and to continue hostilities in concert with them, but Alexander had been too quick for them: he had come upon them by the desert route before either they or the Oxydracae could do anything to help each other. Nor is this the only point in which popular tradition is at fault: for instance, it is generally said that the final battle with Darius, in which he fled for his life until he was caught and killed by Bessus, with Alexander pressing hard upon his heels, took place at Arbela, while the previous battle was fought at Issus, and the one before that, the first – cavalry – battle, on the Granicus. Now it is true enough that there was a cavalry engagement on the Granicus and that the next encounter with Darius took place at Issus, but the historians have stated that Arbela was, at the largest estimate, seventy-five and, at the smallest, rather more than sixty miles from the scene of the final battle between Darius and Alexander. Actually, both Ptolemy and Aristobulus declare that this battle was fought at Gaugamela near the river Bumodus. Now Gaugamela was only a large village, not a town; it was not a well-known place, and the name itself has a somewhat unpleasing sound, and I fancy that it was for these reasons that the town of Arbela was allowed to have the honour of being the scene of this great battle. How absurd! If we are expected to believe that the battle was fought at Arbela, miles and miles from its actual scene, we might as well pretend that the sea-fight at Salamis took place at the Isthmus of Corinth, or that the engagement at Artemisium in Euboea took place at Aegina or Sunium.

Again, all writers agree that Peucestas was one of the men who held his shield over Alexander during those critical moments, but there is no agreement either about Leonnatus or Abreas. One story is that Alexander reeled and fell from a blow on the helmet with a club, but got to his feet again and was then shot in the breast, the arrow piercing his corselet; but Ptolemy, son of Lagus, states that he was shot in the breast only. The most glaring error of all is, in my opinion, the statement of some writers about Alexander's campaigns to the effect that Ptolemy, son of Lagus, went up the ladder with Alexander, accompanied by Peucestas, and protected him with his shield when he lay wounded on the ground, thereby winning the title of Saviour, whereas Ptolemy himself has made it quite plain that he was not present at this action at all, but was, at the time, commanding his own division in other actions elsewhere. I think I must be allowed this digression; these events are of the highest importance, and what I have said should help future historians to record less carelessly the facts connected with them.

For some time Alexander was kept where he was, under medical treatment, and the first report to reach the base camp was that he had died of wounds. The bad news swiftly spread, and the whole army was in the deepest distress. Recovering from the first shock of grief, the men were plunged into helpless despair: who would be their new commander – as both in Alexander's view and in their own a number of officers had an equal reputation for ability? How could they get safely home, encircled as they were by many warlike tribes, some of which had not yet submitted and seemed likely to fight hard for their freedom now that the dread of Alexander's name was a thing of the past? They were, or so they thought, hemmed in by impassable rivers, and every difficulty seemed hopelessly insoluble without Alexander to get them through. When at last the news came that he was alive, they could hardly believe it, and were unable at first to persuade themselves that he would really recover. Then he wrote them a letter saying that he would soon be visiting them at headquarters, but such was their state of mind that they could not believe it was genuine, and most of them thought it had been forged by his officers and Guards.

Alexander's first thought on learning of this state of affairs was to prevent a breakdown of discipline among the men; so at the first possible moment he had himself carried to the Hydraotes, and proceeded to travel down-stream. The troops were in camp at the junction of the Hydraotes and the Acesines, where Hephaestion was in charge of the land forces and Nearchus had the fleet, and when his vessel had nearly reached them, he ordered the awning over the stern to be taken down so that everyone might see him. Even then the troops were incredulous, and supposed that what they saw on board was Alexander's body. At last, however, the vessel was brought in to the river-bank; Alexander raised a hand in greeting to the men, and immediately there was a shout of joy, and arms were stretched towards him in welcome or lifted to heaven in thankfulness. So unexpected was the sense of relief that many, despite themselves, burst into tears. As he was being moved from the ship, a party of Longshields brought him a stretcher; but he refused it and called for his horse. He mounted, and at the sight of him, once more astride his horse, there was a storm of applause so loud that the river-banks and neighbouring glens re-echoed with the noise. Near his tent he dismounted, and the men saw him walk; they crowded round him, touching his hands, his knees, his clothes; some, content with a sight of him standing near, turned away with a blessing on their lips. Wreaths were flung upon him and such flowers as were then in bloom.

We are told by Nearchus that he was annoyed with some of his friends, who blamed him for exposing himself in advance of his men and taking risks which no commander ought to take; and I fancy that his resentment was due to the fact that he was well aware that their criticism was justified. The truth is that he was fighting mad, and such was his passion for glory that he had not the strength of mind, when there was action afoot, to consider his own safety; the sheer pleasure of battle, as other pleasures are to other men, was irresistible. Nearchus goes on to say that a Boeotian soldier, an oldish man whose name he does not mention, aware of Alexander's resentment at his friends' criticism and observing the glum expression on his face, came and said to him in his rustic dialect: 'Action is a man's job, my lord'; and then quoted a line of verse – something to the effect that 'he who acts bravely must expect his meed of suffering'. The fellow's stock went up immediately, and from that time on he enjoyed Alexander's warm approval.

Representatives of the remaining Mallians now came to Alexander with the offer of surrender. A similar offer came at the same time from the Oxydracae, the deputation consisting of the governors of their various towns and districts, accompanied by 150 other dignitaries, all acting as plenipotentiaries to discuss a settlement and bringing with them the most precious Indian gifts. They urged that their failure to treat with him earlier was a pardonable offence, as, like certain other tribes though in a greater degree, they desired to be independent and to keep the freedom which they had enjoyed from the time when Dionysus visited India right up to the present day. However, as it was generally believed that Alexander, too, was of divine descent, they were willing, if that were his pleasure, to accept any governor he should appoint, pay any tribute he should please to demand, and give as many hostages as he should require. Alexander asked for a thousand of their leading men and said he would either keep them as hostages or, if it proved more convenient, make them serve in his army until the end of his Indian campaign. The men were duly sent, all being chosen for their influence and importance, and with them, as an unsolicited gift, 500 war chariots with their drivers. Alexander then appointed Philip as governor of these people and of the surviving Mallians. The hostages he returned, but retained the chariots.

During Alexander's convalescence many new river-craft had been built, and now, when the matters just mentioned were satisfactorily settled, he ordered aboard 1,700 of the mounted Hetaeri, the same number as before of the light infantry, and about 10,000 regular infantry, and set off down the Hydraotes. Actually, the voyage down the Hydraotes was a short one, for at its junction with the Acesines it takes the name of the latter river – so it was down the Acesines that he found himself sailing as far as its junction with the Indus.

Four great rivers, all navigable, pour their waters into the Indus –

but some of them lose their original names before they get there: the Hydaspes joins the Acesines, by which name, after the junction, the united streams are known; the Acesines keeps its name after its meeting with the Hydraotes, and also after receiving the tributary waters of the Hyphasis, until its junction with the Indus, when it surrenders it. From that point on I can well believe that the Indus before it splits into its delta is as much as twelve or thirteen miles wide, and perhaps more in its lowest reaches, where it is more like a lake than a river.

Alexander waited at the junction of the Acesines and Indus until the arrival of Perdiccas' contingent. Perdiccas, on his way to rejoin, had subdued the Abastani, an independent people. About this time, too, the fleet was reinforced by the addition of some new galleys and cargo vessels, built for Alexander in the territory of the Xathri – another independent tribe which had submitted to him – and envoys from the Ossadians, also an independent people, presented themselves with an offer of surrender. He fixed the Acesines and Indus, where they converge to their point of meeting, as the boundaries of Philip's province, and left under his command the whole Thracian contingent and such troops from the other units as seemed sufficient to garrison the country. He instructed Philip to found a settlement at the actual junction of the two rivers, in the hope that the place would grow and become a world-famous town. He also ordered the construction of dockyards there.

During this period he was visited by Oxyartes the Bactrian, father of his wife, Roxane; he conferred upon him the governorship of the Parapamisidae in place of Tiryaspes, the former governor, whom he removed from office on a report of mismanagement.

Before moving on he sent Craterus over to the left bank of the Indus with the elephants and most of the troops, as it appeared to be easier going for an army with heavy equipment on that side and the neighbouring tribes were not everywhere friendly; then he set off down-stream for the royal palace of Sogdia. There he built and fortified a new settlement, had dockyards constructed and his damaged vessels repaired. He appointed Oxyartes and Peitho to govern the country from the junction of the Indus and Acesines to the sea, together with the whole coastal region of India.

Having given Craterus orders once again to proceed by land, he then went on down the river to the kingdom of Musicanus, which according to report was the richest in India. Musicanus had not as yet presented himself with an offer of submission, nor had he sent representatives to establish relations; he had, indeed, ignored Alexander, neither sending him such tokens of courtesy as might befit a great king, nor making him any sort of request. Alexander's voyage down the Indus was so rapid that before Musicanus even knew that he had started he was on the boundaries of his kingdom. This was something of a shock; and Musicanus, in consequence, hastened to present himself before Alexander with all his elephants and such gifts as are considered by Indians to be of the greatest value. He offered the submission of himself and his people and acknowledged the error of his previous conduct. With Alexander to acknowledge an error was always the best way to get what one wanted, and the case of Musicanus was no exception: Alexander freely pardoned him. He admired his country and his capital city, and permitted him to retain his sovereignty. Craterus received orders to fortify the inner stronghold of this city, and the work was done and a garrison established there while Alexander was still present; for the neighbouring tribes needed watching, and this seemed a convenient base from which to control them.

The governor of this district, a man named Oxycanus, had not yet made any contact with Alexander, either in person or by sending a deputation with offers of surrender. Alexander accordingly undertook an expedition against him with a force consisting of the archers, the Agrianes, and the cavalry he had brought with him down the river. The two largest towns in Oxycanus' province he took by assault without much trouble, and in one of them Oxycanus himself was taken prisoner. All the plunder Alexander distributed among his men; the elephants he added to his own force. Other towns in this district surrendered at his approach, and there was no attempt at resistance – an indication of the extent to which the Indians had been cowed by the unbroken chain of Alexander's success.

His next move was against Sambus, whom he had himself appointed governor of the Indian hill-tribes. Sambus and Musicanus were at enmity, and a report had come in that Sambus had fled on learning that Alexander had treated Musicanus with leniency and allowed him to retain his kingdom. The gates of Sindimana, the capital of Sambus' territory, were opened at Alexander's approach; Sambus' relatives made an inventory of his treasure and came out to meet him with the elephants, and pointed out to him that the reason why Sambus had abandoned his capital was not hostility to Alexander, but alarm at his clemency towards Musicanus. Alexander captured another town in the course of this expedition; it had thrown off its allegiance, and he executed the Brahmins (the Indian teachers of philosophy) who had been responsible for the revolt. The Brahmin philosophy, such as it is, I will discuss in my book on India.

News now came that Musicanus had revolted. The district governor, Peitho, son of Agenor, was dispatched to deal with him at the head of an adequate force, while Alexander proceeded against the various towns in his dominions; some of these he destroyed, selling the people into slavery; others he fortified and garrisoned. He then returned to his base, where the fleet was awaiting him. Musicanus, who had been taken prisoner by Peitho, was brought there, and Alexander had him hanged in his own country, together with the Brahmins who had instigated his rebellion.

Alexander was also visited at the base by the ruler of Pattala, the territory which, as I have already mentioned, consists of the delta of the Indus – larger in extent than the Nile delta in Egypt. He offered surrender of the whole territory and put himself and all he possessed into Alexander's hands. Alexander sent him back to his country with instructions to make all necessary preparations for receiving the army, and then ordered Craterus to proceed to Carmania by way of Arachotia and Zarangia with the brigades of Attalus, Meleager, and Antigenes, some of the archers, and the men of the Hetaeri and other Macedonian units whom he was already sending home as unfit for further service. Craterus was also given charge of the elephants, and Hephaestion was put in command of all the remaining units except those which were not going with Alexander down the Indus to the sea. Peitho with the mounted javelins and the Agrianes was ordered across the river – the opposite side to Hephaestion – with further instructions to settle the towns which had already been fortified and to deal with any trouble which might occur in the neighbourhood, before joining Alexander at Pattala.

On the third day of Alexander's passage down-stream news was brought that the Indian chief in charge of Pattala had made off with nearly all his people, leaving his territory empty and undefended. Alexander, in consequence, redoubled his speed and found, on reaching

Pattala, that the town was indeed deserted and that not a labourer was left working on the land. He at once sent his lightest units in pursuit of the fugitives, caught a few of them, and sent them off to tell their friends to come back to their homes without fear, as they were at liberty to live in their town and cultivate their lands as before. Most of them took Alexander at his word and returned.

Hephaestion was then ordered to construct a fortress in the town, and parties of men were sent out to dig wells where there was a shortage of water and to make the surrounding country fit to live in. While the men were at work, they were set upon by natives; the attack was unexpected and a few were killed, but the natives suffered heavy losses and made their escape into the wilds. The working party was then able to finish its task, with the assistance of fresh troops which Alexander sent out to lend a hand as soon as he heard of the attack.

At Pattala the Indus divides into two mighty streams, both of which retain the name of Indus till they reach the sea. At the point of division Alexander began the construction of a harbour and dockyards, and as soon as the work was well under way he decided to sail down the right-hand, or westerly, stream as far as its mouth. Leonnatus with 1,000 mounted troops and about 8,000 light and heavy infantry was ordered to move on to the delta – or island – of Pattala, ready to follow by land the progress of the flotilla down the river, and the voyage began. Alexander had selected for the purpose his fastest vessels – all the thirty-oars, the one-and-a-half-bankers, and some of the light galleys; but, as the natives of these parts had all made off, he was unable to procure a pilot, and this resulted in serious difficulties. The day after he started it blew very hard, and the wind being against the tide raised a steep hollow sea which gave the vessels a thorough shaking; most of them were badly strained, and some of the thirty-oars had their timbers started. However, they managed to run them ashore before they actually fell to pieces.★

A party of light infantry was then sent out to bring in some prisoners from the country adjacent to the river, and for the remainder of the passage these men acted as pilots. But their troubles were not over, for near the mouth of the river, where it attains its greatest breadth of

★ Arrian adds: 'others, therefore, were built'. But this seems so unlikely that I have omitted it. He had other vessels at the base. (Translator's note.)

some twenty-five miles, they encountered a hard wind blowing in from the open sea, and the water was so rough that it was hardly possible to lift the oars clear of the crests and they were compelled to run for shelter into a small creek, under their pilots' direction. Lying in the creek, they were caught by the ebb tide and left high and dry. The tide is, of course, a regular feature of the ocean, but the ebb came as a surprise to Alexander's men, who had had no previous experience of it, and it was an even greater surprise when, in due time, the water returned on the flood and the vessels were refloated. Some of them had settled on soft mud; these were floated again without sustaining any damage and were able to continue their voyage; but others, which had been caught on a rocky bottom and were not evenly supported when the tide left them, did not fare so well: as the flood came in with a rush, they either fell foul of one another or bumped themselves to pieces on the hard bottom.

Alexander effected such repairs as circumstances permitted, and sent two light pinnaces down-stream with a party of men to take a look at the island – called Cilluta – where his native pilots said he would find an anchorage on his passage to the sea. The men reported that there was, indeed, good shelter, and that the island itself was large and well supplied with fresh water; the rest of the flotilla, accordingly, brought up there, while Alexander himself went on beyond it with some of his fastest vessels, to get a view of the river-mouth and to find out if there was a practicable passage into the open sea. They went on some twenty-five miles below Cilluta, and then observed, out at sea, another island, whereupon they put back to Cilluta, and Alexander, bringing his vessel to under a headland, offered sacrifice to those gods which he liked to say Ammon had instructed him to honour. On the following day he sailed down to the second island – beyond the mouth of the river – brought up there, and once more offered sacrifice, this time to other gods and with a different ritual, though still, by his own account, in accordance with the oracular utterance of Ammon. Then, leaving the estuaries of the Indus behind him, he set sail for the open ocean, with the professed object of finding out if there was any other land near by – though I dare say his chief object was the mere achievement of having sailed in the Great Sea beyond India. There on the ocean he slaughtered bulls as a sacrifice to Poseidon and flung their bodies overboard, and poured a libation from a golden

cup, and flung the cup, too, and golden bowls into the water for a
thank-offering, and prayed that Poseidon might grant safe conduct to
the fleet which he proposed to send under Nearchus' command to the
Persian Gulf and the mouths of the Tigris and Euphrates.

This done, he returned to Pattala, where he found the construction
of the fortress complete and Peitho already arrived with his mission
successfully accomplished. Hephaestion was ordered to make all
necessary preparations for fortifying the harbour and for the installa-
tion of docks, as it was Alexander's intention to leave a considerable
fleet stationed at Pattala, at the junction of the two estuaries of the
Indus.

He now undertook a second voyage to the Ocean, this time by the
other branch of the Indus, for the purpose of informing himself which
of the two offered the easier passage (the mouths of the Indus are about
225 miles apart). On the way down he came to a great lake; it is really
a part of the estuary, and its vast extent is due to the spreading waters
of the river assisted, possibly, by other tributary streams flowing in
on this side or on that, so that it resembles, in effect, a gulf of the sea.
Moreover, deep-sea fish were to be seen in it, larger than those we
find in our own waters at home.

Alexander came to an anchor at a spot in the lake which his pilots
recommended; then, leaving behind all the light pinnaces and most of
his men in charge of Leonnatus, he proceeded with the thirty-oars
and one-and-a-half-bankers down to the mouth of the river, and so,
once again, out into the open sea. The passage by this branch proved
the easier of the two.

Bringing up close off-shore, he landed and went three days' march
with a party of mounted troops along the coast, making observations
of the nature of the country along which the coasting voyage would
have to be made and arranging for wells to be dug, to provide the
fleet with water. Then he returned to his ships, and having sailed up
to Pattala, sent off a strong working-party to the coast with orders to
rejoin him when the task was complete. This done, he once again
went down-river to the lake, where he had another harbour and more
docks constructed. Finally, leaving a garrison there, he laid in four
months' supplies for the troops and made all other necessary preparations for the coastal voyage.

At the moment, however, it was the wrong time of year for a sea voyage. The monsoon was blowing, and, unlike our own seasonal winds, the monsoon is not a northerly wind, but blows in off the ocean from the south; but according to the information Alexander received conditions were suitable for sailing from the setting of the Pleiades at the beginning of winter to the winter solstice, as throughout that period the heavy inland rains give rise to constant light offshore winds, convenient for a coastal voyage under either sails or oars.

While Nearchus, admiral of the fleet, was waiting at Pattala for weather, Alexander moved on with his whole force to the river Arabius, and then turned towards the coast and proceeded along it in a westerly direction, taking with him half the total number of Longshields and archers, the brigades of footguards, the picked regiment of the mounted Hetaeri, a squadron from each of the other cavalry regiments, and all the mounted archers. His object was, first, to have wells dug in order to ensure a good supply of water for Nearchus' men during their coastal passage, and, secondly, to make a surprise attack on the Oreitae, a local Indian tribe which had long been independent and had hitherto made no gesture of friendship towards Alexander and his army. Hephaestion had command of the troops left behind at Pattala.

The Arabitae, another independent tribe near the Arabius, did not appear to Alexander worth the trouble of an attack; they did not, however, surrender when they learned of his approach, but made off into the wilds. Alexander, accordingly, crossed the river, which was hardly more than a shallow stream, crossed in the course of the night the greater part of the uninhabited country, and by dawn found himself close to the occupied regions again; then, instructing his infantry to follow in marching order, he entered the Oreitan territory with his mounted troops, dividing them into squadrons to enable them to cover as much ground as possible. All the natives who attempted resistance were killed; many were taken prisoner. He then made a temporary halt near a small stream, and as soon as he was rejoined by Hephaestion continued his advance as far as the village called Rambacia, the largest settlement in the Oreitan territory. The site of this place impressed him favourably, and feeling that if a town were built there it might well become great and prosperous, he left Hephaestion on the spot to put the work in hand.

His next objective was the frontiers of the Oreitae and Gedrosians, and thither he now proceeded with a force consisting of one half of the Longshields and Agrianes, his crack cavalry regiment, and the mounted archers. A report had come in that the approach was by a narrow pass, and that the combined forces of these two peoples had taken up a position in front of it with the purpose of stopping Alexander from getting through. This was, in fact, true; but as soon as they knew of his approach most of them abandoned their post and left the pass undefended, while the chiefs of the Oreitae came to Alexander with an offer of surrender for themselves and their people. Alexander ordered them to round up the scattered members of their tribe and send them back to their homes, adding an assurance that they should come to no harm. As governor there he appointed Apollophanes, and left Leonnatus, officer of the Guard, in the territory of the Orians to support him; he put under Leonnatus' command all the Agrianes, certain units of archers and cavalry, and a number of Greek mercenary troops, both horse and foot, and added instructions that he was to wait for the arrival of the fleet off the coast in those parts to attend to the new settlement and help to introduce such order and discipline among the Oreitae as might induce them to be more obedient to their governor. Then, when Hephaestion had rejoined him with the troops left behind at Rambacia, he moved forward with the greater part of his army towards Gedrosia, mostly through desolate and uninhabited country.

In this wild region (Aristobulus records) myrrh grows in great abundance, the trees being larger than the common species; the Phoenicians who accompanied the expedition for what they could make out of it, used to collect the gum and load their pack-animals with it – it was, indeed, extremely plentiful, for it had never been collected before and the trunks which exuded it were of such uncommon size. The country also produces nard, both abundant and sweet-smelling, and this, too, was gathered by the Phoenicians. This grew in such profusion that much of it was trampled underfoot by the marching men, and the crushed plants spread a delicious fragrance for miles around. Other trees grow there too; one, with a leaf like laurel, is found growing below high-water mark on the sea-shore: this tree is left high and dry by the ebb tide, and on the succeeding flood looks as if it were growing in the sea. Some of them, growing in hollows which do not dry at low tide, are never out of the water, but even so take no harm from the constant immersion of their roots. Some trees are as much as forty-five feet in height and were in blossom when Alexander saw them; the flower is rather like the white violet, but much more fragrant. The region also produces a sort of thistle with great strong spikes – sometimes, as the men rode by, the spikes would catch their clothes, and so tough were they that rather than break off they pulled the rider from his horse. It is said that passing horses get these thorns entangled in their fur; and indeed they used to be caught in this way, as birds are with lime or fish with hooks. The stem of this plant could be easily cut through; and when it was, it exuded juice, more in quantity and more pungent than that of early figs.

From there Alexander marched through Gedrosian territory. The route was a difficult one, and no supplies were to be had; worst of all, in many places there was not even water for the men. They were forced to cover great distances at night, going a long way inland, in spite of the fact that Alexander was anxious to work along the coast in order to see what possible anchorages there were and, so far as he could in the brief time at his disposal, to assist the fleet by digging wells, clearing spaces, and doing what could be done to provide shelter for the ships.

There was nothing of any kind to be had in the whole southern strip of Gedrosia, so he sent Thoas, son of Mandrodorus, down to the sea with a party of mounted troops to find out if there was any sort of shelter for ships thereabouts, or any fresh water near the coast, or anything else which might be of use to the fleet. Thoas brought back a report that he had found a few fishermen on the beach living in stifling huts built of shells and roofed with the backbones of fish; they made do with very little fresh water, getting what they could by scraping away the shingle, and even this little was brackish.

At last Alexander reached a part of Gedrosia where provisions were more or less plentiful. He had what he was able to obtain distributed among the baggage-trains, put his personal seal upon it, and gave orders that it should be taken down to the coast; but during the stage of his march which brought him nearest to the sea, the men, including the guards, in spite of the fact that the provisions were officially sealed, took them for their own purposes and shared them out among those of their fellows who were suffering most acutely from hunger. So

great was their distress that the future prospect of Alexander's anger
and the chance of punishment was, not unreasonably, of less concern
to them than the opportunity of averting the death which stared them
in the face. As it happened, Alexander pardoned them when he
realized the severity of the need which induced them to disobey his
orders.

To provision the troops who would be sailing with the fleet, Alexander by scouring the country got together what he could, and sent
Cretheus of Callatis to see to its safe delivery; the natives, too, were
ordered to bring to the coast from the inland districts as much ground
grain as they could, together with a supply of dates and sheep for the
army to purchase. Telephus, an officer of the Hetaeri, was sent to
another place with a small supply of flour.

The next objective was the capital town of Gedrosia, situated in a
district named Pura. The march thither from Oria occupied in all
sixty days. Most historians of Alexander's campaigns have stated that
the sufferings of his men on that march were out of all proportion
greater than anything they had had to endure in Asia. Alexander did
not choose that route because he was unaware of the difficulties it
would involve (Nearchus is our one authority for this); he chose it
because, apart from Semiramis on her retreat from India, no man, to
his knowledge, had ever before succeeded in bringing an army safely
through. Even Semiramis, according to local tradition, got through
with no more than twenty survivors, and Cyrus, son of Cambyses,
with only seven – for it is a fact that Cyrus came here with the intention of invading India, but found the going so bad and the country so
wild and barren that he lost nearly all his men before he could do so.
Alexander heard these old stories; they inspired him to go one better
than Cyrus and Semiramis, and that was the reason, combined with
the hope of being able to keep contact with the fleet and procure
supplies for it, why, according to Nearchus, he marched by that
route.

The result was disastrous: the blazing heat and the lack of water
caused innumerable casualties, especially among the animals, most of
which died of thirst or from the effects of the deep, burning, sun-
baked sand. Sometimes they met with lofty hills of sand – loose, deep
sand, into which they sank as if it were mud or untrodden snow;
sometimes, climbing or descending, the mules and horses suffered

even greater distress from the uneven and treacherous surface of the track. Not the least hardship was the varying length of the marches, as the fact that they never knew when they would find water made regular, normal marches impossible. It was not so bad when they found water in the morning after covering the requisite distance during the night; but when there was still further to go, and they found themselves plodding on and on as the day advanced, the double distress of heat and raging thirst was almost intolerable.

Casualties among the animals were very numerous; indeed, most of them perished. Often they were killed deliberately by the men, who used to put their heads together and agree to butcher the mules and horses, whenever supplies gave out, and then eat their flesh and pretend they had died of thirst or exhaustion. As every man was involved, and the general distress was so great, there was no one to bring actual evidence of this crime, though Alexander himself was not unaware of what was going on; he realized, however, that the only way to deal with the situation was to feign ignorance, which would be better than to let the men feel that he connived at their breach of discipline. It was, moreover, no easy task, when men were sick or fell exhausted in their tracks, to get them along with the rest; for there were no transport animals left and even the wagons were being continually broken up as it became more and more impossible to drag them through the deep sand. In the earlier stages of the march they had often been prevented for this reason from taking the shortest route and compelled to seek a longer one which was more practicable for the teams. So there was nothing for it but to leave the sick by the way, and any man rendered incapable by exhaustion or thirst or sunstroke. No one could give them a helping hand; no one could stay behind to ease their sufferings, for the essential thing was to get on with all possible speed, and the effort to save the army as a whole inevitably took precedence over the suffering of individual men. Most of the marching was at night, and many men would fall asleep in their tracks; the few who had strength left to do so followed the army when they woke up again, and got safe through; but the greater number perished – poor castaways in the ocean of sand.

There was yet another disaster, perhaps the worst for all concerned, men, horses, and mules. In Gedrosia, as in India, it rains heavily during the monsoon; the rain falls not on the plains but on the mountains, the summits of which arrest the clouds carried thither by the wind and cause them to condense in rain. It so happened that the army bivouacked by a small stream, for the sake of the water it afforded, and about the second watch of the night it was suddenly swollen by rain. The actual rain was falling far away out of sight, but the stream nevertheless grew into such a torrent that it drowned most of the camp-followers' women and children and swept away the royal tent with everything it contained, and all the surviving animals, while the troops themselves barely managed to escape, saving nothing but their weapons – and not even all of those. Another trouble was, that when plenty of water happened to be found after a hot and thirsty march, most of the men drank so immoderately that the result was fatal to them, and for this reason Alexander usually made his halts a couple of miles or so from water, to stop his men from flinging themselves indiscriminately upon it to their own destruction and that of their hearts, and to prevent those who had least self-control from plunging right into the spring or stream, or whatever it was, and so spoiling the water for the others.

At this point in my story I must not leave unrecorded one of the finest things Alexander ever did. Where it actually took place is uncertain: perhaps here, perhaps, as some historians have declared, in the country of the Parapamisidae some time previously. The army was crossing a desert of sand; the sun was already blazing down upon them, but they were struggling on under the necessity of reaching water, which was still far away. Alexander, like everyone else, was tormented by thirst, but he was none the less marching on foot at the head of his men. It was all he could do to keep going, but he did so, and the result (as always) was that the men were the better able to endure their misery when they saw that it was equally shared. As they toiled on, a party of light infantry which had gone off looking for water found some – just a wretched little trickle collected in a shallow gully. They scooped up what they could in a bladder and hurried back, with their priceless treasure, to Alexander; then, just before they reached him, they tipped the water into a helmet and gave it to him. Alexander, with a word of thanks for the gift, took the helmet and, in full view of his troops, poured the water on the ground. So extraordinary was the effect of this action that the water wasted by Alexander was as good as a drink for every man in the army. I cannot praise this act too highly; it was a proof, if anything was, not only of his power of endurance, but also of his genius for leadership.

To add to their difficulties, the time came when the guides admitted that they no longer knew the way; all the marks, they declared, had been obliterated by the blown and drifting sand. There was nothing in the vast and featureless desert to determine what course they should take – no trees, as elsewhere, by the roadside, no hills of solid earth rising from the sand. Moreover, the guides had never practised the art of finding their direction by the stars at night and by the sun in the day-time, as sailors do – the Phoenicians setting their course by the Little Bear, the rest of us by the Great Bear. Alexander, accordingly, took the matter into his own hands; feeling that the route should be more towards the left, he rode ahead with a small party of mounted men. The horses soon began to succumb to the heat, so he left most of his party behind and rode off with only five men. At last they found the sea, and scraping away the shingle on the beach came upon fresh, clear water. The whole army soon followed, and for seven days marched along the coast, getting its water from the beach. Finally the guides once more recognized their whereabouts, and a course was set for the interior again.

At the capital city of Gedrosia the troops were given a rest. Alexander, finding that Apollophanes, the governor, had failed to carry out any of his instructions, dismissed him and appointed Thoas in his place. Thoas subsequently died and was succeeded by Sibyrtius, who had recently been made governor of Carmania, where, on being given control of both Arachotia and Gedrosia, he was succeeded by Tlepolemus, son of Pythophanes.

Alexander was already on his way to Carmania when a report reached him of the death of Philip, governor of India: the mercenaries had hatched a plot to assassinate him, and his Macedonian guards had executed the assassins, some caught red-handed, others after subsequent arrest. Alexander accordingly sent written orders to Eudamus and Taxiles in India to take charge of the territory formerly administered by Philip until he sent out a new governor.

After his arrival in Carmania, he was rejoined by Craterus with the troops under his command, and the elephants. Craterus also brought Ordanes with him, under arrest for disaffection and trouble-making. A number of other officers and officials here presented themselves:

Stasanor, governor of Areia; the governor of Zarangia; Pharismanes, son of Phrataphernes, governor of Parthia and Hyrcania; and the officers left with Parmenio in command of the troops in Media, Cleander, Sitalces, and Heracon, with most of their men. Both the natives and the army had brought a number of charges against Sitalces and Cleander and their personal friends, alleging that they had plundered temples, disturbed ancient tombs, and committed other crimes of a violent and tyrannical nature against the people of the province. Immediately he received the report, Alexander had both officers executed, as an example to other government officials of whatever rank, who would thenceforth realize that if they were guilty of similar irregularities they would suffer the same punishment. If there was one thing more than another which conduced to orderliness and obedience among the numerous and widely separated peoples which found themselves, either by conquest or alliance, under Alexander's sway, it was this: that under his empire no sort of oppression by local government officials was ever permitted. The other officer, Heracon, was cleared for the time being; but soon afterwards some people at Susa had him convicted of robbing the temple there, and he, too, was executed.

Stasanor and Phrataphernes, on learning that Alexander was marching to Gedrosia, correctly foresaw the difficulties he would encounter in the desert, and had brought with them, in consequence, a number of draught-animals, including camels; their arrival was certainly fortunate, and the camels and mules were a most timely addition; in due proportion to their number Alexander distributed them among his forces – among the officers individually, and so many to each squadron, company, and platoon.

Certain writers have told the improbable story that Alexander made a progress through Carmania in a sort of double-sized chariot, specially constructed, in which he reclined with his intimate friends, listening to the music of flutes, while the troops accompanied him making merry as on holiday and with garlands on their heads, and that the people of the country, all along the route of the procession, had provided food and every imaginable luxury for their delectation. All this is supposed to have been Alexander's notion of imitating the Dionysiac Revels, or triumphal marches, in accordance with the legend that Dionysus, after his conquest of India, traversed the greater part of Asia with this sort of pomp and ceremony – *Thriambus* (or Triumph) was one of the titles of Dionysus, and the same word *thriambi* – triumphs – was used to describe his ceremonial processions after victories in war. There is no mention of this either in Ptolemy, son of Lagus, or in Aristobulus, or indeed in any other writer whom one might consider to give reliable evidence in such matters. In any case, there is the story; I do not believe it – and that is all I propose to say. I do, however, put on record (on Aristobulus' authority) that while he was in Carmania, Alexander offered sacrifice in gratitude to heaven for his conquest of India and the escape of his army from the desert of Gedrosia, and that he held a festival with public competitions in athletics and the arts. He promoted Peucestas to be a member of his personal guard – he had already decided to make him governor of Persia, but in view of the special service he had rendered in the battle with the Mallians, he wanted him to enjoy this mark of honour and confidence before taking over his governorship. Up to that time Alexander's personal guards were seven in number: Leonnatus son of Anteas, Hephaestion son of Amyntor, Lysimachus son of Agathocles, Aristonous son of Pisaeus (all four from Pella); Perdiccas son of Orontes, from Orestis; Ptolemy son of Lagus and Peitho son of Crateas from Eordaea. Now there was an eighth – Peucestas, the man who held his shield over Alexander's prostrate body.

Meanwhile Nearchus had completed his voyage along the coasts of the Orians, Gedrosians, and Ichthyophagi, and arrived at the inhabited parts of the Carmanian seaboard. From there he made his way inland with a few companions and gave Alexander his report of the ocean voyage. Alexander sent him back to the fleet with orders to continue his voyage as far as Susia and the mouths of the Tigris. I propose to give a detailed account of his voyage from the Indus to the mouth of the Tigris in the Persian Gulf in a separate volume, basing it on Nearchus' own story; this book, like the present one, will be a Greek history written in Alexander's honour. It will be a work for some future date, when I am in a proper mood, and the spirit moves me to embark upon it.

Alexander now ordered Hephaestion to proceed to Persia with the elephants, the baggage-train, and the greater part of the army. His instructions were to take the coastal route, because it was now winter and he would find in the coastal regions of Persia both warm weather and an abundance of supplies. At the same time he moved forward himself with the lightest infantry units, the mounted Hetaeri, and some regiments of archers, along the road to Pasargadae. Stasanor he sent home. Arrived at the Persian frontier, he found that Phrasaortes, the governor, had died while the Indian campaign was still going on; the reins of government were in the hands of Orxines, who had not, indeed, been regularly appointed, but considered himself, in the absence of any other governor, a proper person to serve Alexander by keeping Persian affairs running smoothly. At Pasargadae, Alexander was visited by Atropates, governor of Media; he brought with him a Mede named Baryaxes, whom he had arrested for wearing his cap upright in the royal fashion and proclaiming himself King of the Medes and Persians. With him, also under arrest, were his associates in the attempted *coup*. They were all executed.

Aristobulus relates that Alexander found the tomb of Cyrus, son of Cambyses, broken into and robbed, and that this act of profanation caused him much distress. The tomb was in the royal park at Pasargadae; a grove of various sorts of trees had been planted round it; there were streams of running water and a meadow with lush grass. The base of the monument was rectangular, built of stone slabs cut square, and on top was a roofed chamber, also built of stone, with access through a door so narrow that only one man at a time – and a little one at that – could manage, with great difficulty, painfully to squeeze himself through. Inside the chamber there was a golden coffin containing Cyrus' body, and a great divan with feet of hammered gold, spread with covers of some thick, brightly-coloured material, with a Babylonian rug on top. Tunics and a *candys* – or Median jacket – of Babylonian workmanship were laid out on the divan, and (Aristobulus says) Median trousers, various robes dyed in amethyst, purple, and many other colours, necklaces, scimitars, and inlaid earrings of gold and precious stones. A table stood by it, and in the middle of it lay the coffin which held Cyrus' body. Within the enclosure, by the way which led up to the tomb, a small building had been constructed for the Magi who guarded it, a duty which had been handed down from father to son ever since the time of Cyrus' son, Cambyses. They had a grant from the King of a sheep a day, with an allowance of meal and wine, and one horse a month to sacrifice to Cyrus. There was an inscription on the tomb in Persian, signifying: 'O man, I am Cyrus son of Cambyses, who founded the empire of Persia and ruled over Asia. Do not grudge me my monument.'

Alexander had always intended, after his conquest of Persia, to visit the tomb of Cyrus; and now, when he did so, he found that all it contained except the divan and the coffin had been removed. Even the royal remains had not escaped desecration, for the thieves had taken the lid from the coffin and thrown out the body; from the coffin itself they had chipped or broken various bits in an attempt to reduce its weight sufficiently to enable them to get it away. However, they were unsuccessful and went off without it.

Aristobulus tells us that he himself received orders from Alexander to put the monument into a state of thorough repair: he was to restore to the coffin what was still preserved of the body and replace the lid; to put right all damage to the coffin itself, fit the divan with new strapping, and to replace with exact replicas of the originals every single object with which it had previously been adorned; and, finally, to do away with the door into the chamber by building it in with stone, covered by a coat of plaster, on which was to be set the royal seal. Alexander had the Magi who guarded the monument arrested and put to the torture, hoping to extort from them the names of the culprits; but even under torture they were silent, neither confessing their own guilt nor accusing anybody else; so, as they could not be convicted of any sort of complicity in the crime, Alexander released them.

He then went to the palace of the Persian kings, which on a previous occasion he had set on fire, as I have already related. I remarked, when I mentioned this act, that I could not commend it, and Alexander himself regretted it when he saw the place for the second time.

As for Orxines, who took charge of Persian affairs after Phrasaortes' death, a number of damaging stories were told about him by the Persians, and he was convicted of robbing temples and royal tombs and of illegally putting many Persians to death. He was accordingly hanged by Alexander's agents. Peucestas, of Alexander's personal Guard, was appointed governor, in recognition of his exceptional loyalty on all occasions – and especially on the occasion of his heroic act during the fight with the Mallians, when at the risk of his own life he helped to save Alexander. Apart from this, he was also a suitable person for the post, as he liked Oriental ways. He showed this clearly enough immediately he was appointed, being the only Macedonian to adopt the Median dress; he also learned the Persian language, and in all other ways took to living as the Persians lived. Alexander thoroughly approved of this conduct, and the Persians themselves were gratified to find that he preferred their manner of life to that of his own country.

BOOK SEVEN

ON reaching Pasargadae and Persepolis, Alexander had a sudden impulse to sail down the Euphrates and Tigris into the Persian Gulf; he had already seen something of the mouths of the Indus and of the waters beyond them, and now he wished to do the same with the Tigris and Euphrates. We find in some writers the statement that he intended to sail right round Arabia, Ethiopia, and Libya, pressing forward past the Nomads beyond Mount Atlas to Gadeira, and so into the Mediterranean; thus, had he added Libya and Carthage to his conquests, he could with full justification have claimed the title of King of All Asia, unlike the Median and Persian kings, who, ruling as they did only a fraction of that continent, could not properly call themselves Great Kings at all. Some authorities say that he proposed subsequently to sail into the Black Sea and on to Scythian territory by the Sea of Azov; others, that he meant to make for Sicily and southern Italy to check the Romans, whose reputation, being greatly on the increase, was already causing him concern.

Personally I have no data from which to infer precisely what Alexander had in mind, and I do not care to make guesses; one thing, however, I feel I can say without fear of contradiction, and that is that his plans, whatever they were, had no lack of grandeur or ambition: he would never have remained idle in the enjoyment of any of his conquests, even had he extended his empire from Asia to Europe and from Europe to the British Isles. On the contrary, he would have continued to seek beyond them for unknown lands, as it was ever his nature, if he had no rival, to strive to better his own best.

I have always liked the story of the Indian sages, some of whom Alexander chanced to come upon out of doors in a meadow, where they used to meet to discuss philosophy. On the appearance of Alexander and his army, these venerable men stamped with their feet and gave no other sign of interest. Alexander asked them through interpreters what they meant by this odd behaviour, and they replied: 'King Alexander, every man can possess only so much of the earth's surface as this we are standing on. You are but human like the rest of us, save that you are always busy and up to no good, travelling so many miles from your home, a nuisance to yourself and to others. Ah well! You will soon be dead, and then you will own just as much of this earth as will suffice to bury you.' Alexander expressed his approval of these sage words; but in point of fact his conduct was always the exact opposite of what he then professed to admire. On another occasion he is said to have expressed surprise at a remark made by Diogenes of Sinope: he was marching somewhere in the Isthmus with a contingent of Longshields and footguards, and chancing to see Diogenes lying in the sun, he stopped and asked him if there was anything he wanted.

'Nothing,' replied the philosopher; 'though I should be grateful if you and your friends would move to one side, and not keep the sun off me.'

One must admit, then, that Alexander was not wholly a stranger to the loftier flights of philosophy; but the fact remains that he was, to an extraordinary degree, the slave of ambition. In Taxila, once, he met some members of the Indian sect of Wise Men whose practice it is to go naked, and he so much admired their powers of endurance that the fancy took him to have one of them in his personal train. The oldest man among them, whose name was Dandamis (the others were his pupils), refused either to join Alexander himself or to permit any of his pupils to do so. 'If you, my lord,' he is said to have replied, 'are the son of God, why – so am I. I want nothing from you, for what I have suffices. I perceive, moreover, that the men you lead get no good from their world-wide wandering over land and sea, and that of their many journeyings there will be no end. I desire nothing that you can give me; I fear no exclusion from any blessings which may perhaps be yours. India, with the fruits of her soil in due season, is enough for me while I live; and when I die, I shall be rid of my poor body – my unseemly housemate.' These words convinced Alexander that Dandamis was, in a true sense, a free man; so he made no attempt to compel him. On the other hand, another of these Indian teachers, a man named Calanus, did yield to Alexander's persuasion; this man, according to Megasthenes' account, was declared by his fellow teachers to be a slave to fleshly lusts, an accusation due, no doubt, to the fact that he chose to renounce the bliss of their own asceticism and to serve another master instead of God.

I have mentioned this because no history of Alexander would be

complete without the story of Calanus. In India Calanus had never
been ill, but when he was living in Persia all strength ultimately left
his body. In spite of his enfeebled state he refused to submit to an in-
valid regimen, and told Alexander that he was content to die as he
was, which would be preferable to enduring the misery of being
forced to alter his way of life. Alexander, at some length, tried to talk
him out of his obstinacy, but to no purpose; then, convinced that if
he were any further opposed he would find one means or another of
making away with himself, he yielded to his request, and gave instructions for the building of a funeral pyre under the supervision of
Ptolemy son of Lagus, of the Personal Guard. Some say Calanus was
escorted to the pyre by a solemn procession – horses, men, soldiers in
armour, and people carrying all kinds of precious oils and spices to
throw upon the flames; other accounts mention drinking-cups of
silver and gold and kingly robes. He was too ill to walk, and a horse
was provided for him; but he was incapable of mounting it, and had
to be carried on a litter, upon which he lay with his head wreathed
with garlands in the Indian fashion, and singing Indian songs, which
his countrymen declare were hymns of praise to their gods. The horse
he was to have ridden was of the royal breed of Nysa, and before he
mounted the pyre he gave it to Lysimachus, one of his pupils in
philosophy, and distributed among other pupils and friends the drinking-cups and draperies which Alexander had ordered to be burnt in
his honour upon the pyre.

At last he mounted the pyre and with due ceremony laid himself
down. All the troops were watching. Alexander could not but feel that
there was a sort of indelicacy in witnessing such a spectacle – the man,
after all, had been his friend; everyone else, however, felt nothing but
astonishment to see Calanus give not the smallest sign of shrinking
from the flames. We read in Nearchus' account of this incident that at
the moment the fire was kindled there was, by Alexander's orders, an
impressive salute: the bugles sounded, the troops with one accord
roared out their battle-cry, and the elephants joined in with their shrill
war-trumpetings.

This story and others to a similar effect have been recorded by good
authorities; they are not without value to anyone who cares for evidence of the unconquerable resolution of the human spirit in carrying
a chosen course of action through to the end.

About this time Alexander sent out Atropates to his province. He had himself gone on to Susa, where he had Abulites arrested and put to death for abusing his office as governor. Abulites' son Oxathres shared the same fate. In the various countries subdued by Alexander there had been a great many irregularities on the part of government officials, acts of violence against individuals, and robbing of temples and tombs. The reason is not far to seek, for Alexander had been away for a very long time in India, and nobody really felt he was ever likely to return from the innumerable hostile nations of the East – not to mention the elephants! – but would find a grave somewhere beyond the Indus, Hydaspes, Acesines, and Hyphasis. Again, the disasters in the Gedrosian desert were a further encouragement to the governors of these more westerly parts to shrug off the idea of his ever getting safely home. None the less, it must be admitted that, by all accounts, Alexander at this period had become readier to accept as wholly reliable the charges which were made to him against officials, and to inflict severe punishment even for minor offences, in the belief that the sort of attitude which allowed an official to commit some petty irregularity might also lead him to serious crime.

Here at Susa he held wedding ceremonies for the high officers of the Hetaeri; he also took a wife himself – Barsine, Darius' eldest daughter, and, according to Aristobulus, another as well, namely Parysatis, the youngest daughter of Ochus. He had already married Roxane, daughter of Oxyartes of Bactria. To Hephaestion he gave Drypetis, another of Darius' daughters and sister of his own wife Barsine, as he wanted to be uncle to Hephaestion's children; to Craterus he gave Amastrine, daughter of Darius' brother Oxyartes, and to Perdiccas a daughter of Atropates, governor of Media. The bride of Ptolemy (of the Guard) was Artacama, daughter of Artabazus, and Eumenes, the King's secretary, had her sister Artonis; Nearchus was given the daughter of Barsine, and Mentor, Seleucus, the daughter of Spitamenes of Bactria. Similarly, the other officers – to the number of eighty all told – were given as brides young women of the noblest Persian and Median blood. The marriage ceremonies were in the Persian fashion: chairs were set for the bridegrooms in order of precedence, and when healths had been drunk the brides entered and sat down by their bridegrooms, who took them by the hand and kissed them. The King, who was married just as the others were, and in the same place, was the first to perform the ceremony – Alexander was always capable of putting himself on a footing of equality and comradeship with his subordinates, and everyone felt that this act of his was the best proof of his ability to do so. After the ceremony all the men took their wives home, and for every one of them Alexander provided a dowry. There proved to be over 10,000 other Macedonians who had married Asian women; Alexander had them all registered, and every man of them received a wedding gift.

This also seemed a fitting occasion to clear off the men's debts, and Alexander ordered a detailed schedule to be prepared, with a promise of settlement. At first only a few entered their names, suspecting that the order might be a scheme of Alexander's for detecting the spendthrifts who had failed to make do with their army pay. Alexander was annoyed when he learned that most of the men were refusing to enter their names and concealing their possession of covenants to pay, and told them in no uncertain terms what he thought of their suspicions; a King, he declared, is in duty bound to speak nothing but the truth to his subjects, who, in their turn, have no right to suppose that he ever does otherwise. He had tables set up in the army quarters, with money on them, and instructed the clerks in charge to pay off the debts of every man who produced an I.O.U. without even registering their names. After that the troops could not but believe in Alexander's good faith, and they were even more grateful for the concealment of their names than for having their debts payed. This gift to his men is said to have amounted to 20,000 talents – over £4,000,000.

He also made a number of other money awards for distinguished conduct in the field, or in recognition of a man's reputation for good service generally. A special decoration consisting of a gold crown was granted to certain officers for conspicuous bravery: the recipients were Peucestas – for saving the King's life; Leonnatus – also for saving the King's life, for hard service in India, for his victory in Oria, for facing and defeating in battle, with the forces left under his command, the rebellious Oreitae and their neighbours, and his satisfactory settlement of affairs in general in Oria; Nearchus (now also arrived at Susa) for his voyage from India along the coasts of the Indian ocean; Onesicritus, master of the royal galley; and, finally, Hephaestion and the other members of the Personal Guard.

Here in Susa, Alexander received the various officials in charge of

affairs in the newly built towns and the governors of the territories he
had previously overrun. They brought with them some 30,000 young
fellows, all boys of the same age, all wearing the Macedonian battle-
dress and trained on Macedonian lines. Alexander called them his
Epigoni – 'inheritors' – and it is said that their coming caused much
bad feeling among the Macedonians, who felt it was an indication of
his many efforts to lessen his dependence for the future upon his own
countrymen. Already the sight of Alexander in Median clothes had
caused them no little distress, and most of them had found the Persian
marriage ceremonies by no means to their taste – even some of the
actual participants had objected to the foreign form of the ceremony,
in spite of the fact that they were highly honoured by being, for the
occasion, on a footing of equality with the King. They resented, too,
the growing orientalism of Peucestas, Governor of Persia, who, to
Alexander's evident satisfaction, had adopted the Persian language and
dress, just as they resented the inclusion of foreign mounted troops
in the regiments of the Hetaeri: Bactrians, Sogdians, Arachotians;
Zarangians, Areians, Parthians, and the so-called Euacae from Persia
were all introduced into the crack Macedonian cavalry regiments,
provided they had some outstanding personal recommendation, such
as good looks, or whatever it might be. Besides this, a fifth mounted
regiment was formed; it did not consist entirely of oriental troops, but
formed an addition to the total cavalry strength and had a certain
number of foreign troops posted to it. Foreign officers were also
posted to the Guard – Cophen son of Artabazus, Hydarnes and Arti-
boles sons of Mazaeus, Sisines and Phradasmenes sons of Phrataphernes, the satrap of Parthia and Hyrcania, Histanes son of Oxyartes
and brother of Alexander's wife Roxane, Autobares and his brother
Mithrobaeus. The command was given to Hystaspes, a Bactrian, and
the orientals were all equipped with the Macedonian spear in place of
their native javelin. All this was a cause of deep resentment to the
Macedonians, who could not but feel that Alexander's whole outlook
was becoming tainted with orientalism, and that he no longer cared a
rap for his own people or his own native ways.

Hephaestion now received orders to move down to the Persian
Gulf with more than half the total number of infantry divisions. The
fleet had already come up the Gulf to the territory near Susa, and
Alexander embarked for a voyage down the Eulaeus to the sea. He

took with him the Longshields, the Guard, and a few squadrons of the mounted Hetaeri. He left most of his ships, including all which were in need of repair, just inside the mouth of the river, and went on with the fastest he had along the sea-coast from the Eulaeus to the mouths of the Tigris; the rest of the fleet returned up the Eulaeus to the canal which joins it with the Tigris, and passed through.

The Tigris and Euphrates, as everybody knows, enclose a portion of Syria called, for that reason, Mesopotamia by the people who live there. The Tigris flows through much lower-lying country than the Euphrates; it receives the water from a number of cuts from the Euphrates and also from many tributary streams, and consequently increases in volume until, by the time it reaches the Persian Gulf, none of its water having been drawn off for purposes of irrigation, it is a river of considerable size and at no point fordable. The river, indeed, cannot be used for irrigation of the surrounding country at all; for such cuts or canals as there are, connecting it with other rivers, flow into, not from it, as the land on both banks is above the level of the stream. The Euphrates, on the contrary, runs through higher country, and throughout its course flows flush and full; consequently at many points the water is led off through cuttings, some of them permanent and a regular source of supply to the natives on either side; others are dug to provide water for the land during a temporary shortage. There is little rain in this part of the world, so this is a necessary procedure. For these reasons the Euphrates becomes, near its mouth, a more or less shallow swamp.

Alexander sailed offshore along the stretch of coast between the Eulaeus and the Tigris, and then proceeded up the Tigris to the place where Hephaestion and the whole army were encamped. From there he went further up the river to Opis, a town on its bank. During the passage up-stream he had the weirs demolished, thus restoring the river to the same continuous level throughout; the weirs had been constructed by the Persians to prevent a victorious naval force from coming up the river to invade their country – a remarkable piece of engineering for a non-maritime people. Their existence, at frequent intervals, made the passage up-river a very awkward business. Alexander declared that no power which enjoyed military supremacy would ever bother with such contrivances; in his own case a safeguard of that sort was pointless and irrelevant; and indeed, the very ease with which he destroyed these works which the Persians had laboured so hard to complete was sufficient proof that they were not worth much.

At Opis he summoned an assembly of his Macedonian troops and announced the discharge from the army of all men unfit through age or disablement for further service; these he proposed to send home, and promised to give them on their departure enough to make their friends and relatives envy them and to fire their countrymen with eagerness to play a part in similar perilous adventures in the future. Doubtless he meant to gratify them by what he said.

Unfortunately, however, the men already felt that he had come to undervalue their services and to think them quite useless as a fighting force; so, naturally enough, they resented his remarks as merely another instance of the many things which, throughout the campaign, he had done to hurt their feelings, such as his adoption of Persian dress, the issue of Macedonian equipment to the Oriental 'Epigoni', and the inclusion of foreign troops in units of the mounted Hetaeri. The result was that they did not receive the speech in respectful silence, but, unable to restrain themselves, called for the discharge of every man in the army, adding, in bitter jest, that on his next campaign he could take his father with him – meaning, presumably, the god Ammon.

Alexander was furious. He had grown by that time quicker to take offence, and the Oriental subservience to which he had become accustomed had greatly changed his old open-hearted manner towards his own countrymen. He leapt from the platform with the officers who attended him, and pointing with his finger to the ringleaders of the mutiny, ordered the guards to arrest them. There were thirteen of them, and they were all marched off to execution. A horrified silence ensued, and Alexander stepped once again on to the rostrum and addressed his troops in these words: 'My countrymen, you are sick for home – so be it! I shall make no attempt to check your longing to return. Go whither you will; I shall not hinder you. But, if go you must, there is one thing I would have you understand – what I have done for you, and in what coin you will have repaid me.

'First I will speak of my father Philip, as it is my duty to do. Philip found you a tribe of impoverished vagabonds, most of you dressed in skins, feeding a few sheep on the hills and fighting, feebly enough, to keep them from your neighbours – Thracians and Triballians and Illyrians. He gave you cloaks to wear instead of skins; he brought you down from the hills into the plains; he taught you to fight on equal terms with the enemy on your borders, till you knew that your safety lay not, as once, in your mountain strongholds, but in your own valour. He made you city-dwellers; he brought you law; he civilized you. He rescued you from subjection and slavery, and made you masters of the wild tribes who harried and plundered you; he annexed the greater part of Thrace, and by seizing the best places on the coast opened your country to trade, and enabled you to work your mines without fear of attack. Thessaly, so long your bugbear and your dread, he subjected to your rule, and by humbling the Phocians he made the narrow and difficult path into Greece a broad and easy road. The men of Athens and Thebes, who for years had kept watching for their moment to strike us down, he brought so low – and by this time I myself was working at my father's side – that they who once exacted from us either our money or our obedience, now, in their turn, looked to us as the means of their salvation. Passing into the Peloponnese, he settled everything there to his satisfaction, and when he was made supreme commander of all the rest of Greece for the war against Persia, he claimed the glory of it not for himself alone, but for the Macedonian people.

'These services which my father rendered you are, indeed, intrinsically great; yet they are small compared with my own. I inherited from him a handful of gold and silver cups, coin in the treasury worth less than sixty talents and eight times that amount of debts incurred by him; yet to add to this burden I borrowed a further sum of eight hundred talents, and, marching out from a country too poor to maintain you decently, laid open for you at a blow, and in spite of Persia's naval supremacy, the gates of the Hellespont. My cavalry crushed the satraps of Darius, and I added all Ionia and Aeolia, the two Phrygias and Lydia to your empire. Miletus I reduced by siege; the other towns all yielded of their own free will – I took them and gave them you for your profit and enjoyment. The wealth of Egypt and Cyrene, which I shed no blood to win, now flows into your hands; Palestine and the plains of Syria and the Land between the Rivers are now your property; Babylon and Bactria and Susa are yours; you are masters of the gold of Lydia, the treasures of Persia, the wealth of

India – yes, and of the sea beyond India, too. You are my captains, my generals, my governors of provinces.

'From all this which I have laboured to win for you, what is left for myself except the purple and this crown? I keep nothing for my own; no one can point to treasure of mine apart from all this which you yourselves either possess, or have in safe keeping for your future use. Indeed, what reason have I to keep anything, as I eat the same food and take the same sleep as you do? Ah, but there are epicures among you who, I fancy, eat more luxuriously than I; and this I know, that I wake earlier than you – and watch, that you may sleep.

'Perhaps you will say that, in my position as your commander, I had none of the labours and distress which you had to endure to win for me what I have won. But does any man among you honestly feel that he has suffered more for me than I have suffered for him? Come now – if you are wounded, strip and show your wounds, and I will show mine. There is no part of my body but my back which has not a scar; not a weapon a man may grasp or fling the mark of which I do not carry upon me. I have sword-cuts from close fight; arrows have pierced me, missiles from catapults bruised my flesh; again and again I have been struck by stones or clubs – and all for your sakes: for your glory and your gain. Over every land and sea, across river, mountain, and plain I led you to the world's end, a victorious army. I married as you married, and many of you will have children related by blood to my own. Some of you have owed money – I have paid your debts, never troubling to inquire how they were incurred, and in spite of the fact that you earn good pay and grow rich from the sack of cities. To most of you I have given a circlet of gold as a memorial for ever and ever of your courage and of my regard. And what of those who have died in battle? Their death was noble, their burial illustrious; almost all are commemorated at home by statues of bronze; their parents are held in honour, with all dues of money or service remitted; for under my leadership not a man among you has ever fallen with his back to the enemy.

'And now it was in my mind to dismiss any man no longer fit for active service – all such should return home to be envied and admired. But you all wish to leave me. Go then! And when you reach home, tell them that Alexander your King, who vanquished Persians and Medes and Bactrians and Sacae; who crushed the Uxii, the Arachotians, and the Drangae, and added to his empire Parthia, the Choras-mian waste, and Hyrcania to the Caspian Sea; who crossed the Cau-casus beyond the Caspian Gates, and Oxus and Tanais and the Indian Stream, which none but Dionysus had crossed before him, and Hydaspes and Acesines and Hydraotes – yes, and Hyphasis too, had you not feared to follow; who by both mouths of the Indus burst into the Great Sea beyond, and traversed the desert of Gadrosia, untrodden before by any army; who made Carmania his own, as his troops swept by, and the country of the Oreitans; who was brought back by you to Susa, when his ships had sailed the ocean from India to Persia – tell them, I say, that you deserted him and left him to the mercy of bar-barian men, whom you yourselves had conquered. Such news will indeed assure you praise upon earth and reward in heaven. Out of my sight!'

As he ended, Alexander sprang from the rostrum and hurried into the palace. All that day he neither ate nor washed nor permitted any of his friends to see him. On the following day too he remained closely confined. On the third day he sent for the Persian officers who were in the highest favour and divided among them the command of the various units of the army. Only those who were related to him by blood were now permitted to give him the customary kiss.

On the Macedonians the immediate effect of Alexander's speech was profound. They stood in silence in front of the rostrum. Nobody made a move to follow the King except his closest attendants and the members of his personal guard; the rest, helpless to speak or act, yet unwilling to go away, remained rooted to the spot. But when they were told about the Persians and Medes – how command was being given to Persian officers, foreign troops drafted into Macedonian units, a Persian Corps of Guards called by a Macedonian name, Per-sian and other infantry units given the coveted title of Hetaeri, Per-sian Silver Shields and Persian mounted Hetaeri, including even a new Royal Squadron, in process of formation – they could contain them-selves no longer. Every man of them hurried to the palace; in sign of supplication they flung their arms on the ground before the doors and stood there calling and begging for admission. They offered to give up the ringleaders of the mutiny and those who had led the cry against the King, and swore they would not stir from the spot day or night unless Alexander took pity on them.

Alexander, the moment he heard of this change of heart, hastened out to meet them, and he was so touched by their grovelling repentance and their bitter lamentations that the tears came into his eyes. While they continued to beg for his pity, he stepped forward as if to speak, but was anticipated by one Callines, an officer of the mounted Hetaeri, distinguished both by age and rank. 'My lord,' he cried, 'what hurts us is that you have made Persians your kinsmen – Persians are called "Alexander's kinsmen" – Persians kiss you. But no Macedonian has yet had a taste of this honour.'

'Every man of you,' Alexander replied, 'I regard as my kinsman, and from now on that is what I shall call you.'

Thereupon Callines came up to him and kissed him, and all the others who wished to do so kissed him too. Then they picked up their weapons and returned to their quarters singing the song of victory at the top of their voices.

To mark the restoration of harmony, Alexander offered sacrifice to the gods he was accustomed to honour, and gave a public banquet which he himself attended, sitting among the Macedonians, all of whom were present. Next them the Persians had their places, and next to the Persians distinguished foreigners of other nations; Alexander and his friends dipped their wine from the same bowl and poured the same libations, following the lead of the Greek seers and the Magi. The chief object of his prayers was that Persians and Macedonians might rule together in harmony as an imperial power. It is said that 9,000 people attended the banquet; they unanimously drank the same toast, and followed it by the paean of victory.

After this all Macedonians – about 10,000 all told – who were too old for service or in any way unfit, got their discharge at their own request. They were given their pay not only up to date, but also for the time they would take on the homeward journey. In addition to their pay they each received a gratuity of one talent – £140. Some of the men had children by Asian women, and it was Alexander's orders that these should be left behind to avoid the trouble among their families at home, which might be caused by the introduction of foreign women and half-caste children; he promised to have them brought up on Macedonian lines, with particular attention to their military training, and added that when they grew up he would himself bring them back to Macedonia and hand them over to their fathers. It was a somewhat vague and unsatisfactory promise; he did, however, give the clearest proof of how warmly he felt for them, and of how much he would miss them when they had gone, by his decision to entrust them on their journey to the leadership and protection of Craterus, the most loyal of his officers and a man he loved as dearly as his own life. When he said good-bye to them, his eyes and the eyes of every man among them were wet with tears.

Craterus' instructions were to take them home and, on arrival there, to assume control of Macedonia, Thrace, and Thessaly and assure the freedom of Greece. Antipater received orders to bring out fresh drafts to replace the men sent home; Polysperchon was sent with Craterus as his second in command – Craterus was in poor health, and thus Alexander ensured that if anything happened to him during the journey the men should have someone to take charge of them.

There was always plausible and malicious people ready to start whispering campaigns about Court secrets – and the more secret the better they like it – and to put the worst possible interpretation upon what appear to most of us perfectly straightforward actions. So it was in this matter of Alexander and Antipater. The rumour was, that Alexander was beginning to be influenced by his mother's calumnious statements about Antipater, and for that reason wished to get him out of the country. It may well be, however, that his recall was in no way meant to discredit him, but was merely to prevent the quarrel between him and Olympias from reaching a point beyond Alexander's power to heal. Both of them were constantly writing to Alexander; Antipater's letters were full of the Queen's violent temper and her determination (most unsuitable for Alexander's mother) to have a finger in every pie – indeed, the stories of her behaviour gave rise to a much-quoted remark of Alexander's, to the effect that she was charging him a high price for his nine months' lodging in her womb. Olympias, for her part, continually complained that Antipater's position and the respect to which it entitled him made him insufferably arrogant; he no longer remembered, she wrote, who had put him where he was, but claimed absolute pre-eminence among his fellow countrymen and the rest of Greece. It cannot be denied that the stories which tended to blacken Antipater's good name did seem to gain more and more influence over Alexander, for such things would naturally alarm anyone in his position; nevertheless we hear of nothing he either did or said, which would serve as ground for the conclusion that he did not continue to regard Antipater as highly as ever.★

... Eumenes was ready for a reconciliation, and this argument was enough to induce Hephaestion, though against his will, to make up the quarrel.

It was in the course of this journey that Alexander is said to have seen the plain called the plain of Nysa where the royal mares were pastured. Herodotus tells us that the mares were always known as Nysaean. There were once about 150,000 of them, but when Alexander saw them there were not more than 50,000, as most of them had been stolen.

There is a story that while Alexander was there, Atropates, the governor of Media, sent him a hundred women, who he declared were Amazons. They were equipped like cavalrymen, but carried axes instead of spears and light targes instead of the ordinary cavalry shield. According to some writers, their right breasts were smaller than their left, and were bared in battle. Alexander sent the women away to avoid trouble; for they might well have met with unseemly treatment from the troops, Macedonian or foreign. However, he told them to inform their Queen that he would visit her one day and get her with child. This story is not to be found in Aristobulus or Ptolemy, or, indeed, in any other reliable writer; personally I doubt if the Amazons still existed at that date – indeed Xenophon, writing before Alexander's time, never mentions them, though he has references to Phasians and Colchians and other barbarian peoples which the Greeks encountered on either side of Trapezus, where they would have certainly found Amazons had there still been any. I cannot, however, bring myself to believe that this race of women, whose praises have been sung so often by the most reputable writers, never existed at all: there is the tradition, for instance, that Heracles was sent to them and brought back to Greece a girdle belonging to their Queen Hippolyta; and that Theseus and his Athenians were the first to defeat them in battle and prevent their invasion of Europe. There is a picture, too, by Cimon of the battle between the Amazons and the Athenians, just as there is of the battle between the Athenians and Persians. Herodotus, moreover, has frequently referred to these

★ A page has been lost here.

women, and all Athenians who have pronounced eulogies on those who fell in war have made particular mention of the fight with the Amazons. If Atropates really did present some female cavalry troopers to Alexander, I should imagine they must have been women, of some nationality or other, who had been taught to ride and equipped in the traditional Amazon style.

At Ecbatana, Alexander offered sacrifice, as it was his custom to do to celebrate a happy occasion. He also held a festival with literary and athletic contests, and drank deep with his closest friends. About this time Hephaestion fell sick. On the seventh day of his illness it so happened that there was a big crowd at the stadium to watch the boys' races, which were then taking place. During the races a message was brought to Alexander that Hephaestion's condition was serious; he hurried away, but his friend was dead before he could reach him.

The accounts of Alexander's grief at this loss are many and various. All writers have agreed that it was great, but personal prejudice, for or against both Hephaestion and Alexander himself, has coloured the accounts of how he expressed it. Many writers have told us of things which were beyond all bounds of propriety; those friendly to him apparently wishing us to believe that whatever he said or did in his grief for this friend whom he loved better than all the world, could but enhance his glory; his critics, on the other hand, indicating that such excesses were discreditable, and unfitting not only for a great potentate like Alexander, but for any King. We are told, for instance, that he flung himself on the body of his friend and lay there nearly all day long in tears, and refused to be parted from him until he was dragged away by force; and again, that he lay stretched upon the corpse all day and the whole night too. Some have said that he had Glaucias, the doctor, hanged for giving the wrong medicine; others, because he had seen Hephaestion drinking too much and had made no attempt to stop him. I do not, however, think it unlikely that Alexander cut his hair short in mourning for his friend, for he might well have done so, if only in emulation of Achilles, whose rival he had always felt himself to be, ever since he was a boy. Then there is the story – to me quite incredible – that he personally drove for a short distance the funeral carriage with Hephaestion's body in it; and, again, that he ordered the shrine of Asclepius in Ecbatana to be razed to the ground – a thing one might have expected from an Oriental despot, but utterly uncharacteristic of Alexander. Indeed, it reminds one of the absurd story of Xerxes, who, with his reckless disregard of what men hold sacred, 'punished' the Hellespont by pretending to bind it with chains. Another story, to me a not wholly improbable one, is that on the road to Babylon Alexander was met by a number of deputations from Greece, with some representatives from Epidaurus among them. Alexander granted the Epidaurians' requests, and gave them something to take home and dedicate as an offering to Asclepius in his shrine. 'And yet,' he said, 'Asclepius has not treated me kindly; for he did not save the friend I valued as my own life.'

Most authorities have said that he ordered sacrifice to be always offered to Hephaestion as a demi-god, and some declare that he sent to inquire of Ammon if he would permit sacrifice to be offered to him as a god; but Ammon refused.

All the accounts, however, agree in telling us that for two whole days after Hephaestion's death Alexander tasted no food and paid no attention in any way to his bodily needs, but lay on his bed now crying lamentably, now in the silence of grief. He had a funeral pyre prepared in Babylon at a cost of 10,000 talents – or more, if we can believe some accounts – and ordained a period of mourning throughout the East. Many of the Hetaeri, out of respect for Alexander, dedicated themselves and their arms to the dead man, a gesture initiated by Eumenes, who, as I mentioned just now, had quarrelled with him. His object, no doubt, was to prevent Alexander from thinking that he was glad to have him gone. Alexander made no fresh appointment to the command of the mounted Hetaeri; he wished Hephaestion's name to be preserved always in connexion with it, so Hephaestion's Brigade it continued to be called, and Hephaestion's image continued to be carried before it. Alexander held Funeral Games in his honour, with contests in literature and athletics; the festival was far more splendid than ever before both in the number of competitors and in the money spent upon it. In all, 3,000 men competed in the various events – and these same men took part soon afterwards in the Games at Alexander's own funeral.

Alexander's distress was long drawn out; but at last he began to get over it, and the proffered consolation of his friends to have more effect. Once he was himself again, he undertook an expedition against the Cossaeans. These people, neighbours of the Uxians, were a war-like tribe of mountaineers, living in village strongholds high in the hills; on the approach of an enemy, their practice was to abandon their positions, either all together or in small parties as occasion offered, and slip away, thus frustrating any attempt by an organized force to get at them; then, when the enemy was gone, they would return to their normal life of brigandage. Alexander, however, destroyed them. It was winter when he made his raid, but Alexander was never held up by either bad weather or bad country – and the same may be said of Ptolemy son of Lagus, who was in command of part of the army on this expedition. Alexander, indeed, once he was embarked upon any of his enterprises, never found anything to stop him from carrying it through.

On the way back to Babylon he was met by representatives from Libya, who with congratulatory speeches offered him a crown in recognition of his sovereignty over Asia; Bruttian, Leucanian, and Tyrrhenian envoys also arrived on the same mission from Italy. It is said that Carthage, too, sent a delegation at that time, and that others came from the Ethiopians and European Scythians – not to mention Celts and Iberians – all to ask for Alexander's friendship. It was the first time that Greeks and Macedonians had ever heard the names of these peoples or set eyes upon their unfamiliar dress and equipment. We are told that they even appealed to Alexander to arbitrate in their domestic quarrels, with the result that then, if ever, both he and his friends felt that he was indeed master of the world. Two of the writers on Alexander's career, Aristus and Asclepiades, declare that Rome sent him a delegation, and that when he met the delegates and observed the proud freedom of their bearing, their obvious devotion to duty and order, and had learned the nature of their political principles, he prophesied something, at least, of the future greatness of their country. I record the story, which may or may not be true; but the fact remains that no Roman has ever made any reference to this delegation, any more than the two writers on Alexander who are my principal authorities, Aristobulus and Ptolemy son of Lagus. Moreover, it would have been out of character for the republican Romans who enjoyed at that date entirely free institutions, to send a delegation to a foreign King, especially at such a distance from their own country, when they had nothing either to fear or to gain from him, and were of all people in the world the most violently averse to Kings, the very word being anathema to them.

After these events Alexander sent Heracleides, son of Argaeus, with a party of shipwrights to Hyrcania with orders to fell timber in the hills and build warships, some decked, some undecked, on the Greek model. The reason for this order was the fancy which had taken him to extend his geographical knowledge by the exploration of the Caspian (or Hyrcanian) Sea; he wished to determine what other sea it was connected with – whether it joined the Black Sea, or whether it was merely a gulf of the great Indian Ocean to the eastward. The Persian – or Red Sea, as it is sometimes called – he had proved to be a gulf of the ocean, and it might, he thought, turn out to be the same with the Caspian. The limits – or origins – of the Caspian had never yet been discovered, in spite of the fact that its shores are inhabited by a considerable number of peoples and navigable rivers flow into it: from Bactria, for instance, the Oxus, the greatest river of Asia outside India, runs into it, and also the Jaxartes after following its course through Scythia, and, as is generally supposed, the Araxes after passing through Armenia. Apart from these three great rivers, there are also many tributaries which join them, and thus discharge their waters, too, into the Caspian; some of these were discovered by Alexander's armies, others, of course, are far to the north in the wholly unknown country of the Nomad Scythians.

On his march to Babylon, Alexander, after crossing the Tigris, was met by some Wise Men of the Chaldaeans, who drew him aside and begged him to go no further, because their god Bel had foretold that if he entered the city at that time it would prove fatal to him. Alexander replied by quoting to them the line of Euripides:

'Prophets are best who make the truest guess.'

'My lord,' said the Chaldaeans, 'look not to the West; do not march westward with your army; but turn about and go eastward.' But this was not easy for Alexander to do, as the country to the east was impracticable for troops. The truth was that fate was leading him to the spot where it was already written that he should die.

Who knows? Perhaps it was better for him to make his end while his fame was unimpaired and the world most grieved for his loss, and before he was overtaken by the ill fortune which, at one time or another, is the lot of all men. That, doubtless, was why Solon advised

Croesus to 'look to the end' of a life, however long, and never to say
that a man is happy till that end had come. Even in Alexander's case,
Hephaestion's death had been no small calamity, and I believe he
would rather have been the first to go than live to suffer that pain,
like Achilles, who surely would rather have died before Patrochus
than have lived to avenge his death.

Alexander had some suspicion that the Chaldaeans' attempt to prevent him from marching to Babylon on that occasion was not, in fact,
based upon a prophecy of impending disaster at all; on the contrary,
its object, he felt, might well be to secure their own advantage. In
Babylon stood the great temple of Bel, a huge edifice of baked bricks,
set in bitumen. Like the other shrines in the city, it had been destroyed
by Xerxes on his return from Greece, and Alexander had proposed to
restore it. According to some accounts, he intended to rebuild upon
the original foundations, and for that reason the Babylonians had had
instructions to clear the site. Others say he intended a still larger building than the old one. The workmen, however, once he was out of the
way, dawdled over their job, so he proposed to set all his own troops
to work upon it. Now a great deal of land and considerable treasure
had been devoted by the Assyrian kings to the god Bel, and from this
the temple, in the old days, used to be maintained and the sacrifices
offered to the god. But at the time of which I am speaking the Chaldaeans themselves had the disposal of the god's property, as there was
nothing upon which the income could be spent. For these reasons it
had occurred to Alexander that they might not want him to enter the
city, lest the rebuilding of the temple might be rapidly completed
and they, in consequence, lose the benefit of the money. Nevertheless,
Aristobulus tells us that Alexander, so far as changing his direction was
concerned, was ready to yield to their wishes; on the first day he
halted his men on the Euphrates, and on the next advanced, keeping
the river on his right hand, with the intention of first passing the
western section of the city and then wheeling to the eastward. But it
turned out that by this route the going was too bad for the army to get
through, as anyone approaching the west side of the city and then
turning east is bound to get bogged down in swampy land. The result
was that Alexander disobeyed the divine command – half deliberately,
and half because he could not help it.

In Aristobulus' account we find the following story about Apollo-

dorus of Amphipolis. Apollodorus, one of the Hetaeri and closely
associated with Alexander, was in command of the force which had
been left with Mazaeus, the governor of Babylon. After Alexander's
return from India, he had not been long in his company before he
observed the severity with which he was punishing the various provincial governors. He accordingly wrote a letter to his brother Peithagoras, a seer who practised divination by the entrails of animals
offered for sacrifice, asking him to use his art to foretell whether or
not any danger threatened himself. Peithagoras asked in reply who
was the principal cause of the foreboding which made him desire the
service of divination, and he wrote another letter in which he said
that it was the King and Hephaestion. Peithagoras then proceeded to
offer sacrifice, first to secure a prophesy in the case of Hephaestion;
and, as no lobe could be found on the victim's liver, he sent a sealed
message to Apollodorus in Ecbatana, assuring him that Hephaestion
would soon be out of their way and that there was, therefore, nothing
to fear from him. Aristobulus declares that Apollodorus received this
communication the day before Hephaestion's death. Peithagoras then
offered a second sacrifice, this time for information about Alexander;
once again the victim's liver had no lobe, and Peithagoras wrote another letter to his brother in similar terms to the first. Apollodorus
made no attempt at concealment, but told Alexander what the letter
contained, in the belief that he would be doing him a good turn if he
warned him to be on his guard against impending danger. Alexander
thanked him, and on his arrival at Babylon asked Peithagoras the
nature of the warning sign which had induced him to write to his
brother as he did.

'The victim's liver,' was the answer, 'had no lobe.'

'What,' Alexander asked, 'does that sign portend?'

'Something,' Peithagoras replied, 'of the utmost gravity.'

Far from being angry with Peithagoras, Alexander treated him
with all the more consideration for having told him the truth without
concealment.

This story Aristobulus declares he heard from Peithagoras' own
lips. He adds, moreover, that Peithagoras, on a later occasion, practised his art of divination to foretell the fates of Perdiccas and Antigonus; in each case the same warning sign appeared, and in each case
the warning proved true; for Perdiccas was killed in his campaign

against Ptolemy, and Antigonus was killed in the battle of Ipsus against Seleucus and Lysimachus.

There is a similar story of Calanus, the Indian Wise Man. According to this, on the way to the pyre where he was to meet his death he made his farewells to Alexander's personal friends, but refused to speak any word of the sort to Alexander himself, saying that he would give him his greetings when they met in Babylon. At the time nobody paid much attention to this incident; but when, later on, Alexander died in Babylon, all who had been present on the occasion remembered what Calanus had said, and realized that his words were inspired by some mysterious foreknowledge of Alexander's death.

In Babylon, Alexander was visited by delegations from Greece, for purposes which have not been recorded; most of them, I fancy, were to offer him the victor's crown and congratulate him on his many successes, especially his triumphant campaign in India, and to express their pleasure in his safe return. We are told that he received the envoys graciously and paid them all the honours due to their position before dismissing them; he also entrusted to their care the statues, images, and other votive offerings which Xerxes had taken from Greece and brought either to Babylon or Pasargadae or Susa or any other Asian city, and this was the means by which the bronze statues of Harmodius and Aristogeiton and the Celcaean Artemis were restored to Athens.

Aristobulus writes that the fleet was in Babylon when Alexander arrived there. Nearchus' squadron had sailed up the Euphrates from the Persian Gulf, the others – two Phoenician quinqueremes, three quadriremes, twelve triremes, and about thirty light galleys – had come over from the Phoenician coast; they had been taken to pieces and transported overland to Thapsacus on the Euphrates, where they were re-assembled and sailed down the river to Babylon. Apparently Alexander was having a new flotilla built as well, and for this purpose was felling the cypresses in Babylonia; cypress being the only sort of timber of which there is an abundance in Assyrian territory, which is otherwise badly off for ship-building material. Man-power and crews for the new vessels were supplied by shell-divers and others whose work was connected with the sea, from Phoenicia and the neighbouring seaboard. He also by dredging operations had a harbour constructed at Babylon; it was large enough for 1,000 warships to lie in, and was equipped with yards. Miccalus of Clazomenae was sent to Phoenicia and Syria with a sum of 500 talents to hire or purchase more men familiar with ships and the sea. The fact is, Alexander had ideas of settling the seaboard of the Persian Gulf and the off-shore islands; for he fancied it might become as prosperous a country as Phoenicia. The naval preparations were directed against the Arabs of the coast, ostensibly because they were the only people in that part of the country who had sent no delegation to wait upon him, or shown their respect by any other normal act of courtesy; actually, however, the reason for the preparations was, in my opinion, Alexander's insatiable thirst for extending his possessions.

Report has it that Alexander had heard that the Arabs worshipped only two gods, Uranus and Dionysus, the former because he is seen to contain within himself not only the stars but the sun too, the greatest and clearest source of blessing to mankind in all their affairs, and the latter, Dionysus, because of the fame of his journey to India. Alexander accordingly felt it would not be beyond his merits to be regarded by the Arabs as a third god, in view of the fact that his achievements surpassed those of Dionysus; or at least he would deserve this honour if he conquered the Arabs and allowed them, as he had allowed the Indians, to retain their ancient institutions. Moreover, the wealth of their country was an additional incitement – the cassia in the oases, the trees which bore frankincense and myrrh, the shrubs which yielded cinnamon, the meadows where nard grew wild: of all this report had told him. Arabia, too, was a large country, its coast (it was said) no less in extent than the coast of India; many islands lay off it, and there were harbours everywhere fit for his fleet to ride in and to provide sites for new settlements likely to grow to great wealth and prosperity.

He was further informed of the existence of two islands off the mouth of the Euphrates. One of them lay fairly close, at a distance of, perhaps, fifteen miles from that point on the shore where the river joins the sea. This, the smaller of the two, was densely wooded, and contained a temple of Artemis the regular service of which was performed by the islanders themselves. Deer and wild goats found pasture there, and as they were held sacred to the goddess it was unlawful to hunt them except for the purpose of sacrifice. For this reason only was the ban upon taking them removed. Aristobulus tells us that

Alexander decreed that this island should be called Icarus after the Aegean island of that name, upon which the legendary Icarus, son of Daedalus, fell when the wax melted with which his wings were fastened – it melted, the story goes, because he disobeyed his father and, instead of flying low, soared aloft in his folly until the heat of the sun softened the wax, and falling to his death he bequeathed his name to the isle of Icarus and the Icarian Sea.

The second of the two islands, called Tylus, lay off the mouth of the Euphrates at about the distance a running ship can cover in a day and a night. It was of some size, most of it neither wild nor wooded, but fit to produce all sorts of cultivated crops in their proper seasons.

Some of this information Alexander got from Archias, who was sent out in a galley to reconnoitre the coast for the proposed expedition against the Arabs. Archias reached Tylus, but did not venture beyond; Androsthenes, who went in command of another galley, got further, sailing round a part of the Arabian peninsula, and Hiero, the shipmaster from Soli, made greater progress than either. Alexander put him in charge of a third galley and gave him instructions to circumnavigate the whole peninsula as far as the Egyptian town of Heroopolis on the Red Sea. But even he found his courage fail him, though he had sailed round the greater part of the Arabian coast; he turned back, and stated in his report to Alexander that the peninsula was of immense size, nearly as big as India, and that a great headland ran far out into the ocean. This headland had, indeed, been sighted at no great distance by Nearchus' men on their voyage from India, before they altered course for the Persian Gulf, and they were on the point of crossing over to it, as Onesicritus the pilot advised them to do; Nearchus, however, says in his account of the voyage that he refused his permission, as after completing his survey of the coast of the Persian Gulf he would have to report to Alexander on the object of the voyage, and that object was not to explore the ocean, but to examine the coast and collect information about the coastal peoples and how they lived, the fertility or otherwise of the various districts, and the places where anchorages and fresh water were to be found. And this, he adds, was what enabled Alexander's army to come through in safety; it would have been quite useless to take his fleet across to the desert coast of Arabia, for to do that is said to have been the object of Hiero's turning back.

While the new warships were under construction and the work of dredging the harbour proceeded, Alexander sailed from Babylon down the Euphrates to the river known as Pallacopas, about 100 miles down-stream from the city. The Pallacopas is not actually a river rising from an independent source, but a canal leading off from the Euphrates. Now the Euphrates, which rises in the mountains of Armenia, is in winter a shallowish river and runs well within its banks, but in spring, and especially round about the summer solstice, its volume is greatly increased by the melting of the snow in the Armenian mountains, so that the water, rising above the level of its banks, floods the neighbouring Assyrian plains. At least, this flooding would inevitably occur were it not for the cutting by which its waters are diverted along the Pallacopas into the marshes and lakes which continue from that point almost into Arabia, and passing thence over a vast area of swampy land, finally reach the sea by a number of ill-defined channels.

In autumn, after the snows have melted, the level of the Euphrates drops, yet even so much of its water continues to find its way along the canal into the lakes; thus, unless the canal were closed by a sluice, to block the entrance of the river-water and allow it to flow along its proper channel, it would, at this season of the year, empty the Euphrates completely, and so prevent the irrigation of the Assyrian plains. The construction of such a sluice was undertaken by the governor of Babylonia; it proved a tremendous task and the result was unsuccessful, as the soil at that point is mostly soft, wet clay which is easily penetrated by the water of the river. Consequently it was no easy matter to keep it from percolating into the canal, though for three months over 10,000 Assyrian workmen were kept on the job.

When these facts came to Alexander's knowledge, he was anxious to do something to improve Assyria's prospects. Accordingly, he proposed to construct a really efficient sluice at the junction of the canal and the river; however, at a spot some four miles lower down he observed that the soil was of an harder and stonier nature, and it occurred to him that if a new cutting were carried from that point into the Pallacopas canal, the problem might be better solved, for the water would be unable to penetrate the hard, impermeable ground, and could easily be shut off by the sluice at the proper times.

This, then, was the project which took Alexander to the Pallacopas, and down the canal to the lakes in the direction of Arabia. Happening to observe a good site, he built and fortified a new town and settled some of the Greek mercenaries in it, making up the numbers with volunteers and men who were either incapacitated or too old for active service.

It now seemed that he had proved the Chaldaeans' prophecy to be nonsense. They had foretold disaster in Babylon; none had occurred. He had marched safely out of the city before any mischance could catch him. Accordingly, with renewed confidence he sailed again for the lakes, proceeding to the southward. Some of his ships went astray among the narrow channels through the lakes and swamps, and he had to send them a pilot to get them back into the main stream.

The greater number of the tombs of the Assyrian kings were built in the lakes and marshland, and the story goes that Alexander, while his vessel with himself at the helm was passing through, was wearing a sun hat, bound with the diadem or band, signifying royalty. Suddenly a strong gust of wind blew the hat off, which fell into the water, but the light band went flying away and caught on a reed in a reed-bed near one of the ancient royal tombs. This in itself was a presage, but there was more to come: one of the sailors swam off after the hat-band and, finding when he had taken it off the reed that he could not bring it back in his hands without wetting it as he swam, he bound it round his head. Most historians state that Alexander gave the man a talent by way of reward for his willing service, and then had him beheaded in obedience to the prophecy which warned him not to leave untouched the head which had worn the diadem. Aristobulus, however, though he confirms the gift of money, says that the punishment for putting on the band was only a flogging. He adds that the man concerned was one of the Phoenician sailors. Some writers say it was Seleucus, and declare that the incident portended Alexander's death and Seleucus' inheritance of his vast empire – and Seleucus was, in actual fact, the greatest king among Alexander's successors. There can, I think, be no two opinions about this: he had the royallest mind of them all, and, after Alexander himself, ruled over the greatest extent of territory.

Returning to Babylon Alexander found Peucestas back from Persia with 20,000 Persian troops; the force also included a considerable number of Cossaean and Tapurian fighting men, as it was generally supposed that of all Persia's neighbours these peoples produced the best soldiers. Here too he was joined by Philoxenus with troops from Caria, by Menander from Lydia and by Menidas with the cavalry which had been serving under his command. Successive delegations from Greece also presented themselves, and the delegates, wearing ceremonial wreaths, solemnly approached Alexander and placed golden chaplets on his head, as if their coming were a ritual in honour of a god. But, for all that, his end was near.

He took this opportunity of thanking the Persian troops for their loyalty and obedience to Peucestas, and of congratulating Peucestas himself on his orderly and successful government. The Persians were then enrolled in the various Macedonian units, so that the 'decad' – or section – now consisted of a Macedonian leader, two of his compatriots, one of them a 'double-pay' man, the other a 'ten-stater' man (so called from the pay he received, which was less than that of the 'double-pay' soldiers but more than that of the ordinary rank and file), twelve Persians, and, last, another Macedonian 'ten-stater'. Four Macedonians, that is – the section-leader and three others on extra pay – and twelve Persians. The Macedonians wore native equipment; the Persians were armed either with bows or light javelins.

Fleet exercises were constantly held at this time. There was much rivalry between the trireme crews, besides the few quadriremes which were on the river, what with frequent rowing races and trials of skill for the ships' masters, and prizes for the winners.

Some time before this Alexander had sent special envoys to the shrine of Ammon to inquire what honours he might with propriety pay to the dead Hephaestion. The envoys now returned with the news that Ammon permitted sacrifice to be offered him as to a 'hero' or demi-god. Alexander was much pleased, and from that day forward saw that his friend was honoured with a hero's rites.

About this time he wrote a letter to Cleomenes, an official with a bad criminal record in Egypt. In so far as this letter showed his love for Hephaestion, a love which persisted even beyond the grave, I can find no fault with it; but there were other things in it which, I think, were highly reprehensible. The letter contained instructions for the erection of a shrine in Hephaestion's honour in the city of Alexandria, and another on the island of Pharos, where the lighthouse is, both to be of great size and built regardless of expense. Cleomenes was to see

to it that the island was named after Hephaestion and that all mer-
cantile contracts should bear his name. So far, so good – except that
too much feeling was wasted upon matters of too little importance. It
is what followed that I cannot approve. 'If,' the letter went on, 'I find
that everything connected with Hephaestion's shrines in Egypt is in
proper order, I will grant you free pardon for your former crimes,
and henceforward you will suffer no punishment at my hands for anything you may do, however heinous.' A remark of this kind, in a letter from a great king to the governor of a large and populous country
– and a scoundrel at that – is, to my mind, shocking.

Alexander's end was now rapidly approaching. Another portent of
what was so soon to come is mentioned by Aristobulus: while the
King was engaged in incorporating in the various Macedonian units
the troops which had come from Persia with Peucestas and from the
coast with Philoxenus and Menander, he happened to feel thirsty, and
getting up from where he was sitting moved away and left the royal
throne empty. On either side of the throne stood couches with silver
feet, on which his attendants had been sitting, but they had got up and
gone away with the King, and only the guard of eunuchs was left
standing round the throne. Now some fellow or other – some say a
prisoner under open arrest – seeing the throne and the couches un-
occupied, made his way up through the eunuchs and sat down on the
throne. The eunuchs, according to some Persian custom, did not turn
him off, but began to tear their clothes and beat their breasts and faces
as if something dreadful had happened. Alexander was at once told,
and ordered the man to be put to the torture in an endeavour to find
out if what he had done was part of a prearranged plot. However, all
they could get out of him was, that he acted as he did merely upon
impulse. This served to strengthen the seers' forebodings of disaster.

A few days later Alexander was sitting at dinner with his friends
and drinking far into the night. He had previously celebrated the customary sacrificial rites in thanks for his success, adding certain other
offerings in obedience to his seers' advice, and had also, we are told,
distributed wine and sacrificial victims among the various units and
sections of the army. According to some accounts, when he wished to
leave his friends at their drinking and retire to his bedroom, he happened to meet Medius, who at that time was the companion most
closely in his confidence, and Medius asked him to come and continue

drinking at his own table, adding that the party would be a merry one.

The royal Diaries confirm the fact that he drank with Medius after his first carouse. Then (they continue) he left the table, bathed, and went to sleep, after which he supped with Medius and again set to drinking, continuing till late at night. Then, once more, he took a bath, ate a little, and went straight to sleep, with the fever already on him.

Next day he was carried out on his bed to perform his daily religious duties as usual, and after the ceremony lay in the men's quarters till dark. He continued to issue orders to his officers, instructing those who were to march by land to be ready to start in three days and those who were going with himself by sea to sail one day later. From there he was carried on his bed to the river, and crossed in a boat to the park on the further side, where he took another bath and rested. Next day he bathed again and offered sacrifice as usual, after which he went to lie down in his room, where he chatted to Medius and gave orders for his officers to report to him early next morning. Then he took a little food, returned to his room, and lay all night in a fever. The following morning he bathed and offered sacrifice, and then issued to Nearchus and the other officers detailed instructions about the voyage, now due to start in two days' time. Next day he bathed again, went through his regular religious duties, and was afterwards in constant fever. None the less he sent for his staff as usual and gave them further instructions on their preparations for sailing. In the evening, after another bath, his condition was grave, and the following morning he was moved to the building near the swimming-pool. He offered sacrifice, and, in spite of his increasing weakness, sent for his senior officers and repeated his orders for the expedition. The day after that he just managed to have himself carried to his place of prayer, and after the ceremony still continued, in spite of his weakness, to issue instructions to his staff. Another day passed. Now very seriously ill, he still refused to neglect his religious duties; he gave orders, however, that his senior officers should wait in the court, and the battalion and company commanders outside his door. Then, his condition already desperate, he was moved from the park back to the palace. He recognized his officers when they entered his room but could no longer speak to them. From that moment until the end he uttered no word. That night and the following

day, and for the next twenty-four hours, he remained in a high
fever.

These details are all to be found in the Diaries. It is further recorded
in these documents that the soldiers were passionately eager to see
him; some hoped for a sight of him while he was still alive; others
wished to see his body, for a report had gone round that he was already dead, and they suspected, I fancy, that his death was being concealed by his guards. But nothing could keep them from a sight of
him, and the motive in almost every heart was grief and a sort of helpless bewilderment at the thought of losing their king. Lying speechless
as the men filed by, he yet struggled to raise his head, and in his eyes
there was a look of recognition for each individual as he passed. The
Diaries say that Peitho, Attalus, Demophon, and Peucestas, together
with Cleomenes, Menidas, and Seleucus, spent the night in the temple
of Serapis and asked the God if it would be better for Alexander to be
carried into the temple himself, in order to pray there and perhaps recover; but the God forbade it, and declared it would be better for him
if he stayed where he was. The God's command was made public,
and soon afterwards Alexander died – this, after all being the 'better'
thing.

The accounts of both Ptolemy and Aristobulus end at this point.
Other writers have added that the high officers most closely in his
confidence asked him to name his successor, and that Alexander's reply was 'the best man'. There is also a story that he went on to say
that he knew very well there would be funeral 'games' in good
earnest after he was dead.

I am aware that much else has been written about Alexander's
death: for instance, that Antipater sent him some medicine which had
been tampered with and that he took it, with fatal results. Aristotle is
supposed to have made up this drug, because he was already afraid of
Alexander on account of Callisthenes' death, and Antipater's son
Casander is said to have brought it. Some accounts declare that he
brought it in a mule's hoof, and that it was given Alexander by Casander's younger brother Iollas, who was his cup-bearer and had been
hurt by him in some way shortly before his death; others state that
Medius, who was Iollas' lover, had a hand in it, and support that view
by the fact that it was Medius who invited Alexander to the drinking-
party – he felt a sharp pain after draining the cup, and left the party in

consequence of it. One writer has even had the face to declare that when he knew his death was imminent he went out with the intention of throwing himself into the Euphrates, in order to disappear without trace and make it easier for posterity to believe that one of the gods was his father and he had gone away to join them. His wife Roxane, this writer continues, happened to see him as he left the building, and stopped him, whereupon he gave a great cry and bitterly reproached her for grudging him the eternal fame of divine birth. I do not wish to appear ignorant of these stories; but stories they are – I put them down as such and do not expect them to be believed.

Alexander died in the 114th Olympiad, in the archonship of Hegesias at Athens. He lived, as Aristobulus tells us, thirty-two years and eight months, and reigned twelve years and eight months. He had great personal beauty, invincible power of endurance, and a keen intellect; he was brave and adventurous, strict in the observance of his religious duties, and hungry for fame. Most temperate in the pleasures of the body, his passion was for glory only, and in that he was insatiable. He had an uncanny instinct for the right course in a difficult and complex situation, and was most happy in his deductions from observed facts. In arming and equipping troops and in his military dispositions he was always masterly. Noble indeed was his power of inspiring his men, of filling them with confidence, and, in the moment of danger, of sweeping away their fear by the spectacle of his own fearlessness. When risks had to be taken, he took them with the utmost boldness, and his ability to seize the moment for a swift blow before his enemy had any suspicion of what was coming, was beyond praise. No cheat or liar ever caught him off his guard, and both his word and his bond were inviolable. Spending but little on his own pleasures, he poured out his money without stint for the benefit of his friends.

Doubtless, in the passion of the moment Alexander sometimes erred; it is true he took some steps towards the pomp and arrogance of the Asiatic kings: but I, at least, cannot feel that such errors were very heinous, if the circumstances are taken fairly into consideration. For, after all, he was young; the chain of his successes was unbroken, and, like all kings, past, present, and to come, he was surrounded by courtiers who spoke to please, regardless of what evil their words might do. On the other hand, I do indeed know that Alexander, of all the monarchs of old, was the only one who had the nobility of heart to be sorry for his mistakes. Most people, if they know they have done wrong, foolishly suppose they can conceal their error by defending it, and finding a justification for it; but in my belief there is only one medicine for an evil deed, and that is for the guilty man to admit his guilt and show that he is sorry for it. Such an admission will make the consequences easier for the victim to bear, and the guilty man himself, by plainly showing his distress at former transgressions, will find good grounds of hope for avoiding similar transgressions in the future.

Nor do I think that Alexander's claim to a divine origin was a very serious fault – in any case, it may well have been a mere device to magnify his consequence in the eyes of his subjects. In point of fact I account him as great a king as Minos or Aeacus or Rhadamanthus, whose claims to be sons of Zeus were not felt by the men of old to be in any way dangerously arrogant; and the same may be said of Theseus' claim to be the son of Poseidon and Ion's to be son of Apollo. Surely, too, his adoption of Persian dress was, like his claim to divine birth, a matter of policy: by it he hoped to bring the Eastern nations to feel that they had a king who was not wholly a foreigner, and to indicate to his own countrymen his desire to move away from the harsh traditional arrogance of Macedonia. That was also, no doubt, the reason why he included a proportion of Persian troops (the so-called 'Golden Apples', for instance) in Macedonian units, and made Persian noblemen officers in his crack native regiments. As for his reputed heavy drinking, Aristobulus declares that his drinking bouts were prolonged not for their own sake – for he was never, in fact, a heavy drinker – but simply because he enjoyed the companionship of his friends.

Anyone who belittles Alexander has no right to do so on the evidence only of what merits censure in him; he must base his criticism on a comprehensive view of his whole life and career. But let such a person, if blackguard Alexander he must, first compare himself with the object of his abuse: himself, so mean and obscure, and, confronting him, the great King with his unparalleled worldly success, the undisputed monarch of two continents, who spread the power of his name over all the earth. Will he dare to abuse him then, when he knows his own littleness and the triviality of his own pursuits, which, even so, prove too much for his ability?

It is my belief that there was in those days no nation, no city, no single individual beyond the reach of Alexander's name; never in all the world was there another like him, and therefore I cannot but feel that some power more than human was concerned in his birth; indications of this were, moreover, said to be provided at the time of his death by oracles; many people saw visions and had prophetic dreams; and there is the further evidence of the extraordinary way in which he is held, as no mere man could be, in honour and remembrance. Even today, when so many years have passed, there have been oracles, all tending to his glory, delivered to the people of Macedon.

In the course of this book I have, admittedly, found fault with some of the things which Alexander did, but of the man himself I am not ashamed to express ungrudging admiration. Where I have criticized unfavourably, I have done so because I wished to tell the truth as I saw it, and to enable my readers to profit thereby. Such was the motive which led me to embark upon this History; and I, too, have had God's help in my work.